AspergerWorld

To Carne Ross,

I hope my book
empowers you.

J. Williams

AspergerWorld

My Fairy Jam Jar

Joely Williams

Matador
9 Priory Business Park,
Wistow Road, Kibworth Beauchamp,
Leicestershire. LE8 0RX
Tel: 0116 279 2299
Email: books@troubador.co.uk
Web: www.troubador.co.uk/matador
Twitter: @matadorbooks

ISBN 978 1838595 302

British Library Cataloguing in Publication Data.
A catalogue record for this book is available from the British Library.

Printed and bound in the UK by TJ Books Limited, Padstow, Cornwall
Typeset in 11.5pt Garamond by Troubador Publishing Ltd, Leicester, UK

Matador is an imprint of Troubador Publishing Ltd

This book is dedicated to the people in my life who have always empowered, supported, and taught me life's most valuable lessons…

To my Mum, Joy Colmer; My best friend who motivates me. The one who taught me how to fly; my guardian Angel. Thank you for always empowering me, by encouraging my story writing, and art. Thank you for your sleepless nights, and the hours you spent on the phone to get me the support I needed. Thank you for teaching me the values of self acceptance and love. Thank you for never giving up and teaching me my disabilities quirks.

To my Dad, Robert Colmer; My most cheerful supporter, my biggest fan. The one who has always believed in me; who helped un clip my wings. Thank you for teaching me the joy of family, and for sacrificing your time, so we children had everything we needed. Thank you for the bear hugs, the trips down memory lane, and for teaching me the art of compassion, good food, specialist topics and the ability to appreciate my disability.

To my Sister, Corinna Colmer; The one whose golden heart beams, and smile lights up the room. The brightest ray of sun shine, within a delicate silver locket; A gift, a memory, I'll always treasure. Thank you for your understanding of how to help me, thank you for inspiring me, organising me, teaching me the joys of friendship, and swimming. Thank you for always being there, and for dedicating so much time and effort into helping me on "My Fairy Jam Jar" journey.

To my Brother, Keith Colmer; Whose kindness shines, glittering in his suit of armour as he protects and empowers; adventurous and fun. There is no equation that can symbolize how much I admire you. Thank you for always helping me when I needed you, thank you for teaching me the joys of loyalty, self-worth. Thank you for helping me with my maths work at school., and looking out for me. Thank you for our adventures together; those teenaged parties and countless childhood games of football and garden obstacles courses.

To my Partner, Macrae Williams; My perfect star, whose kindness and sense of fun knows no boundaries, making me laugh, and count my blessings everyday. You are 'the one'; the one who literally followed me half way across the world to show me how much you love me. Your soul shimmers, with a caring outlook that appreciates my disabilities quirks; enabling me to overcome my psychological barriers to love you back. Thank you, for teaching me to live happily; thank you simply for being you.

Key

A.S.D – Autistic Spectrum Disorder
A.S – Asperger's syndrome
Aspie – Someone with Asperger's
Autie – Someone with Autism

Contents

Introduction

I have a gift; a gift that hinders me with many hidden hardships, but also walks hand in hand, snug as a glove, with the very things that I love most about myself.

You see, my disability is my gift; my gift is Asperger's syndrome.

My name is Joely Colmer, and I am currently 25 years old (2017). Living with Asperger's is like being a little fairy, stuck inside a quaint jam jar; witnessing the world from a different angle, powerless to escape and deaf to certain language.

I have to say though; I rather like my fairy jam jar!

You see, my gift enables me to experience the rich, vibrant tapestry of life in all its glorious detail. Tell me, when you were a small child, did you ever lay in a luscious green meadow, surrounded by the tall shoots of grass sheltered by the splintered trees, and gaze upon the interesting mechanics of the flowers in your surroundings? 10 years on, would you be able to accurately describe everything you saw? Everything from the scientific names and values of the flowers, clouds and insects to the number and shades of colours upon the leaves scattered upon the floor? I can. I am able to remember all these insignificant facts and details about most places I visit, due to my disability.

This is one aspect of my gift that is unique, positive and empowering. On the flip side, can you envisage how observing such great detail can be ever so exhausting as an everyday experience? Indeed, the frustrations of constantly being aware of so much detail and information can become unbearable. This is because I could walk into a room and notice every little thing at the same time. I could notice every cobweb, every grain of detail on the brick walls, every speck of grime, textures, and anything big or small. Usually I notice all of these things and I find it very difficult to not look at everything, because of this my concentration is badly affected giving me sensory overloads. A classic example of this is when I am at school. In a classroom there is a multitude of things to look at, that other people don't notice. I find these things so consuming that I spend my time looking at them rather than listening to what the teacher has to say. I always try to listen, but because the distractions are so intense I find it difficult to take in anything the teacher is saying. This means that learning anything is very difficult.

Asperger's syndrome is a wonderful disability on the higher end of the Autistic spectrum. My disability may be complicated, but I smile with great pleasure through my difficulties. This is because my disability has given me so much understanding for the diverse beauty of the human race and I love that about myself. I believe there are far more positive than negative aspects; for my disability makes me caring, honest, loyal, passionate, and motivated. I shall now explain a bit about the difficulties that come with Asperger's.

People with Asperger's syndrome have difficulties with social interaction and understanding spoken language as we take everything people say literally. Due to my Asperger's I also have quite a difficulty with fine motor skills and I have a complete lack of social imagination. Having a lack of social imagination means I have grave difficulty with working out a solution to a problem if my routine has unexpectedly changed. It also means I find it really hard to organize myself and get from one place to another.

The BIG question... What is 'normal'?

I felt somewhat compelled to try and be normal but it is very difficult when you have little understanding of what normal is- this still remains a slight mystery- I mean what is deemed as 'normal' nowadays?

In my head I am just a 'normal' girl. I have many interests that are similar to other 'normal' young people my age. Interests such as hanging out with my friends and having fun, working, volunteering (Ok, so according to my mates volunteering is not something most young people would call a hobby) shopping, festivals, art, clubbing and reading and writing books. I do all these things and a lot of people say I don't appear to have any disability at all. I don't look like I have a disability (and as they say), it is fairly hidden, but trust me, once you get to know me you'll notice my disability.

My disability is hidden, but a lot of other disabled people's are not hidden. For example, people with physical disabilities. Unfortunately a lot of people make judgements and then discriminate about the things they know little about, it sounds silly, but it's true. This is why disability needs to be widely recognised and understood better within communities. It would make our lives a lot easier if we can educate the general public about different types of disabilities, they will have a better understanding of how to treat us- with a bit more respect and justice. In this way I am somewhat fortunate because I look 'normal' and don't stand out as different to other people, because of this more people accept me for who I am.

I am the happiest I have ever been, due to the incredible support I have received from my family and the voluntary sector. I am a firm believer that without support and help, we are all like old autumn leaves, old and decaying, unable to show the world our usual bright colours. Yet with help and support, our bright colours glow through, and people can see our quirks, and why we are so clever. It is much the same for people understanding our disability, if people understand us, life is so much easier. We are not so 'difficult' and our powerful personality can seep through our difficulties and showcase a world of beauty and hilarity to those in the know. I have not always been this happy, as life has not always treated me so kindly. To achieve my dreams of making positive change happen, I have various voluntary projects on the go, which aim to make real positive differences. I give speeches and teaching presentations to professionals to help spread awareness and build an in depth understanding of disabilities on the Autistic spectrum. I talk more about my voluntary work in the chapter – Infinity and Beyond.

I write this book, because I wish to share insight into my wondrous splendour captured within My Fairy Jam Jar. I wish to help introduce an understanding of Asperger's syndrome, from childhood through to teenaged and adult life, living with the ever affecting disability. I want to create a swell of understanding within our communities, and a promise to society that we will accept our differences in people, and try to make life wonderful. Within this book, I aim to help support your understanding of the depths of this unique disability, so that you can best help others with Asperger's, whether you have, or are interested in, this brilliant disability.

I shall end my introduction with this; Life is incredible, to be alive, disabled or not, is an amazing adventure of incredible strength. This is why all life deserves the right to be listened to, respected, understood and helped, to aid in making life's adventure as supported and wonderful for everyone as we can. Difference within people is good and having a disability certainly does not make them inferior, a freak, stupid or difficult. I hope I have piqued some of your interests and I trust you will read on, to learn more about Aspergers Syndrome to better expand your intellectual curiosity.

Remember, all diversity in people is amazing, we are mammals of intellect, friendship, justice, love and most importantly; we are mammals of difference. Like a sprinkle of fairy dust, may you also be enchanted by My Fairy Jam Jar.

My AspergerWorld

I see myself as a Fairy living in AspergerWorlds Jam Jar for a reason; because my brain is its own world of possibilities. Wonderful in its own unique way; allowing me to use my worlds diverse abilities and different view point's to give insight into a world so different to what is sometimes considered the 'norm'.

You see, my AspergerWorld has beautiful beaches with soothing waves; sometimes the sand is too sensitive on my skin, but the waves allow me to calm myself. My AspergerWorld has a tall, magnificent forest, with every tree branching out, every specific narrow interest shoots through the bark; each vein a sparkling mass of colour and information. Tree branches lit up, bright, colourful, unique, and spanning out, growing taller each day; an insight to behold with each new fact I have been enabled to learn. In my AspergerWorld, I also have over whelming water crashing down from picturesque waterfalls, surrounded by a thick misty fog, which gives me brain fog and severe confusion of how I can problem solve, concentrate or get myself from A to B with such startling white noise distracting me. Meadows of luscious crops spread out like a patchwork of colours; each colour represents a different ability or skill. With support from my environment, my crops of abilities can grow; However shutdowns wreak havoc with my ability, colours fading to grey, my crops of abilities can no longer be grown or used. All I need then is support from my environment to allow me to recover; I need the warm glow from my worlds family suns, and showers of understanding rain, to empower my crops of abilities to grow, and permit me to survive again. My AspegerWorlds peaceful countryside is trip wired by volcanoes and chaotic whirlwinds. I am easily overwhelmed, making panic sizzle throughout me. A bit like a Volcano; stimuli bubbles on the surface of my mind like lava, until my brain is ready to explode at the slightest overload, or life skill. Lava pouring over, with new information, thoughts, creativity and a never ending surge of memories and analyzed anxiety. Then the shaking earthquakes control me when I have to problem solve, trembling me to the ground, forcing me to cover my ears and protect myself from all the angst, screaming out in terror as meltdowns take control, trapping me in a frightfully overwhelming burning hot, skin prickling, core.

It takes time for my little island to become safe and enabling again, and a lot of support to help me through such difficulties. In these ways, there are many aspects of my disability; many hidden hardships, and quirks, and I am going to try and explain them in a bit more detail for you.

Gifts and Quirks for those who have an Autistic Disability

Average or Above Average IQ
This is generally true for those with specifically Asperger's Syndrome; I have an IQ of 125 according to my last assessment – not that I trust that grading; I imagine my IQ is far lower. I feel so daft, so much of the time!

The main difficulty with having an higher IQ when you also have Asperger's is that it's really hard to express or communicate intelligence. Due to problem solving and other associated difficulties; judgments can sadly be made that those with Asperger's don't have an high IQ at all; and they can become victims of bullying as a result, either because the bully is jealous of a high IQ, or does not understand the difficulties of expressing an higher IQ. None of these things are faults in the victim, but are faults in the bully.

Additionally, what struck me as most unfair and odd, was at school I would be placed in all the bottom sets of learning. However my level of understanding was far greater, and my intelligence levels were higher, so sometimes, I was not challenged enough. Additionally, the lower sets of learning would mean I was forced to 'learn' with all the noisy and disruptive students as well as those students who had special educational needs or otherwise struggled in that subject. The support that would sometimes be provided would not be adequate to help me at the level I needed it. The most frustrating thing is that because of my Aspergers, and because the support I needed could only assist me in a lower setting – I would be bullied and called stupid because I would be placed in a lower setting; where as in reality my intelligence did mean that I should have been in a much higher setting. Why an earth can the support I desperately needed not be paid to go into a higher setting – if the higher setting is where my intelligence and understanding showed I should have been placed? It makes zero sense that those who need support all have to be in the bottom sets in order to gain their support. How exactly is that challenging those who should be in a higher setting?

Vast Amount of Knowledge about a Specialist Topic or Specific Narrow Interest

Some people call those with Asperger's 'walking encyclopaedias' for a reason, you know, because of the abilities to retain all or most factual information regarding their specific narrow interest. A fascination can be so strong that people with Asperger's may only want to think, talk and do things that are related to their specialist topic. I think this is wonderful, an ability to feel safe and comfortable, within the outside world of chaos, whilst being under appreciatively clever, and passionate about their interests.

Good Memory

As I mentioned, those with Asperger's are sometimes known as a walking encyclopedia; This is due to an remarkable ability to remember facts, dates and other information The thing with having amazing memory, is that it can often means you notice and remember loads of irrelevant details, which means there is often no room for any important information (important information here means things like life skills – for example the ability to catch a bus, remembering what to do when in a shop, asking for help, etc). Those on the Spectrum are unable to back stream irrelevant information that we notice, so if we are sat in a class room, trying to learn something we often remember everything in the classroom and the indents in the desk in front of us more than the additional information that teacher is trying to teach. Good memory also means we are more likely to be able see the patterns in daily life (patterns here mean an ability to understand how things work – cause to affect, structure and so on). Recognizing such patterns in daily life and daily activities, are the skills that helps us grow and develop. Such patterns are easily recognisable to those who don't have our disabilities which means we have to try a lot harder to develop than others do – hence our fabulous memory. If we can seek and understand patterns, by using our fabulous memory, it means we are more likely to be able to use the patterns and learn and develop even further. My fantastic memory is one of the reasons I see my disability as a total gift.

Obsessive Behaviours – Routines

Those with Asperger's can generally thrive within the comfort of a well structured routine. This obsession with truth and doing things the same way, the right way, is because not only do those with Autistic Spectrum Disorders find the facts and correct realities comforting, but the truth helps those with Autistic Spectrum Disorders learn what reality and truth really is. This ability to do really exceptionally well, when in a structured routine, becomes an ability to maximise potential and development. I love that as a result of my obsessive behaviours, I will always be punctual. My obsessions can be very good indeed, making me very honest and less likely to manipulate and tell lies, because my obsession with routine, correction and structure does not allow me to be impromptu.

Abide by the Rules / Laws

Will not intentionally break any laws, rules or boundaries. Any jobs will be done 'by the book' which means that they will do everything exactly the right way -sticking to rules as much as humanely possible. Will do their best – wont do anything deliberately wrong or take any 'short cuts' that could compromise the 'truthful' and 'correct' result. Those with Autistic Spectrum Disorders can obsess over truth, justification and doing the 'right' and 'correct' thing. Due to these obsessions someone with Asperger's will try to follow social protocol 'the right way' , and behave lawfully, and with kindness, always keen to do the 'right' and 'correct' thing, and be truthful, justified and honest as much as their environment can enable them too.

Will try to be a Good Friend

Although communication, empathy and making friends can be hard, those with Autistic Spectrum Disorders are often good, honest and loyal friends – as much as they can be at times of overloads or high stress. We will be less likely to lie or manipulate and although we find it hard to express it, we will be very caring. We do make very good friends indeed, we just need a fighting chance and friends that understand and accept us and our quirks!

Trustworthy

Those with Asperger's are well known to be able to keep a secret, but most importantly if you ask them to do a job, they will do that job to the best of their ability. They are likely to be punctual, presuming they have routines in place to help them. Any jobs will be done 'by the book' which means that they will do everything exactly the right way -sticking to rules as much as humanely possible, so you can trust they won't do anything deliberately wrong or take any short cuts. Due to the rules, routine and truth necessary to perform well in daily life, you can trust that someone with Asperger's, will try to follow social protocol and behave in a manner that points in the direction of justice, kindness and truth, as much as their environment can enable them too.

Not Selfish

Despite this common misconception. The simple truth is that those with Asperger's find it impossible to lie, and hate un-justice, lack of structure and things that are 'in-correct'; with this also comes the necessity for those with Asperger's to try and be 'correct'- selfless, caring and trustworthy just like other people. The reality is that this is very hard to do; it is very complicated living a life behind glass, misunderstood by so many of the human beings that we walk past in the street – feeling like an alien is rather horrid. The thing to remember is that it is the disability causing the seemingly 'selfish' behaviour – and NOT the other way around.

Passionate and Motivated to Learn

Especially when in relation to their specialized topic or interest. Very good at learning, and soaking up information, and can be very hardworking, when in a supportive and appropriate environment with suitable teaching methods.

Ability to Communicate Specifically about their Personal Specialized Topic

Due to difficulty communicating, those with Autistic Spectrum Disorders tend to use their specialized topics as a point of conversation and are very good at communicating this way.

Likely to have an Ability to Notice lots of Details Others Don't Realize are There

Although this leads to overloads and meltdowns, this also means that those with Autistic Spectrum Disorders are also able to remember details that others are swift to forget – sometimes this can be very helpful.

Sensory Issues

Many people with disabilities on the Autistic spectrum suffer with very sensitive skin. I don't mean that we necessarily come out in a rash and have to be careful which skin care products we use. I merely mean that we can be easily agitated by our surroundings, such as labels on clothes and being overly hot or too cold. I can do. This is a story I have got to tell. You see, although I have sensory difficulties they are not as bad for me as they may be for other people. Here is a quote to begin my explanation.

> "I love it. Everyone is so weird and wacky, everything is brilliant and everyone is different and I feel... I feel normal."
> *Me, first time at Glastonbury Festival. 2007*

My happiest place in the world is this festival. I absolutely love it there and it makes me feel happy, safe, exhilarated and absolutely normal. It is brilliant and I will never have the grace to describe how much so. This festival is currently the biggest and the best festival in Europe. This festival is filled with the most incredible things to look at, constant noise, and constant strain on the senses. It usually has a fair bit of mud too, not to mention the sheer volume of people. My goodness, apparently in those fields of Glastonbury, there is as many people as there are in my town (some people call my town a city though, so this can tell you how many people there are crammed into those fields). I can imagine it sounds horrendous to some of you, but you have got to see the beauty of it all, this is a festival which I have been for seven years in a row, I have never once seen a fight and rarely hear people swear it is purely all about peace, happiness, caring for our environment and music. It is so fun at this festival. The overloads are worth it because the things I am overloaded by are beautiful and arty.

After a few days of this fabulous Festival, I do begin suffering with sensory overloads and extreme fatigue. Sometimes despite wanting to explore more, I do have to take cat naps within the days to pull myself through. It may sound silly but Glastonbury is my second home, a lot of effort has been made by my family to make me happy at Glastonbury- we always camp in the same camping area by the same fence, the general systems and routines are always the same, even in a place full of change, I still have my routines to maintain my sanity. Despite the sensory nightmare Glastonbury portrays to us sensitive few, it is absolutely brilliant.

I also love clubbing and going to pubs with my mates, I just love hanging out having a laugh with friends dancing and the expression of freedom all of this entitles me to. Sometimes all the chaos, the noise, the busyness and the many sights to ponder over make it so worthwhile. When I am out all I do is smile, it's just the way I am. My neutral facial expression would be a little smile because I am usually very happy to be there. I love having the ability to see so much and really put my senses to good use by being in such overwhelming places like this it makes me feel empowered and like I can really learn from the people whom I meet at these places.

My mum worries about me when I am out and about like this, I can think I am independent and safe, but in reality I am a very vulnerable person. Consequently my mother does not sleep until she has heard from me; her mobile phone is usually right beside her all through the night just in case I contact her. My family have taught me all the basics- what to do in various situations, just in case certain scenarios come to light. An example is that a night out rarely turns out as planned, one night I was meant to stay in one night club with all my mates for a birthday party; this did not happen and I got abandoned by mates who did not understand my disability and the effect this would have on me, and I ended up completely alone in the midst of town centre in the early hours of the morning. Needless to say I rang mum and she came to collect me.

So I can imagine you pondering over this. I can imagine yourself telepathically asking me "let me get this straight, you like clubbing, you like Festivals, you like Pubs….. You enjoy socializing… you like sensory overloads? How? What disability do you have again?"

I can imagine you would ask such a question based on the judgment that because I have sensory overloads due to my disability means I would avoid these things all together. Well, you're not too wrong if you think this. The thing is that I am rather silly and tend to do these things regardless. In fact I have been encouraged to do so by my family. They want me to experience 'normal' day to day life, I am glad that I have been encouraged to do this because these are all things that have taught me how to deal with various life situations which I can't avoid. I also have grown to love these activities too. Yet, sometimes it is incredibly difficult dealing with these things and I do get overwhelmed with everything very quickly, and suffer greatly with Autism Shutdowns; leading to a sensory meltdown, causing me to feel ill, tired and mentally and physically drained for days afterwards.

Sometimes when I get overwhelmed in a social situation, all I need is a break, I could be in a club dancing and suddenly I will get over loaded and will start to feel dizzy, it is hard to cope and my eye sight will start to go crazy and out of focus. My hearing becomes distorted and I either hear everything or nothing at all. I feel like all I want to do is run outside to a grassy patch and lie down and smell the fresh night scent of the grass, to let my senses be calmed by the clear sanity of the night. Sometimes I would be sick or feel like I am going to faint. It has been known for me to run outside into the pouring rain and just spin round and round dancing in the rain until I have calmed down. Fun times, I tell you. On a good day, when I am feeling generally better in myself, I will be able to just shut out the noise and whatever is causing the overloads would be calmed down by having a little break.

I dislike sensory overloads but I don't avoid them so much anymore – I embrace them as a part of me, because I usually get sensory overloads doing something I enjoy – Why an earth should I stop doing the things I love because of the risk of suffering a Anxiety attack? It is unpleasant yes, but it should not prevent me from living a life I enjoy. To the readers with a disability, I hope having these feelings do not prevent you from doing the things you enjoy too. Providing you are safe and have an option to get out of that situation, you should try to embrace things that you want to achieve- all it takes is practise, support from family and friends (just a phone call away) and a safe place to calm yourself down. The most important thing is always to be safe. Some people may disagree, but in my eyes, life is for enjoying; not being afraid of.

I used to go out all the time and always have sensory overloads and high Anxiety, things were really difficult and after a while it did somewhat prevent me from accessing what I loved. Sadly I stopped going clubbing entirely, I avoided all places that were noisy and filled with people such as Pubs and I even stopped going to big supermarkets for food shopping. Supermarkets are really bad for me. Seriously I walk in sometimes and feel like I will faint after barely two minutes, purely because the lights were flickering, the amount of noise, people and the glaring white walls. These overloads have prevented me from accessing the things I love. Not so much anymore, because I have learnt how best to cope with them. I pulled through my sensory overloads and started to go back out again. You see, after a while I got sick of feeling sick all of the time, it got so ridiculous and I could not stand not being able to do the things I loved any longer. I figured that the only way to be happy was to pull through and force myself to be happy; by starting to do the things I love, one thing at a time. If I felt overloaded at any point I would just take a break, literally just sit down and drink some water (I always carry a bottle of water with me for this purpose) and sometimes I put my head phones in if possible to listen to my playlist of happy calming songs that would make me feel better (all of which specifically picked for these moments of enhanced stress).

The sense of touch
When I was a child I used to dislike cuddling, however minimal the hug. I still hated it and thought it was rather pointless. Things have somewhat changed now, as now I believe it shows respect and sentiment to someone that you care about. My mother took great care and effort teaching me the ways of young teenage girls, who run up to each other shrieking and then spend a few

minutes hugging each other in excitement. At first this seemed like a rather alarming scenario to witness, due to the shrieks and the quite exaggerated displays of affection (sometimes quite rough, my friends used to spin each other round, dance and all sorts) but soon I was taught that girls just like to do this and it shows how much they like the person they are hugging. As I was saying, my mum took a long time teaching me how to hug and teaching me how to hug without awkwardly patting the person on the back as I used to do when faced with an unfamiliar person hugging me. After months of arguing with my mother asking "why do these teenage girls shriek and hug like that?! Why..?" my mum explained that this is just what the teen girls do, and that is what you will have to accept- go with it, learn how to hug too, it's nice once you get used to it. It took me a long time to get used to hugging, but now, it is rather nice hugging my friends and family, just like my mother promised.

Thankfully, I hug my friends and my family now and see it as completely normal – I hug everyone whom I love. I enjoy hugging it makes me feel safe and shows we care about each other (we as in the people that are hugging). Hugging is no longer an embarrassment or an awkward thing for me anymore. Also, hugging makes you feel more part of the group, so to an outsider watching, they may think that you are just a normal teen in a normal group. There's nothing wrong with that. Little do they know it has taken months (years actually) to learn such a simple task.

As a child, I use to also dislike that game adults play with children – it's called 'Round and round the Garden like a Teddy Bear'. It's a funny little game where someone strokes the palm of the child's hand round in a circle, when you get to the 'Tickle you under their' bit the person would tickle the child under their arm or on their belly. I used to hate that because it tickled the palm of my hand dreadfully and then the anticipation of the tickle under my arms made it rather dreadful and quite a dire consequence for the adult playing it with me as I would probably shriek and jolt away viciously trying to escape such nasty tickles. I find this amusing as the intention of such a game is meant to make a child laugh by tickling them. The effect was always lost on me because I hated the thought of being touched and tickled by any one, I believe I used to scream and push away.

My skin always feels itchy, hot and like my skin is on fire. It is not like skin conditions, I think maybe our neural networks are high wired and our nerve endings allow us to feel more heat or cold than others without our disability. This burning sensation on my skin takes over my thoughts and forces me to behave in certain ways. Agitation and frustration takes over, and as a child unable to cope with my painful skin, I used try and control the sensory input (itchy and painful skin) with sensory output. I did this by moving a lot, running a lot and being my general 'whirl wind' self. A lot of children try to control their sensory input, with (what is considered by those with little understanding), 'bad' behaviour, by flailing their arms and legs about, almost aggressively, striking out in times of high stress, although usually, they are merely coping, not being aggressive on purpose. Of course, every individual is different. However, you have to remember this one thing; it is the disability causing the behaviour, not the behaviour causing the disability.

When I was really young and overloaded to the point of having a complete meltdown, I have learnt that I need to change clothes into something baggy really ultra soft and comfortable. Unless my skin can calm down there is no way I can de-stress.

Sense of touch – sensory overload

When I am having a sense of touch sensory overload, I begin to feel itchy, clammy and whatever I am wearing or touching starts to feel rougher than it would normally. When things get too much for me, I admit my sensory overloads can be quite alarming. I still handle things badly when alone, I literally shake my hands and cover my ears; if my hands are covering my ears then they are not touching the things causing the sensory overload. I know this makes me look crazy, but it really helps. It usually only takes 2 minutes to calm down before I can continue with what I was doing. I am a strange girlie sometimes.

Clothes

What fond memories I have of screeching and getting increasingly agitated that my clothes were itchy or had labels (In case you couldn't tell I was being sarcastic, those were not fond memories at all). I used to have really soft clothes because even the slightest bit of roughness would distress me. Other people would stroke the fur on some clothes and say "Oh it is ever so soft", but I would cringe because I could feel how rough it was. I think that the roughness of some clothes is just another distraction for me. This is because the clothes are constantly on my skin and you can't get away from them. I imagine a lot of other children with A.S.D were like that too.

Advice to Parents – Clothes
Clothes must be comfortable. Labels need to be completely cut out and the inside seams must be soft. Denim is usually too stiff but this gives with time.

The sense of sight

I have big problems with this daily. I walk into rooms and everything literally starts to rotate and turn into patterns every which way I look, it is rather disorientating. This is because, much like many other people on the Autistic spectrum, we see in a great deal of detail. Objects appear larger (or smaller) and change in size (despite the physical being of the object not changing in size at all) and I find it hard to focus my attention on one thing, at any one moment (I can't help but focus on lots of things at any one moment). Some places I used to avoid because they are too busy, too loud and too frustrating to even look at, places like bowling. Do you know what it is like walking into a Bowling Alley and every tiny detail suddenly screams at you "look at me." I won't be able to cope with the hideous mess of patterns that is in a Bowling Alley. Oh my, those numerous patterns on the floor, the flashing lights- all the bright colours everything is just screaming at me to have a sensory overload and I would start feeling so sick and achy.

Sensory overload – what happens to my sense of sight?

The room would start to spin, whatever it is I look at would start to zoom in and out of focus and often get larger or smaller. Walls start to appear like they are breathing (moving in a wavy fashion) if I try to read anything the words would stumble over themselves, much like dyslexia I guess. Lights would hurt my eyes, and migraines would last for days. I feel nauseas. I just start to feel damn terrible really quickly.

The sense of hearing

I have noticed that many people who have a disability on the Autistic spectrum have sensitive hearing. To be honest so do I. I used to be partially deaf in one ear, so it is surprising how much I can hear nowadays. Or not, as it would seem sometimes.

Here is a classic example of which happens all the time to me. This is a conversation between me and my friend a few years ago. She had been saying my name and trying to talk to me and I was completely oblivious and had not heard her talking to me. The conversation goes as follows:

My friend saying loudly (shouting apparently) – "Joely, Joely. I'm trying to talk to you... Joely. Joely?! ... How can she not hear me?!"

My friend, who had gained no response, tried again – "Joely, I am talking to you"

Me- "Oh, are you? Sorry I didn't hear you..."

My friend laughs and shakes her head looking rather confused.

My friend then said – "How could you not hear me, I have been repeating your name in your ear, for like, ever now."

Me- "Oh, you have? Ummm sorry, I guess that it's so noisy here that I'm, listening to all the other noises and because I did not know that I was supposed to be listening out for your voice, I did not hear you..."

My friend – "Eh? What you chatting about?"

Me – "Oh....never mind..."

I don't blame my friend for not understanding, because from an outsider's point of view it would be a hard concept to grasp. I would be confused too, if I were her. In reality, there are so many other thing that I am concentrating on and am distracted by (other noises and visuals) it makes it harder for me to listen out for unexpected conversations. There are a million different noises going off at once, so for me to concentrate on the noises that are important I have to learn to filter out the unimportant noises. If I don't my brain will go bang. (Not literally, kids). Sometimes when this filtering process is too difficult I get confused between important and unimportant noises. All of these noises happening at the same time often become too much and I go into sensory overload. It happens to me a lot. Even now.

A person with Asperger's does not expect that they need to listen to you straight away, especially if the conversation is not already present – they won't have 'listening to voices' in their main hearing stream and so they will just filter the voices straight through to back ground noises. It is a subconscious habit, I believe so anyway. I think we do it without realising as a part of our body's natural coping strategy for lots of noise. So please don't think someone with Asperger's is being rude and purposely not listening or answering you because they are not responding to your voice – it is likely not to be their fault.

Hearing and listening

There is a big difference between hearing and listening. At any given time, there are many different noises and sounds. Despite the mixture of noises and sounds most people can 'tune in' to a particular sound they need to concentrate on. The noises you are concentrating on are the noises you are listening to, while the background sounds are the noises you hear.

For example, I once went into a cafe with my friend and made a note of everything I could hear. Here is my little list:

1.   Lights buzzing
2.   The sound of a ceiling fan that was making a screechy noise every time it rotated past 180 degrees
3.   A hiss of bacon/sausages, or whatever was frying in the cafe's kitchen area.

4. The sound of spitting fat as the chef flipped the bacon. As it was breakfast this happened a lot. Nearly everyone was ordering bacon, sausage, eggs and mushrooms, a lot of fried stuff
5. The general lull of laughter and other peoples conversation
6. People clicking and using the buttons on their mobiles phones
7. Other people's 'bad' taste in music seeping out from their head phones- I could hear and identify 3 different songs from different people, but I won't mention them because I don't want to offend anyone by calling their music bad
8. The sound of scratchy material of the person sat behind me every time they move, that abrasive material they were wearing rubs against the chair and makes an annoyingly grating rough noise
9. The sound of padding and creaking as people sit or shift their weight on the chairs
10. Some person persistently tapping against the table- very annoying
11. The radio buzzing because the reception was all crackly
12. Boiling water. Bubble bubble
13. The screech of chairs being pulled out and being moved about
14. Crashes from the kitchen as chefs and waitresses prepared food (or dropped the cutlery at one point)
15. The sound of cutlery on plates and cups being placed on tables
16. The sound of my friends jaw clicking as she chewed on some sausage- and whatever else it was that needed chewing – the whole breakfast effectively
17. The sound of coffee machines and other such food machines like microwaves whirring, beeping and buzzing and goodness knows what else
18. The weather outside, wind and leaves scuttling along the floor
19. The traffic roaring past
20. Tyres screeching
21. One car outside has a broken fan belt because I can hear it squeaking and wailing
22. I could hear another car engine that would pop every time it accelerated. Either a fabulous engine- or they have a good straight through exhaust- or a hole in their exhaust that has ripped their flexi pipe. I am no expert; it's just what it sounded like
23. Another car has bad breaks because every time they slow down there is a long squeak and tap
24. The traffic lights beeping
25. The blood pumping round my body

26. The sound of my ear drum. It sounded like there was a crackle of fire in my ear because I had an ear infection and the ear wax is shifting (hmmm..... Nice) I can hear it and yes it is gross
27. The sound of me eating
28. A big dog growling at a small dog. I couldn't see the dogs but I could tell by the sound, depth and loudness of the different types of barks as to which one was being victimised and the probability of it being a smaller dog
29. Footsteps and different types of shoes. I can often tell the shoe in which the person is wearing as they walk past without looking at their feet. Just by merely listening to the sounds their shoes make
30. The squeal of the air conditioning shrieking in the corner
31. The sounds of the electricity burring through the room.

Most people in the cafe are able to concentrate on the conversation they are having and block out back ground noises. Yes, they can hear all of the other sounds, but they are choosing not to concentrate or listen to them. Imagine being me, and not always being able to block out those irrelevant background noises. Trust me; it makes it hard to concentrate on what is important.

This is a quote from my wonderful dad which I think summarises the concept perfectly.

"Listening means you chose to listen to something, hearing means you chose not to listen to it-it becomes back ground noise"

I believe many people with Asperger's suffer with similar sense of hearing. I believe this is one of the main reasons why people with Asperger's find themselves in the lower sets of learning at school. Not because of their intelligence levels, but because they find it hard to concentrate on what the teacher is saying, due to being un able to back stream irrelevant noises and getting heavily distracted.

Sensory overloads – What happens to my sense of hearing?
When I go into sensory overload, it seems like the volume has been turned up. The noises are empathised and louder than normal and some noises feel like they are quite literally clawing at my ear drums from the inside. It is nasty. I would be forced to try and block out all of the noise because it is simply too much for me to bear. After a few minutes I start to hear less and less, to

the point where I hear nothing at all. Obviously this is not a good thing. The reason I can't hear anything is usually because I feel so dizzy and I am going to pass out, or I'm starting to shutdown from the pressure of overloads. That is rather scary and so sometimes I have panic attacks and would start breathing funnily and heavily. As the agitation continues I begin to react physically. I start either blocking my ears; slapping my ears and then I bury my head in my arms. Normally, by doing this, the sensory overload will pass and I can relax.

The sense of speech

Apparently I speak very well, but, I have found that a lot of people with a disability on the Autistic spectrum can find it difficult to talk. Even though people say I speak well, I get my words mixed up, I say things that would appear to be strange to others and would mix up the past and present tense. I am especially prone to this when I am tired. I end up stuttering and slurring over my words – honestly sometimes it sounds like I have had one or two alcoholic drinks. I tend to put emphasise on the wrong word which can alarm a few people as I have unwittingly changed the meaning of the whole sentence. But to me, I am just talking.

The sense of smell

I have a rather amusing sense of smell, a friend once called me 'a typical pregnant lady.' This is because I smell everything in more depth than most people and apparently that is similar to that of a pregnant woman. As I have never been pregnant, I can't really confirm if my friend's statement is accurate. So yeah, basically I smell a lot of scents. This is rarely problematic unless the person is ill, let me tell you why.

I can often smell when someone is ill. Smelling illnesses, I'm being serious. I know it sounds bizarre and please don't question how this is possible, because I have less than no idea on how I do it. Yet, sometimes I can smell if someone is ill. Some people when they are really ill smell of wet dogs, a wet dog that has not been washed (no offence if you are ill right now- usually no one else notices such smells so don't get self conscious, it's just me I'm sure). I have found it is usually when the person has a chesty cough. It's a smell that clings to the clothes like smoke from cigarettes. I hate to say it, but when I can smell this on a person, I feel an instant surge of sickness whirl up with in me. I start coughing and feeling ill. Obviously people often have bad breath when they have a sore throat but it's not that smell. Yes it is strange and it is probably just in my imagination, who knows, but this sense of smell is so strong it gives me a physical reaction.

When I was at school, there was a girl in one of my classes who was always ill. She used to sit in front of me, sneezing and coughing for the whole lesson. Her distinctive wet dog smell would flow back towards me, engulfing me like a cloud of smoke. I don't wish to sound horrid, but all I could think when sat behind her was 'what a horrible wet dog smell'.

Sensory over load – What happens to my sense of smell
When I have a sensory overload usually my sense of smell is stronger than usual. I would pick up on a few smells that don't mix nicely together, sometimes making me sneeze or feel ill. This is just another thing that distracts me from what I am meant to be doing.

Dealing with sensory overloads – Controlling sensory input, with sensory output
I would now like to tell you a story, about how, after a hard day of sensory over loads, I try to manage my emotions. I try to control my negative feelings, created by sensory input, by creating positive sensory output. I do this by dancing, exercising and behaving crazily and being very hyper. At stressful times, it was not unknown for me to go to the gym everyday and exercise for hours on end, or go swimming in the sea every evening... you see, the rage from the day's anxieties, quite literally make me feel so worked up, so wired that my very veins seem to shake with negative spirits – which is why it is understandable that to cope with such panics is very difficult for those with troubles expressing or communicating. It is so difficult, that I end up with lots of energy that has to be safely released. So I let the energy be released through hyperactivity, exercise and dancing in a safe haven or place.

Finding my peace – On my roof top story
I am always so tranquil when able to relax upon my roof top at home. I often climb out there for a moment, after a hard, tiresome day to try and recollect what remains of my rapidly disappearing sanity. This time, the day had been long, difficult and filled with misunderstandings and hardships that I had no control over. The frustration of all sensory input built up, and I regret to say that I found it difficult to cope. So in this example, it was a late beautiful summer's night. It was late, gone 11, and finally the day was slowly celebrating its masterpiece of sunset glory. I gazed at the sky, drenched in the dutiful last bouts of purple

and rosy shades, beckoned by the late day's sunset. As I watched, the frenzy from the day's unjustifications just seemed to melt away. Indeed, along with my wardrobe (As a child, this was a favourite haven of rest, obviously I have grown up since then), Glastonbury festival and my bedroom, my garden roof top is my safe haven where I can escape the nastiness of day to day life. The sky, mingled purple and pink, held fascinating cloud formations, stars twinkling above my head, entire constellations smiling at me in their specialised, entirely captivating, beauty. I could gaze for hours upon the never ending opportunities of our universe surrounding us. I realise that although, life with A.S is difficult (although I don't know how hard because I don't know any different) I can find peace within a struggle, you see, when there is a struggle there is hope for improvement, and when there is confusion or complexities in life there is also lots of room for hope and wisdom to be learnt... Good changes that can be made. For, the complexities our universe betrays, including Asperger's and differences within people, renders us all blubbing like new born babies, striving for the first embrace of their loving mother's breast. As humans, we are all desperately trying to understand the unknown, but there is still little in our world we understand – just like a new born. Yet we have still learnt so much, and are able to learn so much more, about our universe and the things we know little about. I think, despite our incredible developments, none of us could truly experience or ever understand the true depths of our universe.... or indeed, understanding the true depths of a disability. The thought makes me feel at harmony, as I know there is no need to worry. Likewise, Asperger's, on the most part, can never be fully understood by those without such a disability. However, those with Asperger's can be understood by those who know us well, the disability itself, the reasoning behind why we find such things difficult, may always remain a mystery; even to those with the disability. We just have to accept our hardships, and grin, and bare it. When life is complicated or stressful, just imagine how little we are in the greater scheme of things, yes we are all important, disability or not, but such complexities with which we don't understand about our world and universe are both unique, scary and beautiful – just like us. Sometimes, the things we find difficult (like a disability) can walk hand in hand, snug as a glove, with the very asset that people love most about us. Complicated does not always have to be bad. Our complexities can make us kind, good natured people.

Anyway, when I start getting stressed, I tend to go on my roof to be reminded of this therapeutic thought; like I did in this scenario I was writing before I got heavily distracted. It was so peaceful outside- the breeze was fresh, cold on my cheeks, the darkness glimmering with specs of light from houses. It was lovely. The rain, which was oddly distinct in its flavouring, drizzled pleasantly onto my face and I smiled. I relaxed like this for about a minute. Breathing the night scents, allowing the air to pass through my lungs and listening to the calm whistling distribution of carbon dioxide pass through my lips, allowing the night to sooth my frazzled (from sensory overloads) nerves. I could not sit still; I was far to energised from the sensory input making me jittery and on edge. The feelings of unjust raging through my system always made me quite hyper, in order to cope with everything (You know what I say, when sensory input is stressful, which it is, always, you control sensory input with sensory output, which often comes out as behaviour- hyperactivity, or 'lashing out'). I tend to get hyper. To quell my ever exceeding thirst to jump about, I put my head phones in my ears to play my favourite songs. The music started playing and at once, I felt that much better, I started dancing, on my roof top, in the middle of the night. The music thumping through my very soul, made me feel so alive with the jingles that reverberated through my very bones. I danced and I twirled, the world I could see while I span, was also spinning with me, in one beautiful stripe of colour. Patterned light sources spinning around me in long ribbon like streamers that, as I spun in circles, appeared to wrap around me and engulf me in dancing's wonderful charm. I spun round in circles, focussing on a chimney in the distance every time I spun round to tire myself from nausea...... Dancing and relaxing up there in the shade of night, helps quell many of my negative emotions, likewise, so does dancing freely to music. Such a combination is close to perfect when enjoyed together. I am so at ease when I can relax on my roof top, the scene, although not so therapeutic by day, is deliciously beautiful when the dark of night takes my garden under its respectful wing.

Everyone is different, while I go hyper and dance about, other people with Asperger's, may not be able to cope with sensory input so well. Some people with Asperger's may lash out in acts of aggression. Although such behaviour can be difficult, tiresome and frustrating, you have to remember it is not always the person's fault. It is the disability causing the behaviour, and certainly not the other way round. Lashing out like this, is simply just a way of surviving in a world of chaos and misunderstood frustrations. People with Asperger's find communication very difficult, so expressing themselves when dealing with the trials of sensory overloads is extremely difficult, near to impossible. Even though aggression should not be tolerated, I understand how sometimes, this is the only way someone with an Autistic spectrum disorder, or disability, can express themselves during such misunderstood and extremely difficult times. I am lucky that I have learnt to cope with my sensory overloads in a calm and controlled manner. Although I do find any excuse to retreat into my furry blankets and just shut the world and my problems out with a good book, most of the time, I allow my 'whirl-wind' antics from my childhood to take control of my behaviour, and I dance… dance… dance!

Sensory Overloads, Meltdowns and Shutdowns

I have noticed that people often think that meltdowns and sensory overloads are the same thing. Well to me, they are not. I get sensory overloads, which is when I can't cope with any of my senses, and all my senses become so clear that it is impossible to think; everything gets too loud, too detailed and too bright to look at, too smelly, too itchy or rough to the touch. Yet it's only when my sensory overloads get too much to cope with that I have meltdowns. For instance, a sensory overload, will become a meltdown if I am problem solving, trying to do something, multi tasking, coping with change in routine or coping with unexpected stresses. So if I'm having a sensory overload (but I also have to concentrate on doing something else, like problem solving even) something as simple as working out how to make room in a dish washer for a dirty plate causes a meltdown because my brain can't multi task thinking strategies, and because I can't back stream irrelevant information. I become desperate to try and rid myself of the alarming sense of panic that rises within me as a result of sensory overload, turned meltdown.

A lot of people have said that I don't often look like I had many meltdowns, but this is merely because I show it in a different way. When I have meltdowns, all of my difficulties became impossible, and I simply become unable to do anything at all. Problem solving, listening, understanding, communicating, everything becomes impossible to cope with. I end up shaking to the point of finding it hard to stand, clicking my fingers and humming (screeching when it is a really bad meltdown, depending on how difficult the problem solving is) and when I really can't cope I have a complete meltdown which looks like a tantrum, where I can't look or cope with anyone for that moment.

At school, meltdowns happened a lot more than I care to remember, and the only way to cope was to block my senses, and the things that were too much, and the main way I could do that, was through drawing, in a desperate attempt to control sensory input with sensory output.

The difference between a meltdown and a tantrum
Meltdowns can look like tantrums, but they are not tantrums at all; I often screw my eyes, block my ears, make loud noises, stamp my feet and screech loudly. Sometimes I hit myself on the forehead, it just happens and I have no control over it. Often it's the only way I can cope with the mayhem of the worlds in my surroundings. Here are a few vital things that I feel are important for anyone to know in regards to recognising the difference in general cases. Remember I am no expert, this information is formed merely from personal, and countless years of work experience in the matter:

Tantrum
1. **A tantrum is only created to get something or in protest of not getting what they want,** (for instance protesting for being told "no", or "stop")
2. **Someone is in control of their actions while having a tantrum, and will not hurt themselves in the process of trying to get what they want** (or at the least very rarely hurt themselves, remember all people are different)
3. **Usually, someone having a tantrum would behave badly in short bursts because they would occasionally look up to see if the person at whom they are throwing a tantrum is watching them or giving in to their negative behaviour** (giving in to their behaviour by getting them

what they want or saying yes to what they previously said no to). Someone throwing a tantrum may shout, scream, fake cry and often they may pause every now and again, which also proves that they are in control of their actions and able to stop if they really wanted/had to.

Meltdown

1. **A meltdown is not 'created' or even a choice**. A meltdown is not at all deliberate, so certainly not 'created' to get something
2. **Someone having a meltdown has no control over their actions**, and may start hurting themselves. Although it is both distressing, harmful and should be controlled safely, they are simply communicating something is wrong, the very last way they know how to
3. **Someone having a meltdown will usually avoid all contact with others**, including eye, and physical contact. Someone having a meltdown would often screech loudly for long periods of time (or make a noise that has the possibility to drown out all other noises) they are unlikely to stop unless something changes; that change could be a change in sensory stimuli, they could be removed from previous complication and taken somewhere calmer or quieter, when senses had been replaced with 'quieter' beams or they may stop out of sheer exhaustion. Someone having a meltdown is unlikely to stop because they have received anything, even food or drink, you won't often see a pause in a meltdown because it is usually impossible for someone experiencing the chaos of a meltdown to pause.
4. **Meltdowns can often consist of physical excursion too, perhaps continued motion, stamping of feet, rocking or swinging of arms**, this is usually to vent out distressed energies that has been building from the sensory overload, and to overload the other senses by attempting to focus on just one continued motion. You would often see someone having a meltdown continuously repeating one exaggerated motion, rocking backwards and forwards is a good one to look out for. This sort of behaviour is often to try and distract their attention from the other offending senses, by overloading themselves with just one sense, which is better than being overloaded with a million senses, and is then easier to get back to their 'normal' functioning states.

"Stop throwing that tantrum"

I was out walking along the quay not so long ago, it had been a boiling hot day, noisy and very busy with lots of people. It was very pleasant, although I remember at the time how easily I could have had a meltdown of all the senses if I was pressured to do anything or problem solve. Sure enough, as I walked, I had come across a young boy who looked about 11, who clearly to me was having a compete meltdown of all the senses. He was kicking, stamping his feet, screeching and ferociously hitting himself in the face. His carer was there professionally taking care of him. One lady walked past the boy and his carer, rolling her eyes with a look of disgust on her wrinkled face and snarled "stop throwing that tantrum you little brat" as she stalked passed the boy and his carer. I could hardly believe my ears. It was clear to me the boy was having a meltdown which was not his fault. I could not help it, I could not witness unjust behaviour like that, so I walked straight up to this stranger (well, I'll admit that I had to jog to keep up with her quick stride) and I tapped her on her shoulder. My heart was in my mouth, as she turned to glare at me, I am almost certain my heart stopped with Anxiety. Shakily, I said to the lady that this boy she just judged to be a brat clearly has special needs which are not his fault. I then went on to tell her how he was not throwing a tantrum and why. I explained to her the key signs of a tantrum.

"This boy is not throwing a tantrum; to me he is clearly having a meltdown. I know this because I know the difference and I also have a disability and experience the same meltdowns. Also I can assure you meltdowns like this are not deliberate, unlike a tantrum which is entirely deliberate" I said.

The lady looked at me with a glare, as if to say 'how dare you attempt to talk to me about this issue, girl!' My adrenalin kicked in as the look in her eyes made my legs quake with nerves, I steadily continued before I lost my nerve, my voice catching with intense emotional tension

"A tantrum is only created in order to get something, or in protest of not getting their own way. So someone having a tantrum is completely in control if their actions at all times and will not hurt themselves in the process of the tantrum. Whereas someone having a meltdown has no control over their actions or if they are hurting themselves. Does it look like the boy is hurting himself, to you?"

I asked the lady, who was staring at me in bewildered annoyance and didn't even glance at the boy before she snapped at me

"Well of course he's hurting himself, you stupid fool"

I let her nasty comment slide as I continued to explain in a calm manner.

"Yes I can see that, its further proof he is having a non deliberate meltdown and not a tantrum as you put it".

I said slowly, the lady was now staring at me, eyes challenging and darting with annoyance, daring me to continue, so I did.

"Secondly someone having a tantrum will stop as soon as they get their own way and will pause every now and again to see if their tantrum is succeeding in getting them their own way or not. Does it look like the boy is pausing to look at his carer to see if his 'tantrum' is working?"

The lady pursed her lip, expression stony and took a big breath, as if to calm her from shouting at me, and looked at the boy who was now thrashing about in his carers arms, completely avoiding eye contact and not once pausing. The lady shook her head and I smiled

"Does it look like he is stopping his behaviour because his carer has just given him a soft blanket?"

The lady pursed her lips, her eyes staring at me stony and cold. She glanced over at the boy, and shook her head.

"No it doesn't, does it?"

I ventured, wanting her to admit it herself, as the information might sink in more if she admitted it out loud. The lady hesitated as she looked at the boy again and then quietly agreed with my statement, now looking at her feet, sighing. A strange look passed across her face making it suspiciously look like she had just passed wind, although I suspect she was merely frustrated at being so obviously proved wrong. I continued

"This is because someone having a meltdown cannot stop having a meltdown – even if they have been given a favourite soft blanket. A meltdown is not created to get something, a meltdown happens purely because it is the last course of action to take when a sensory overload becomes too much to cope with."

The lady looked over at the boy again; who was still thrashing about, but less violently now, with his carer stroking his soft blanket on his arm as she loudly sung a lullaby as she hugged him close.

"The only thing that will succeed to quell a meltdown is to remove previous complications and sensory stimuli or let the meltdown safely run its course until exhaustion takes its toll. This is why the carer is singing to the boy while sitting on the floor with him and protectively hugging him close. A meltdown does not stop just because the boy is getting something his own way, because a meltdown did not happen with a purpose".

I finished with a smile, the lady stiffly nodded, not meeting my gaze. She looked thoroughly guilty and ashamed of herself; oh how quickly her temper had subsided.

"In future, when you see someone who you think is having a tantrum, please have compassion and remember the difference between a tantrum and a meltdown before you judge. It's not the boy's fault and his behaviour is not intentional and it is certainly not justified or fair for you to make a judgement like that when you clearly know little of the situation".

As I explained this, her face had first clouded with anger, dismissal then confusion, understanding and guilt. With shame plastered upon her face, she admitted that she had been a judgemental hag, (those are her words, not mine) and immediately went over to apologise to the boy and his carer for her harsh words. Although the boy did not notice, as his eyes were tightly shut, and he was clapping his hands together and humming to himself, a lot less aggressive now. The carer was certainly very appreciative and later thanked me when the boy was calmer for standing up for him. The lady then came back to me, and apologetically asked me to explain, if I could and if I had the time, what a meltdown was and what caused them. So I did, we sat down on a splintered bench overlooking the boats docked at the quay, and discussed key areas of what causes meltdowns. I explained as much as I could and eventually we parted to go our separate ways with her carrying my business card snug in the confinements of her purse, vowing she would participate in Autism training to better her understanding for future purposes, and also encourage her husband, family and friends to do so also, as her cousin in law had Autism. I call that, a successful day.

A meltdown is not a tantrum; and if you see someone having a meltdown please don't judge or stare. If you are curious and want to learn more, ask polite and non judgmental or non offensive questions when the situation is better (after the meltdown has been resolved, rather than during!). Meltdowns are out of my control and when they happen there is little I can do to stop them aside from someone calming me down, or removing myself from stressful circumstances. I believe it's the same for other people on the Autistic spectrum too, and even people with other difficulties. I'm hoping that society will stop judging like this woman had. The only way to make meltdowns easier is for those surrounding us to understand and not judge. There's nothing worse than having a meltdown and having some nasty judgemental person make some unpleasant remark about your behaviour.

When you next see someone behaving like this (having a meltdown) in the street please remember the difference between a tantrum and a meltdown. The sooner society remembers the difference and learns compassion and not to judge, the better and easier it will be to cope when meltdowns arise.

Shutdowns – Becoming Bambi

Today, something bizarre happened to me, something that made my Autism disability so much harder to deal with.

I woke up from a nightmare, to find myself transported into a different type of scary reality. I found myself transformed into something I like to call "Bambi". I woke up and dizziness swam within my head and I could hardly open my eyes to my chaotic surroundings. I tried to get out of bed, and was plagued with such an intense pain, agony really, that struck every part of my body, so much so that I couldn't move. Eventually I manage to stand up, and my legs wobbled, and gave away as if I was Bambi skating on Ice.

Pain crashed through me with every step, my legs cramped in agony, my toes feeling like they were curling around each other, weakness threatening to overwhelm me; and believe me, I frequently stumbled and fell over – it was as if my leg were made of jelly. I start to shun myself for leaving my walking stick down stairs... when will I remember that my usually hidden disability can turn physical like this, at a moment's notice?

Autism effects every second of my life, but when I'm Bambi... I lose all my usual ability, and everything becomes near impossible to cope with, or do... becoming Bambi is never easy...

I realize too late that my head was surging with energy; migraine pain crushing my brain, making me feel like my brain was encased in a cage of spikes. I manage to stumble to the bathroom, my surroundings swimming, furniture moving, floor tripping me up, and the pain, the dizziness, flowed through me. My brain misted with an un clearable fog, making it impossible to make simple 'obvious' connections, or problem solve. Such as realizing I need to answer my phone when I hear it ring. Or for instance when I washed my hands in the sink, I didn't realize that water was rushing out the pipe below the sink, and I didn't realize my legs and feet getting wet, means I need to turn the tap off and move... Not only that, but I was so ill, I hadn't even made the connection that my feet were wet, or that the crashing water sound, was actually water flowing out the pipe... We had a Plumber in, tools everywhere on the floor, the broken pipe on display in front of me, but I still didn't make the connection as to what this all meant, or even notice it at all. Autism makes it hard to make connections or problem solve on a good day, but on days like today, it's almost impossible.

My mum comes in, having heard the water, and tidies up whilst I lean, breathing heavy against the wall, unable to move, unable to make the connection that I should help, or at least offer. Eyes squeezed shut from the mass of patterns in front of me, my 'Bambi' legs quaking beneath me. She asks me if I want toast or cereal for breakfast, and in my head I thought, toast, because trying to eat cereal like this, while I was so wobbly and Bambi like, would be too difficult, and would spell disaster. I opened my mouth, desperately trying to form the words, but to no avail. My mum watches, concerned, patient, she's trying to help me, why can't I show my gratitude and answer her? "Thank you, I would really like some Toast, please'. My desperation and frustration bubbles up, I know the answer, why can't I get my words out? What's happening to me?! Eventually I can't even think about answering her, my hand flies to my head and I hit myself once, hard, then I'm too exhausted to even do that anymore, and I start crying.

In fact, anyone asking me a question when I'm like this, will witness me hitting my head in frustration at not understanding what they mean, and not being able to answer them; even if I know the answer. I open my mouth and stutter, dribbling, babbling worthless sounds, desperately trying to portray what I mean, but my shutdown, my exhaustion, the pain, everything, is too strong... I can't control it, no matter how hard I try.

It's a little scary to be honest, to suddenly have everything about you change at a moment's notice.

To think yesterday I had delivered a workshop, and stood up on stage and delivered a speech to 450 people; I felt on top of the world. There was a standing ovation. People asked for autographs. I had been on cloud nine; it had been incredible... What happened to that person? Where was the confident, able bodied person, today?

Overnight, everything about me, completely changed... and it was horrible.

You see, I was riding an Autism Shutdown, an Autism Shutdown that affected me for 3 days straight before some of the pain went away, and my abilities started coming back. This is when my hidden disability becomes very physical, and noticeable, indeed.

What is an Autism Shutdown?
Although I said this change was bizarre, it's actually incredibly common. An Autism shutdown means that your body, and your brain's usual abilities, literally shutdown. Everything I can usually do, I can't. Every difficulty I usually have as a result of my Autism is enhanced to the degree of being impossible to cope with. Shutdowns are a result of unresolved stressful circumstances, usually things that are completely out of control, such as school, work or college... or indeed every day 'un stressful' life. Shutdowns are a type of overload, and even though the two are very different, a Shutdown is also a type of Meltdown. Usually an overload comes first, followed by a Meltdown and then / or a Shutdown. I usually don't get Meltdowns, usually its a Shutdown that grip me, and make my disability hard.

So, what is the difference between an Autism Meltdown and an Autism Shutdown?
I guess the difference is that a meltdown is an uncontrollable physical reaction against an injustice (change of routine, dishonesty, overload or stress), certainly not a fault to be corrected or a tantrum, where as a Shutdown is being completely unable to do anything at all, including physical actions

and speech; unable to think, cope or do anything at all to any usual ability – certainly nothing physical. Someone suffering with an Autism Shutdown often hide themselves somewhere compact, peaceful (I always hid in my wardrobe or out on my roof top – not recommended!) or they lie on the floor; they avoid having their eyes open, make no noise, and don't move, because they are far too over loaded, and exhausted, for any of that. They sit in complete silence, maybe gently rocking, and maybe crying, and unable to stop. Just like an old, over worked computer, someone suffering with consistent stresses will eventually crash, and shut down. Typically, due to how stressful ordinary life with an Autistic disorder is, Shutdowns are quite common, although every person displays differently, not everyone get pains that prevents them from walking, for instance, I am just describing how it affects me, and me alone.

Sensory friendly places

I believe it is not fair that there are barriers for some people with disabilities from accessing certain facilities because of their sensory issues. Certain places have (what I like to call) 'sensory overload barriers'; and consequently some people with disabilities may avoid accessing these places. These places are supposed to be fun for everyone, so I think they should accommodate everyone. Wheel chair ramps are an example of how we try to accommodate people with physical disabilities, so why not do something to make it accessible for people with sensory difficulties? Simply minimising patterns and bright colours would really help.

These things need to be tackled and changed. I think there should be a sensory friendly bowling alley, games arcade and children's centres (the kind with ball ponds and slides) etc in every town. For people without these types of sensory issues, having bright colours and patterns is great. However, for people with sensory issues, less patterns, 'quieter' and lighter colours such as pastels would be preferred. That way the chance of having a sensory overload is weakened and everybody can enjoy the facilities.

I love the fact that change has already started in our society to make town centres more accessible for people with disabilities. Things like 'The Safe Places' scheme which I am helping to develop in Bournemouth and my mini project of making Bournemouth Sea Front more accessible for young people with disabilities.

I think it is brilliant because various cinemas have started having Autistic screenings, which are sensory friendly. I think it's fabulous that the needs of thousands of young people on the Autistic spectrum are finally being met. However I strongly believe more needs to be done. It would be very easy to change the carpet in a Bowling alley to something more neutral. Such a small change would have a massive positive impact for people like me.

Rigid Routines

One of the difficulties, that comes with having a disability on the Autistic spectrum is the desire for routines and for things to remain the same. The reason why has clouded my thoughts and perceptions of what my disability means for many years. After years of my thoughts and theories being shrouded in doubt and confusion, I think I have finally found myself an answer. I shall start with a little explanation of why routines are a necessary part of daily life, and why they are important to me.

Routines are absolutely paramount in the everyday life of someone with A.S.D, and I am certainly no exception. I have a routine for absolutely everything, literally. Right down to what I have to do to emotionally and physically prepare myself to see someone, regardless of who, to what I have to do before, during and after I leave my bedroom (let alone house!). If any part of my routine is disturbed, distracted or interrupted by anything, then I have to start my routine again (regardless of how close to finishing). This is because I get so panicky that I won't be able to complete what I know is correct and the truth. Routines have been practised to perfection therefore I know that the routines I practise are the best I can do. Why change something that works so well?

People with A.S.D, find great comfort in the truth and things that are correct. This is why routines are so important, because the person with A.S.D knows their routines to be correct and true. This also means that everything outside of the routine has the potential to be incorrect or wrong. If something interrupts the correct routine, the routine has to start again, because the interruption has made the routine incorrect.

This obsession with truth and doing things the same way, the right way, is because not only do those with A.S.D find the facts and correct realities comforting but the truth helps those with A.S.D learn what reality and truth really is. The patterns those with A.S.D form, from seeking the truth in reality, actually help to establish and understand the unwritten rules and technicalities of their surroundings. Such rules that the patterns from routines help to understand are the same rules that those without disabilities take for granted and already understand without trying as much. So much of life is misunderstood that we desperately seek the truth wherever we go, routines are vital to teach us how to behave and understand what we see in the world around us. This is why we are obsessed with routines and have to follow correct routines like the law. This is why any change in routine or interrupting routines is greeted with such frustrations or horror. The change throws us out the comfort zone so much that there is no truth or reality that can be understood anymore and there is nothing we can do about it to regain that control. It's nice to be right for a change and we stick to being right within our routines as much as humanly possible.

The consequences of any changes in routines are actually very simple. Here is a list of general reactions

1. Crying
2. Panic attacks / irritability
3. Hiding / refusal to participate / running away from the situation
4. Inability to concentrate, or do things (anything) to usual ability
5. Frequent trips to the toilet – due to tummy pain and sickness

The person will become unable to continue doing anything to their usual ability without first completing their routine. If a routine is compromised, any previous ability to do anything will go out the window. For example, a teacher thinks that a child (who has A.S.D) in their school should take private tutorial lessons in mathematics during their lunch break because the child is really good at maths. The teacher finds the child during their lunch break one day and explains to the child that a maths tutorial has been arranged and that the child has to leave for their first tutorial now. To be honest, that's bad enough to cope with, and usually that would result in crying, have panic attacks, absolute refusal to do as the teachers says (probably resulting in a detention) or running away. However, if the teacher managed to reach the location of private maths tutorial with the child, then the change would still negatively affect what has to happen. The child would be in such a state of panic and angst that they would hardly be able to concentrate or remember anything at all. No matter how clever the child is, no matter how clear their memory usually is, the panic and untruth of change in routine clouds over all other possible thought processes and leaves no room for anything else. Therefore changing routine for the sake of improvements is entirely counterproductive. While changes in routines are sometimes necessary, it is important that this change is approached with great care and consideration. Only then will the person with A.S.D be able to accept the change and possibly form a new routine. Ideally the teacher in the above example would have approached the idea with the child's parents or carers, so they could talk to the child about the potential change. The child would not start the new maths tutorial until the following week, so that the child has time to understand why the change is occurring and how to best cope with the new routine. Important things to consider would be how to get to the new tutorial, what time it finishes and begins, who will be teaching, is the tutor aware of the child's disability, what the child needs to bring, an overview of what will happen during the tutorial and what is expected, what the child does after the tutorial. I know it is a lot of things to take into consideration, but it is entirely necessary if the child is to positively benefit from the situation.

As I mentioned before, I have routines for everything. This includes

1. Getting dressed
2. Before, during and after shower
3. Cleaning my teeth
4. Applying crèmes to face and body
5. How I consider making food and how I make food
6. How I exercise
7. Before I leave the house
8. How I get the bus or transport
9. How I purchase something from the shop
10. Before bedtime

I understand some people have routines that may be similar to this, but my routine are completely rigid and have to be followed exactly. The list of routines I have is endless and range from 'normal' to bizarre. Here is a list of the more bizarre routines I follow

1. How to answer the phone or make a phone call
2. How to emotionally and physically prepare myself to see someone/a group of people
3. How to emotionally prepare myself to leave the house
4. How to handle, and pass a knife or pair of scissors to somebody

5. How to fold anything
6. How to talk and breathe at the same time
7. How to answer the door
8. How to answer a question
9. How to have a conversation with any visual or noise distractions
10. Routines for my routines

While routines are essential for somebody with A.S.D, in the 'real' world change is sometimes unavoidable and constant. So learning to cope with these changes are extremely important. This is why the appropriate support is key.

I have had many situations where a change in routine has become disastrous. It has ruined my whole day and even affected me negatively for the rest of the week. Not only does this affect me, but it also impacts the people around me, for example my family, friends and teachers. As I have got older and the people around me have become more educated and experienced in the matters of A.S.D, such disasters are less frequent. The only reason I can better cope with change in routines, is because the people around me are much more understanding and considerate of my disability.

Countless Collections and Counting...

It is a common stereotype for people with A.S.D to be obsessive over a specialist topic and to have collections, and I am no exception. I love collecting things, and I really am quite obsessed by it.

I believe that people with A.S.D have collections to do with their specialist topics simply as an escape from the world of confusion in their wake; an escape to something that they understand, something they like and prefer. The world of their collections simply means they are safe, free to communicate how they wish to; you may find that some people with A.S.D only know how to talk 'facts' about their specialist topic or collections. Indeed it's how they know to talk, something they are confident to talk about, and so they communicate that way. I find this quite admirable really. In their little world of collections there is no confusion, no change, no difficulty; just their reliable safe world of their favourite topics and everything they understand about it. Sometimes, when people are confusing and life is tough to understand, (which it is for everyone; but dare I say even more so for those with A.S.D coping with the hourly overloads of seemingly 'unstressful' life) it can really make you try anything just to make this crazy life easier. So it's understandable that obsession with anything, including obsessive collections, kicks in.

I used to collect literally anything and everything. Seriously, if I was asked what the most bizarre thing I have collected – I would honestly have a hard time choosing between the weird and wonderful things I used to collect. Usually, collections are to do with the person's specialist topic. Well this is rather amusing, as although I had an extensive collection about Egyptology, I used to have many other collections as well.

I collected Snoopys, Bratz Dolls, Wombles, Beanie Babies and many other cuddly toys. I collected Micro Machines (small cars) and those little racing tracks where you wind a handle and the cars would zoom round the track. I loved it.

I am very bad at throwing things away – I have a habit of keeping everything that I don't need, in the weird belief that I will one day need it (I'm not a 'hoarder' – I have been checked over by a specialist). At the moment I have a collection of wallpaper scraps (different patterns and all sorts of colours) under the impression that I will use them for an art piece. In fact all of my weird collections I have nowadays are to do with me thinking I can create something arty out of it later. I currently have rubbish collections of:

1. Wall paper
2. Materials – soft, rough, leather patterned, fluffy anything
3. Any random pretty things. Flower shaped decoration
4. Beads
5. Paper clips – different patterns
6. Marbles – really nice ones. I got them when I was really young from Poole pottery and they really are beautiful
7. Papier Mache balls which are beautiful
8. Petri dishes – filled with fake 'disease cells'
9. Anything at all I can use for some arty project
10. Really old paint tubes, tubes of paint that have dried out

I am certain I can use all the above to create art pieces one day.

I collected foreign money, which started from my collection of Egyptian money (I will tell you about Egypt later). I have no idea how much I have, but I still have that collection gathering dust somewhere.

I had bottles of sand which I filled up from the beach. I live minutes from the sea so consequently I spent a lot of time at the beach and very quickly became a water baby. As you can imagine all of this time spent at the beach meant I have collected a lot of sand.

Specialist Subjects

If you walked into my house you would have easily guessed what my specialist topics were. Honestly, they are absolutely everywhere. This is because my parents did a wonderful job in encouraging me to learn about my specialist topic. Even now, once a topic has piqued my intellectual curiosity there is little I can do to hinder myself from researching it. For this reason I have done extensive research into the multiplication of cancer cells, small pox and influenza. I now know how the cells spread, what the cells are called and how the whole process works. My other random favourite is the constellation of Gemini (Geminorum).

I would like to tell you a little bit about my specialist topics as a child.

When I was about 4-6 years old, I used to love history, including Greek Mythology, Romans and pillars. My goodness did I love pillars? I loved pillars!

Whenever my family and I were driving in the car, they were forever pointing out pillars to me. I would sit there in the car and stare at the pillars taking in every grain of detail. I would try to draw a picture in my mind's eye so I could draw it when I got back (hooray for photographic memory). I would stare at the pillars with intense concentration until we drove away and until the pillars became small specs in the distance. I loved it because it reminded me of what I had learnt about Roman times; and every time I saw pillars I would imagine all the people surrounding the pillars dressed in Togas, some females wearing Bulla's and other Roman attire. I would imagine old buildings, a busy market place filled with animals and dusty roads. My family had no idea why I loved pillars and what I was imagining when I saw these pillars. This is because I had difficulty communicating my thoughts. Despite this they still took an interest in my bizarre love for pillars. Whoever says kids with Asperger's don't have any imagination I think they're quite wrong- I certainly have a brilliant imagination and I think many others do too. Anyway, back to pillars and specialist topics.

My fascination with Romans and Roman pillars hardly holds a candle against my main fascination as a child... Egyptology.

When I was 6-9 years old I was fascinated by it. Every time someone visited Egypt I would ask them to come home with some Egyptian money for me to keep, some sand and anything else as a souvenir of their journey. I used to own every sculpture, every book, every figurine and every scroll. I had everything I wanted with relation to Egyptology.

It was wonderful. My family were shocked at how much I knew, yet I still don't believe I had a great understanding of Egypt. For example, I couldn't tell you specific dates and events, but because I was very interested in their way of life, I could tell you a lot about their day to day life and belief systems.

I learnt to read and write Hieroglyphics when I was about 7/8 years old. I used to write them regularly covering bits of paper with my 'writing' although it was more likely to be rambles and made little or no sense. At the old age of 22 I still found myself writing in 'Hieroglyphics' like I did when I was 8. All the memories of my fascination came flooding back to me and I can remember what each letter means surprisingly quickly. So it seems that specialists topics never disappear entirely, I think it is like love, once you love something (or someone) for the first time you may never forget your first love.

On that note I absolutely must show you the extent of this slightly crazy obsession. Here is a picture as an example of my writing (hieroglyphics) from when I was 9.

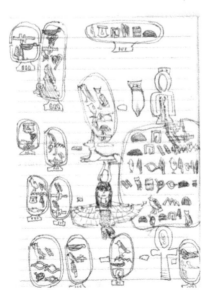

Every specialist topic is different. If you know someone with Asperger's, chances are you know what their topic is. It can be anything that holds a fascination to the person, such as cars, science, rocks and stones, animals, art, the earth, geography, diseases etc. A fascination can be so strong that people with Asperger's may only want to think, talk and do things that are related to their specialist topic. The specialist topics can be so consuming that the person quickly develops a wide knowledge of their subject, and they can relay it relentlessly onto anyone who cares to listen. Some call people with Asperger's 'walking encyclopaedias' for a reason, you know. As bizarre as it sounds, it is true, this is an area in which we (people with Asperger's) can be quite clever indeed.

One of the reasons my parents encouraged me with my specialists subjects was because they could see that when I was researching or thinking about it, I was very calm and happy. I was able to de-stress and disconnect from the world through my specialist topics. They almost saw it as a therapy session for me. I believe that if you want a child or young person with Asperger's to learn something all you have to do is tap into their specialist subject. I believe it is called 'learning through association' and is quite a common practise.

My guess is as good as yours in regards to why people with A.S have such specialist topics. I can only imagine it is because when there is so much difficulty understanding so much of their surrounding world, I guess those with A.S take great comfort in knowing everything, and anything about one subject. Maybe because in most other aspects of life, they may be wrong and confused or misunderstood. It least with having all that difficulty and 'wrong' doings (not their fault, or even wrong), they can be brilliant and really excel in at least one subject where they can remain word perfect. Specialist's topics are usually related to some sort of truth, perhaps computers, devices, engineering or mechanics, history, the weather, space and indeed, collections. This is because the truth is a matter of great importance to those with A.S, I for one am obsessed by truth, justification and fact, and I believe others with disabilities on the Autistic spectrum are too. There is so much deceit about truth in day to day life, so much so that things get altered; there are changes, and even truth and facts can change. With all that change and unsettling misleading truth happening in other aspects of life with many variables, it is nice to find comfort from facts, and truth, with variables that will never change.

A poem about one of my specialist topics
One of my most recent specialist topics, as I previously wrote, is my fascination with space and the constellation of Geminorum. I am utterly spell bounded by space and constellations, because of the beauty and the concept of belittling my problems in such a vast amount of space. I find it fascinating and research such a topic endlessly. I even created a giant hanging textile wall piece that depicts the constellation of Geminorum in as much detail as I could manage (or sew; in the literal sense. It is pictured below if you would like a glimpse). Here, is a poem I once wrote for a magazine article, about how my obsession with space, most particularly the night sky, calms my nerves and makes me feel better.

I called it 'Comfort in the night sky'. Enjoy.

Comfort in the night sky

When sensory overloads, drive me crazy,
Looking up into space, is where you'll find me.
I sit outside, with grass between my toes,
Allowing the calm of night, to melt away my woes.
Gazing up at the stars, so far, so bright,
The wonders of the universe beholds a magical sight.
Twinkling and dancing, the stars shimmer,
Alongside the moon, also glimmers.
Pale speckled splendour, of moonlight streaking,
Light sources gleaming, yet still I'm peeking,
Kinetic, moving, lit upon my freezing skin,
Only in the moons ghostly white sheen,
Can the obscene, be calmed by the tranquil space scene.

In the velvet sky of darkness,
Clouds simmer over the gleam of moon;
Clouds that are bustling, bursting and floating,
Cold air lingering, clouds slide, flailing.
Striding within the moons beautiful tide,
I find myself gazing as the clouds bumble and glide.
Whenever Anxiety wreaks havoc upon my mind,
I confide, that this is the calming sight, I need to find.

Space is a place where my imagination can roam free,
Space holds the key, to my everlasting sanctuary.
My mind, my fabrications, allow me to see such oddities,
And I glimpse a sight, a sensation, and marvel at the prodigy,
What a sight for the creator...can it be true?
In confused splendour, I review, my sight I pursue,
Within the infinite skies of blue,
I think I see a light flicker, a spaceship, and an alien, too!
In a blink of an eye, my vision has gone,
Yet the memory will leave me a smile, that lasts so long.

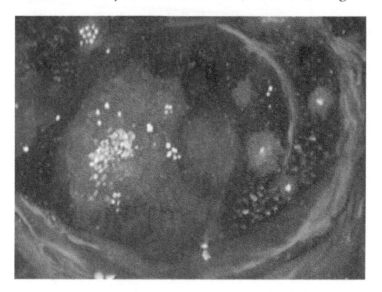

Knowledge and Understanding, Understanding that People have Minds

Gee, how do I explain this one?
It sounds rather odd but I think it happens to a lot of people with A.S.D.
Basically when I was a child I used to think that everyone was the same as
me, but looked different. I thought that if I knew something – everyone else
would know it too. Apparently this is called understanding that other people
have minds. Or in other words, someone with Autism will experience different
theory of mind to those who are neuro-typical.

Example 1
The mystery of the missing pencil case
At my mainstream primary school, one pupil had a pencil case which was really cool. It was in a shape of a Sausage Dog (I remember being really impressed by this pencil case- I used to think to myself 'That sausage dog pencil case is so cool.'). This pupil loved her little pencil case and carried it with her everywhere she went for months. Her mother bought her the pencil case, so it was extra special.

This is how I knew this was a very important pencil case to this little girl. During a lesson one day, the class bully had taken the pencil case and put it in their bag when the teacher's back was turned and the girl who owned it had gone to the toilet (which is stealing and I knew it was wrong). When the girl came back from the toilet no one knew where her pencil case had gone, no one else had seen what had happened so no one knew where it was – apart from me. The poor little girl missing the pencil case then got really upset because she couldn't find her pencil case. I did not know why she was upset – to me, she knew where her pencil case was. For some bizarre reason I thought that she knew it was in the other pupil's bag, I also assumed the teacher knew as well, because I knew. I thought this because I did not make the connection that the girl who owned the pencil case was not there when the other pupil put it in their bag, somehow I thought that because I knew, the girl must know.

So it came to the end of the day and the girl had been crying for ages and I do remember wondering 'why is she crying?' I did not make the connection between her losing her pencil case and her being upset. Consequently it was not until the next day when a teacher asked me "Joely did you see where the pencil case went?" I said "Yes it went in *Hayley's bag".

(*Hayley is a false name by the way, like all the names in this book)

I got told off quite a lot for not saying it sooner because I imagine it would have saved a lot of drama if I had.

Example 2
The not so mysterious case of the 'out of service' bus
I was on an outing with my friend's family to the beach, I was very young and still at mainstream primary school. My friend and I arrived at the Bus Stop

first and were waiting for her parents to arrive. We had been told to wait for her parents and that we were then going to catch a *3 bus down to the beach. A number *3bus went past with a note in the window saying "out of service". The out of the service bus was the bus we needed to get to the beach. My mate hadn't noticed what the note on the bus had said because she was not looking at the bus at the time.

When my friend's parents arrived and asked if a bus had gone past, I said "yes a bus has gone past". However, because they didn't question me further or ask a specific question I didn't tell them the bus that went past was our bus and out of service. I assumed that because they did not specifically ask, they already knew.

We waited a further 24 minutes for another bus to go past again, this number *3 bus also had the note saying "out of service". My friend's parents said "oh darn, our bus is out of service – we will have to walk to the beach, girls". Then my friend's mum looked at me with an unreadable expression probably annoyance/sympathy and confusion and said "Joely, you saw the bus go past earlier – you must have seen it was out of service so why didn't you say anything.? We could have been there by now." I was confused because I thought they knew it was out of service.

The reason I did not say anything about the missing pencil case and the out of service bus is because:

1. No one had asked. If no one asks then clearly (to me) it means that no one wants to know this information- therefore I would not say. Or it means they already know the answer
2. If no one asks a specific question then I will not give a specific answer.
3. I assumed that because I knew they also knew
4. I was unable to realise that because they were not there they didn't witness the event- therefore their knowledge would be different to mine

Many neuro-typical children also find it difficult to make the right connections and also assume that other people know what they know. This is something most children grow out of, but people with A.S.D do not. I think it has something to do with people with A.S.D not making correct connections. Connections like acknowledging how they found out something and acknowledging that other people were not there to find out the same way they had.

I still don't make connections today. Even now people still say to me

"You must have known, so why didn't you say anything?"

Social Imagination

Social imagination is very difficult to describe. 'Why is it so?' is a question I have asked myself multiple times while considering the depths of my disability.

You see most people look at me and say something along the lines of "You appear to have an amazing imagination – writing your fantasy books, drawing and painting your fairies" Then they would pause and say "I thought people with Asperger's are not meant to have an imagination?"

It is amusing because it's true in a sense, we are not supposed to have imagination but it appears evident that a lot of people with Asperger's have quite a vivid imagination indeed. The question then turns to the difference between the imagination we are supposed to *not* have and the imagination we do have. It's actually quite simple really once you know.

So what is the difference?

Social imagination is the type of imagination we (people with Asperger's) don't have as much of, this is a type of imagination that can be developed and maybe taught, with time, effort, patience and understanding. Social imagination means that we find it difficult to think and work out solutions in social situations, usually due to change in a routine. This is called having a lack of a social imagination because I can't think of differing ways to cope, work out and help a situation when things change. This of course is linked to the little problems we (or maybe just I) have in coping with change.

As you know people with Asperger's are very good with routine. When I went to College I knew my routine well. I knew which bus and train to get I knew the timetables and I knew how long it would all take. I was very comfortable with this routine and could carry it out with ease. However, if any part of the routine changed, I would find it difficult or sometime impossible to cope. Even something as simple as the bus being 5 minutes late, road works and / or not being able to find something I need for the day would prove disastrous. Most people would easily be able to cope with this situation and work out the best strategy to help, where as I would find this impossible. There have been countless situations where the change in routine has caused me to have overloads and go into a meltdown. Either I would return home in too much distress to function properly or I would simply hide in a bush wherever I was having a meltdown and wait there, safe and compact until family members found me.

Social imagination can affect daily routine and also my ability to organize a one off 'out of routine' trip. If I suddenly had to travel to town today on a matter of great importance that was not scheduled, I would find it very difficult to organize myself to actually make the travelling possible. Please bear in mind that I travel to town all the time by myself, and when it is part of a routine the process is easy; if not the whole process could become disastrous. I still need a lot of support with:

1. **Transportation**, how to get there, where to go and how to get off that form of transport
2. **How much money I would need**, also knowing what type of money to use (i.e., my mum usually advises me on how to use the money in an easy way. She often tells me to use the pound coins for the bus, use the notes for the train and what type of money would be best for what purchase- this is to prevent me from counting out 10p coins to buy a £9 train ticket as I have done before. She advises me to count my change and she tells me how much change I should expect from each purchase. etc)
3. **Different scenarios to expect**, how to act and how to respond to these scenarios – my mum usually goes through everything possible that may occur to help me cope effectively with the situation (otherwise I can't cope with anything. Thanks to my mum and family I now have the ability to achieve next to anything)
4. **Making sure I had credit and battery on my phone**
5. **How to get to my destination** once I have got off the bus/train
6. **Where to go to get help**
7. **Communication** – what do I say? Who do I approach?
8. **Organizational skills**, decent bag with zip for safety (to keep my phone and purse/money in)
9. **Appropriate clothes**, rain coat etc
10. **Appropriate footwear**, (I don't know about you, but I get terrible blisters on my tootsies.)
11. **Timetables**
12. **Timing**, knowing when to leave, how much time I have to get ready, what time I need to leave to get to a certain place.

You know what? The list goes on, and I love my mum so much for constantly helping me with these things, I really don't think I could leave the house without such support.

Seriously, without this amount of support I would find it exceedingly difficult to travel anywhere, every mole hill would become a mountain for me.

I have some rather amusing examples related to transport, I am about to reveal such very shady territory in which I feel rather embarrassed about.

"It's too early to use your bus pass, girlie"
One time, I had to try and travel to the town center; this is at a time when I had not caught a bus in months. I guess no matter how much I have learnt from catching a bus twice daily for years (school and college) – if I don't practice regularly everything just gets forgotten amongst the other important things I have to remember.

So I walked to the bus stop and saw my bus go past – I had missed it. This freaked me out enough before everything else had happened. At this time I knew that my bus pass did not work before 9:30am. This is not a problem usually. I was waiting at the bus stop to leave for town. I checked the bus time table and it said that the bus that had just gone past was the 9:24am bus and the next available bus for me to catch would arrive at 9:32am. I checked my phone for the time and all the times matched and made sense and I calculated that I had 7-8 minutes wait, before my bus arrived.

The bus arrived at 9:28am, so I got on the bus without checking the time and just assumed the time had passed rather quickly and that it must have been 9.32 am. I smiled brightly at the bus driver as I do with everyone I meet, and handed him my disability bus pass. The bus driver gruffly said,

"It's not 9.30 yet – you have to pay like everyone else"

then refused to accept my bus card. There was less than 2 minutes until it was valid – and the bus had been early – what a cheek, if it had arrived on time (at 9.32) I would not have found myself in such a predicament…

I can't lie, I was in an absolute state, for some reason the change in routine and the change in what was expected of me just made me freak out. Consequently, it took me far too long to understand what he meant, he told me several times that he would not accept my bus pass but he had an accent and I was finding it difficult to understand or hear him amongst the other noises on the bus and road. Due to not hearing him reject my bus pass, I assumed he had thanked me so I thanked him with a smile and started walking on the bus to find myself a seat. That bus driver probably thought I was really cheeky and bad. It was so very embarrassing as then he shouted at me to go back to him, the crowded bus full of people all just went quiet and suddenly there was near silence. I disliked it a lot as everyone appeared to glare at me and I was rather hoping that was just me misreading their cold facial expressions. So I walk back to him and he tells me (probably again) that my bus pass is not valid before 9:30am. He seemed annoyed and was using a tone that I had by then learnt meant he was losing his patience (A lack of patience was there in the first place, may I just add. He could have cut me some slack it's obvious I have a disability because I had a disability I.D card.). I stood in front of him and was fumbling in my bag to find my purse (which unhelpfully was stuck amongst loads of stuff right at the bottom, whereas if I had known I would have to pay I would have had my money and purse in a reachable place so I would have been prepared somewhat) I was looking for my purse for ages trying to find any cash at all and I was panicking a treat. I had no idea how much this bus journey would cost me and the fact that I was panicking so much just slowed me down and freaked me out further. Seriously, I just wanted to run off of that bus and crawl into a cupboard where I could feel safe and compact like I did as a child, the bench at the bus stop was becoming more and more appealing to hide under, the more freaked out I became under the hot glare of the mean busy driver and all the passengers. I eventually found two pound coins and gave them to him, I felt like my head was spinning and I felt like I could be sick he just stared at me with merciless eyes, my legs began to shake as I asked if I had given him enough money. My trembling voice betraying my emotions, and he just stared at me like I was a hated idiot. Eventually after staring at me for what seemed like ages, he asked in a very annoyed tone where I was travelling to. In my absolute rush and utter freak out I had completely forgotten to tell him where I was going. So eventually I told him and quickly sat down, by this time, it was gone 9.30… I was so upset that I couldn't stop crying, and I arrived at my location in so much pain I thought I could pass out.

That change in routine completely stumped me, not only in that incident but it affected my problem solving, ability to cope with change and communicational skills negatively for the rest of the day too. My lack of social imagination made it very difficult to work out how to solve this problem in the heat of the moment. Other than finding money, I could not work out how to act, what to say and all the other necessities and even pleasantries I had learnt.

Here's another example of my lack of social imagination. This occurred when I was very young I believe I had just started secondary school.

Wait, was I meant to get off of the bus then?
What do you say when you teach a person who is young how to catch a bus? I imagine you would say something along the lines of -

-You need to wait at the appropriate bus stop; you need to check which bus goes to the location you wish to travel to. Once the bus arrives you step on, wait your turn to pay. Ask for a child/ adult ticket to the location you are travelling to. Say please, say thank you, blah blah blah…

Everyone explained how to catch the Bus, but no one mentioned to me how to get OFF the bus.

One time I did not get off the bus in time because no one told me to. Typical me. It was my first week of my secondary school I had been practicing how to catch the bus with my family and it had been getting on really well. However, I was travelling home one day from school and although I was aware I was approaching where I lived I should have thought that I needed to get off the bus soon – oh no, not me. I am never that great at making connections. Also, as the bus approached the bus stop I could see my family all waving and smiling at me at the bus stop corner where I was supposed to be getting off; it did not connect that I should get off the bus. I did not even move down stairs. I remained seated upstairs, being excited to see my family distracted me somewhat from the lack of concentration I previously had. So I sat there waving and smiling at them as the bus drove past, suddenly my family all realized at the same moment that I was meant to be down stairs waiting to get off the bus so they all started frantically waving and pointing down. I can't read body language I just assumed that they were being weird, (I mean they are weird and lovely of course) sometimes it is no bad thing. So I just continued to wave at them upstairs completely oblivious to their quite evident panic. All the other girls on the bus could see it but not me. One older girl even asked if I was ok, but because I was ok I said I was fine. Then another one questioned if that was my family and if I had missed my stop I then realized that we were actually quite a bit down the road from where I lived, my family were tiny dots in the distance, and so I ran down the bus stairs. I did not know where to stand as I had not been told where to stand on a bus when getting off so I just stood at the bottom of the stairs. However, I got in the way of another pupil who was coming down stairs to get off so I moved out the way, and followed her off the bus. I got off the bus and the girl snarled at me "I don't get how you forgot to get off the bus even though your folks were waving at you… weirdo". I smiled at her in confusion and panic at not knowing where I was, and she shook her head and grimaced as she turned to leave. I walked back up the road towards my family who were all running down the road towards me shouting and waving a lot still. It must have looked quite amusing to onlookers. I remember thinking that to onlookers who would not be aware of our family bond, I should be running away from the group of crazy people shouting and running towards me, certainly not walking towards them. What an embarrassment.

I think I was just being silly but according to my mum nobody told me how to get off the bus so it was not my fault. These are some of my biggest daily difficulties.

Problem Solving

I have always found it very difficult to make connections and work out solutions to problems; this is due to my lack of social imagination and my inability to process new information that could help. For instance, if I'm trying to work out a solution to a problem, I stare into space, as it is easier and less distracting looking at nothing, than it is looking at someone's face and trying to decipher what their facial expression means and problem solve at the same time. I need to allow my brain space to work out appropriate possibilities to best help for a solution. Also, when there is too much sensory input to focus on, and a problem or unexpected change displays itself to me (which happens constantly) solutions to problems seldom come up because my brain can't think about new possibilities of helping, without first removing the old sensory stimuli. For instance, if the dish washer is filled with dirty dishes and I need to make room in it to put a dirty plate in, I can't work out what to do or how to solve this problem if someone is merely standing there distracting me; I need to remove the distraction (ask the person very politely to leave) so I can solve the problem and work out how to move everything around to make room for the dirty plate. I believe it might have something to do with an inability to cope with new information, incapacity to cope with distractions and difficulty with multi tasking. Maybe it's just me, but I believe that it could be the same with a lot of people with A.S Complexities with problem solving come out as a result.

Even in a very normal, seemingly not stressful circumstance, like being at home doing normal jobs like tidying my room (yes, really mother) if someone was even to stand in the doorway, I would instantly forget what I was doing and freak out. I would then become unable to work out the rest of my routine or remember what I was doing. My concentration would disappear and that job would be over. Something so simple, and easy, becomes a problem that I can't solve. I would then have to start again once they had left, from scratch. This is because they are distracting me by standing there which makes me think about appropriate conversations we might have, when I should be focusing on cleaning my room. Again, it's all about distractions and inability to cope with new stimuli.

It was much the same at school; distractions and changes were a constant pressure at school and problems came up all the time; I could hardly find room in my thinking process to realise potential solutions due to all the distractions.

One time in lesson I had been writing an essay about my favourite subject (History) which as you can imagine meant I had a lot to write. I had one page, which I filled both sides with my detailed writing. Yet needless to say, because of my love of writing, I wrote and wrote, barely covering the main points until there was barely enough room for me to write any more. At this point, I panicked, knowing I had much more that needed to be said, but with no room on the paper to express myself. Instead of making the connection that I had used all the space and realising I needed more paper, I had begun to scrunch my writing up so tiny, that it was unreadable at the bottom of the page. I had not even made the connection that in running out of room to write on the paper meant I needed more paper, where as other people would make the connection and be able to work out a solution to the problem (i.e. get more paper). As it was, the classroom was noisy, when I had realised I would run out of room; there were too many visual and noisy distractions, and so my brain could not cope, and would not allow me to process any new information that could help. This means that even if I had made the connection to look for more paper, my brain would not have been able to focus long enough to process new information. So I would effectively have been looking, but not seeing any solutions. I did not even think about the possibility of new paper, because my brain was too busy thinking about everything else.

I have failed many tests, simply because I had not made the connection that I needed more paper, and had instead missed out huge chunks of vital information to my workings, to ensure everything fitted at the bottom of the page. I just didn't realise there was even a possibility of getting more paper, even if I had been told by a teacher that we could use as much paper as we liked. I just could never make that connection in the heat of the moment. It is a complicated little fairy jam jar in which I live.

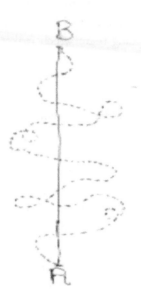

Advice for people who are on the Autistic spectrum
I know I have said that I find it difficult problem solving due to these things, but I don't want you to give up trying, because I will never give up. Just because you may read in a book, that people on the Autistic spectrum can't do this or can't do that, does not means you should not try; you should always try, because improvements can be made. These things do get better and even a little easier as you get older, especially with an understanding support system, a helpful environment and the motivation to keep trying. Good luck, my little fairy.

Advice for people who are not on the Autistic spectrum
Please be patient with someone on the Autistic spectrum, sometimes they may seem like they are not concentrating or listening when you're talking to them. Maybe this is because they don't look at you; but please realise this may be so they can understand what it is you are saying.

Honesty is the Best Policy, People

I am extremely honest, painfully honest sometimes. This is because I have been taught that all honesty is good. However, I am slowly learning this may not always be the case. My honesty can sometimes make other people react differently to me because they don't always like you to be honest with them. I have now learnt to be more tactful when I speak, but I didn't realize I had to be tactful, as a child I was unaware of the consequences, and had no fear of them. This would mean that I would do and say what I thought was right, merely being honest, without thinking what could happen (I have some good examples of this). I believe that this is similar for many people on the Autistic spectrum. The following is an example of when I was honest about something when asked a question, but suspected it was not the desired answer to give. But I was honest anyway.

This particular incident happened when I was 12. I was sat at the front of the school bus going home with my friends, when a girl walked from the back of the bus carrying a sandwich which was oozing with filling. I watched in the reflection of the bus window as she threw the sandwich on the floor, with quite some force. The contents splattered and spilled, grossly gleaming, lumpy and yucky on the dirty bus floor. I turned to look at the sandwich, and then at the girl, who had a twisting smirk on her bright pink painted lips and cold, outlined in black, glaring eyes. She then said, looking directly at me:

"Oi, you shortie – I am your head girl and I am demanding that you pick the sandwich up. Do it NOW."

I recall just staring at her, wondering why she had said that, when she was the one that threw it down there, I wasn't about to be bossed around by some confused bully. So I said

"No, why should I pick it up? You threw it there, so *you* pick it up"

I said in the hope of clearing up the confusion she had felt. At this point she became very angry, but because I couldn't read facial expressions I was not aware of this. I thought I was just answering her question and being honest, I can see now it was not the answer she wanted to hear. She then shouted

"Are you disrespecting my authority? Are ya? Pick the damn sandwich up now."

This is when I became really confused. As, no, I was not intentionally disrespecting her authority, I was merely refusing to pick the sandwich up, because picking it up would be giving in to her bullying. However I still was refusing to do what she wanted me to do because I knew she was trying to bully me. Maybe she thought I was being disrespectful because I was not doing as she asked, I don't know, all I do know is that the question she asked "Are you disrespecting my authority?' was very confusing. How can I be honest, if I am uncertain of what the honest answer is? At this point, I think I realized that if I gave her the truly honest answer, which is "No, I am not disrespecting your authority, you're just abusing your authority to be a bully and I refuse to give in to your taunts' she would have become angrier. So I remained silent. By now, the entire bus had fallen silent and all eyes were on me, and this girl.

She screamed at me again to pick the sandwich up, her face alarmingly close to mine, pointing viciously at the sandwich on the floor. Her features screwing up in ugly anger, causing the layers of orange foundation creams on her face to crease and crack under the pressure of her screeches, but still I remained quiet, still uncertain of the honest answer to give. I shrugged at her starting to feel really scared, and told her quietly.

"Of course I'm not trying to disrespect you… But you dropping that sandwich on the floor has nothing to do with me"

If looks could kill, I think I would have died a few times over in those split seconds as she bent down and picked the sandwich up, glaring at me with daggers.

Suddenly without warning, she lunged forward, throwing the sandwich on my face, my head, and in my hair. My eyes had closed in an instant, but most unfortunately my mouth was still hanging open in shock. She picked apart the sandwich and crushed the foul bread and fillings against my skin; in my eyes, mouth and ears. My senses went into meltdown, as the stinging, sensation and rancid taste overloaded my very being. I spat out the rankest taste and she laughed, curtly, like a hyena as she continued her little attack. She took great delight in smearing the filling all over my face and in my hair, flicking at me the remains of the filling from her fake nailed fingers. The content dripping, slipping, and bumpily gliding over my face; wet, atrociously thick and cringingly smelly, hair hanging down in stinking soaked rags, the filling was utterly grotesque upon my skin. It was horrible. The disgusting texture and appalling smell was too much for my senses to bare and in an instant I could feel myself being sick but I swallowed it down with great distaste. I stared at that bully right in the eyes, and smiled while shaking my head, trying to show how unaffected I was. All I could think was, how pathetic that girl was, and also, how sad her home life must be for her to abuse a position of trust and prey on random girls on the bus. What is her background story, to make her think she can 'justify' treating others so terribly? She had wanted me to cower away from her, to run off and cry, that would have made her feel powerful and superior (because bullies are twisted like that) but I didn't, I stood and made strong eye contact until she blinked and looked away in shame. She stormed off (walked away quickly and angrily – like a storm maybe?) to the back of the bus. The other bullies started calling me nasty names but I didn't care. In my eyes I had just stood up to her, and won. I was really elated and although I was shocked by what had happened, and I still had the remains of that dreaded sandwich in my hair, it taught me a valuable lesson that I still carry with me today, stick up for myself and don't be controlled like that.

However, all though it was nasty at the time and I wanted to lie on the floor under a seat and cry in private, I never had trouble from any of those bullies again. They sat at the back of the bus each day for the whole year, never calling me or my friends nasty names or even looking at us. It was worth standing up to them, just to get some peace, freedom and relief from bullying. Trust me, you do however need support and trustworthy adult guidance to help you say and act in the most effective way.

From all of this I have learnt that honesty is not always the best policy. Had I not antagonized her by answering her question honestly, but instead been tactful, I could have avoided being covered in sandwich. Luckily for me getting covered in sandwich meant that I stood up to the bully and was left alone ever since.

White Lies

I believe it is the classic example of a self-conscious lady in a tight dress that does not suit her large body shape and her asking if she looks fat in the dress. The polite answer would be to say "you look lovely" Which could actually mean her facial beauty rather than actually answering the question – hehe, rather clever I think. However the honest answer is an answer she may not wish to hear. So one could answer honestly but be gentle about it. Like this, the honest answer in the politest form would be to avoid referencing to her size, but to instead offer a solution. For example, "I think you should wear what you are most comfortable in, however I personally think the other dress may suit you and your personality better."

However, it is somewhat typical for a person with Asperger's to answer truthfully but quite bluntly – "Yes you look fat" is the honest answer. In our eyes, she wanted to know if she looked fat, we gave the correct answer and therefore have helped her. We don't always foresee the probability of such a comment crushing her self-image and reducing her confidence to nothing. Nor is skimming round the truth to make her feel better thought necessary because if she did not want to know the full correct truth (such a blunt and honest truth) then she would not have asked in the first place, right? By being blunt, we have helped more than if we skimmed around the truth, because this can give a distorted picture. The truth could be misinterpreted and if a person misinterprets it as something different then it is no longer a truth. By being blunt you cut out the possibility that the truth will be seen wrong by other people.

I still think being polite is best though. You don't have to be blunt when being honest and sometimes if you skim round the bad parts by replacing them somewhat with good parts then you could really save a situation from serious deterioration.

Joely, You've Eaten an 'Asperger's Burger' Again

Did you know that the Latin for Honey Bee is 'Mella'? Mella is my favourite Roman name, I think it is beautiful. Anyway, there I go again. Ramble, Ramble.

I am mentioning this because apparently it's very normal for people with Asperger's to interject facts about their specialist topic into any conversation with a little bit of, (or no) relevance, just merely making conversation because they know they have to (social protocol), in the only way they know how. Usually when I do it, I have no idea I have 'eaten an Asperger's Burger' until half way through... rather an embarrassing predicament to find oneself in.

When I used to ramble on about something or when I had taken something literally, my friend used to say to me

"Joely, you've eaten an Asperger's Burger again"

I believe that people with Asperger's are very intelligent and clever. People just need to help us for it to shine through, although often I have noticed that knowledge is clear from the beginning. Sometimes, when I interject my facts about history into random conversations or when I take things really literally, I get told I have eaten an 'Asperger's Burger'. What my lovely mate meant is that, I was being very Aspergery and I should stop rambling because they got the message. I have quite a few examples of this.

Example 1
My boyfriend and I were watching a T.V show about building houses and it reminded me of something I had learnt about Ancient Egypt; how they built the Pyramids. I explained the process of mixing mud and straw and using a mud mould to construct the correct shape of a brick, I was talking in quite a lot of detail. Half way through talking about how the bricks were sun dried, I suddenly realised that this is rather Aspergery. So I paused and said

"Sorry that had no relevance-
I have eaten another Asperger's Burger."

Fortunately for me my boyfriend was actually interested in what I was saying and allowed me to finish without making me feel like a weirdo like I am normally made to feel.

Example 2

In this example my friend and I were talking about ballet. I then went off on a tangent about Japanese women in the 19th- 20th century. It was in this time period where females in most classes used to have their feet bound painfully tightly, and broken in order to prevent further growth. My understanding is that it was for purposes of beauty – little and narrow feet were considered beautiful; also it was to make a woman's movements more feminine and dainty. So, I was telling my friend this and then I realised I had been talking for a while about Japanese women rather than ballet. I was about 18 at the time, and my friend thought the whole thing was hilarious. Luckily my friends are used to my ramblings now.

Example 3

This time I was with my boyfriend and we were talking about twins, in all honesty we were talking about Geminorium constellation in the sky that contains the twins Castor and Pollux (trust me I have the biggest obsession with this constellation. I love it). The sheer thought of twins led me to the train of thought about triplets and how triplets in Ancient Rome were considered to be very unlucky. They were thought to be so unlucky that the foundations of Rome itself would fall if they were allowed to be together. If they were to remain together their powers would be too strong (like the gods). So, the Romans believed that the best thing to do was to separate the triplets as new born babies and have them grow up in different cites/countries. If they did this then Rome would never fall foul of their dark spell. I realised after too long, that I had been talking about Roman triplets for about four minutes when we were originally talking about Castor and Pollux the twins in Geminorium.

I had gone and eaten another Asperger's Burger again.

So yes, those are just a few examples, I seriously do this all the time; I just randomly pipe up with random facts about history at any given opportunity. Admittedly this is happening more nowadays because I have more of a chance to research and learn about the things I love. Lucky for those who surround me! (That was me trying to use sarcasm, aha!).

Communication and Language

Many times I have been to a specialist for help with my communicational 'skills'; for instance speech and language therapy. Sadly, this proved unhelpful. This is because speech and language assessments would always involve the same unhelpful things; therapist would always get me to read out sentences from a book. Yet because I happen to have a very good reading age and ability to speak my words clearly and well, they told my parents that I needed no more support from the speech therapist, because I could talk...?

My family know the difficulties I have with understanding spoken language and even understand what my own language means to other people who perceive things differently to me. I must need some help, if I can barely understand every sentence people say to me? What these specialists clearly don't understand is that just because I can speak, and speak well, does not mean I can understand what I am saying or, what I am listening to.

I can only describe my difficulty with understanding spoken language as listening to someone talk, and every other word they say is in a different language. Can you imagine that? Listening to someone talk in the same language as you, but then throwing in random unfathomable words in foreign tongues? Can you imagine how much that would impact your understanding of what they were saying, if you were then unable to piece together the rest of the sentence with huge gaping holes, due to the complexities of the rest of your disability. It is very difficult.

It feels like I am talking to people of a foreign language to me purely because of the way people word things. Using unspecific language, literal language and talking in riddles, I find myself enveloped in clouds of confusion when talking to some people because mostly, they don't even understand that what they have said can clearly make no sense to me at all. Even my family who know how best to communicate with me so that I can understand, even they forget the best language to use sometimes.

The noticeable problem is that people tend to talk the same way to everyone, because they assume that everyone has similar understanding as them. They assume that whoever they are talking to understands and know what they mean, without them having to try explaining in simple terms. Because most people do understand as most people don't have a disability.

I have found that often people's lack of understanding of the genuine complexities of Asperger's clouds their judgements and then affects how they treat those they know with such a disability. Due to a lack of understanding, some people may think that people with A.S don't make an effort to listen to conversations (and make a judgement that this is why they don't understand) and they may also think that people with A.S don't make an effort to look at the face when they are being spoken too, (which could create the judgement that they are not making the effort to understand). Perhaps from their point of view, they think that maybe the people with Asperger's are not listening, this belief perhaps reinforced because of the lack of eye contact. Consequently anger settles in, and they would rather not make the effort to someone, who 'clearly' does 'not' make an effort to understand.

People without an Autistic spectrum disorder expect those with Asperger's to start listening, and then understand what they are saying. People without Autistic Disorders don't know that people with Asperger's are listening, to every word they utter because they can't back stream irrelevant noises due to their disability; they're always listening to everything. Rather the problem is that those with Asperger's simply can't understand the language they are using, it really is as simple, and complex, as that. People without Autistic Disorders expect everyone to look at their face and suddenly understand what their face is expressing. This will not happen, Asperger's does not work like that, it can't work like that. The simple reason we avoid eye contact is merely to make processing information easier, to try and enable success at understanding what is being said. Maybe it is a coping strategy that has been developed, maybe it works, maybe it doesn't; but for me it most certainly does help. This is because I have less to focus on when I am not looking at someone's face which means I have more room in my head to understand what is being said.

To try and make things clearer I shall make a list of the things I find difficult to understand in spoken language

1. Literal language
2. Sarcasm
3. Riddles (words used in a different way to the original and literal version e.g. "That was sick" does not mean 'disgusting' any more, it means awesome.... apparently?)
4. Unspecific words or phrases
5. My lack of empathy means I have trouble working out the best response to better help someone.
6. Understanding their expressions, body language
7. Not understanding what they meant when they said something
8. Jokes

I take things very literally, which shouldn't be a problem; it's just people tend to not use literal language in a way it is intended to be understood – in a literal manner; which is odd if you ask me, but hey ho, I can't begin to understand the human race sometimes.

In fact, I think it is unfair for people to make judgements about people with A.S when we take things literally. We merely understand language exactly as people say it, if they are talking in a weird way that does not make sense to someone who is taking things literally, then how an earth is that our fault when we are interpreting the language exactly as it should be? People say things for the sole purpose of their words to be taken literally, why else would you speak using literal language? Yet these people are the ones using inappropriate literal language and expecting it not to be understood as intended. My question is; how is this communicating effectively? Just because people with Autistic disabilities are in the minority we have been labelled the difficult ones and so we are the misunderstood ones. It really does mystify me.

I am pretty bad at understanding sarcasm, people have often used sarcasm on me, and I never usually realise they are being sarcastic at all, which can be embarrassing. For instance, this is something that happened to me the other day while I was out shopping with a friend in a very busy shopping mall, both of us were standing in an entrance to a shop. I have written it in a form of a script, I'm not particularly sure why.

Friend "Joely, I'll meet you at a shop door in two minutes"

Me, already confused, because I'm special like that, had said: "Which door?"

Friend *rolls eyes:* "the door to the moon. That door, over there"

Friend points uselessly in the general direction of four doors; all leading to different shops, one of which she was about to walk into, one of which we were about to go into once we met again, and none of which go to a moon, obviously. My friend was being sarcastic. Anyway back to the script;

Me "Wait a second, which of the four doors am I waiting for you by?"

Friend "Wait by the door with the sign saying 'wait here, Joely.' Seriously Joely, what door do you think? Work it out… I'm going in that shop now, bye."

And off my friend goes, leaving me as confused as ever. Am I meant to wait at the door of the shop she is going in now? Or am I meant to wait at the door of the shop we are about to go into together? So I look over to the doors, examining each and every door for a labelled sign (as instructed to, I took it literally), thinking that perhaps she had previously gone over to a door and put a sign there for me. It was only then that I realised that no, she obviously had put no sign by a door, and she was just being sarcastic and I had taken her literally. I felt like such an idiot, silly me. She had a habit of being unhelpfully sarcastic and literal, that one. Consequently, I waited by the wrong door, as she did not specifically tell me where to wait, I lost her, and had to get a lift home. It freaked my parents out that I had been left with so little instructions like that and for the friend to just tell me to 'work it out' and then leave is extremely unhelpful (especially when she knew of my disability); as the nature of my disability does mean I am often unable to work 'it' out without support. My brain doesn't work like that.

Communicating with others

Then there's the small matter of how I communicate with other people. I tend to say things that I don't understand, use words that I'm not sure of the meaning, or speak using the wrong phrases; for instance, I may say "I was down the shop earlier today" despite knowing that I should say "I went down to the shop earlier today". These things are something I can't control and happen mostly when I am stressed. I know how I should speak, but my words don't come out the way I intend, unless I have practised to perfection, perhaps for a public speaking event. However, most conversations and speaking are entirely spontaneous, with no practising to be had, and so all conversations are stressful and unexpected.

I often tell stories and start at the middle, not the beginning. I miss out important information because I forget that the listeners knowledge of the story is different to mine – understanding that people have minds is a great difficulty of mine. I don't make sense to people. It's a wonder I am writing a book at all, and a miracle if people can understand my ramblings within my book.

I use words in the wrong context, I put emphasis on the wrong words, and suddenly my entire sentence sounds differently to what I was intending. I tend to speak words in the wrong order, usually when I am under pressure or stressed, I develop a stutter, because my mouth can't keep up with what my brain is trying to say (or the other way round, I have not quite worked that out yet), and so my words tumble out, slurred, stuttering, words falling out my mouth in the wrong order, in the wrong context, not making any sense at all.

Communicating in an appropriate way

Understanding what's appropriate to say to people is a big issue for those with A.S.D. The reason has haunted me during my many wakeful hours from desired sleep. Why is it I used to say such inappropriate things in complete innocence? I used to speak in such an inappropriate manner, that people disliked, were uncomfortable or even angry with me. Why is it that those with A.S can't seem to understand the unwritten rule of communication? I find it to be a fascinating concept that someone can have the ability to talk, but have very little idea about what is right, or wrong to say.

I would like to tell you a story about when I realised that communication strategies for people with an Autistic disability can often be rude, insensitive or unsuitable. Yet mostly I learnt from this experience that despite an ability to talk and start conversations did not necessarily mean that communicational skills are 'good'.

Not long ago, I was volunteering at a World War Memorial Festival with a friend of mine who has Asperger's too. My friend and I had a great day volunteering together and it was in that short amount of time that I realised just how 'good' my friend was at starting and maintaining a conversation. How wonderful she is at communicating! She could talk with ease to strangers, start a conversation (without prompting) of mostly relevant topics with ease and little aid. She did not need encouragement and she then continued to show great listening skills too. I marvelled at the difference between us, because there I was, unable to work out a single thing to say to start, let alone maintain, a conversation. Mostly, I am only able to talk to people as part of a routine – perhaps, with a speech or to answer questions and ask questions, nothing spontaneous. I was thinking that anyone who could at least manage to start a conversation must be better at communicating than me. However as time passed at this festival I realised that actually, my friend often says the most inconsiderate and inappropriate of things and she was also clueless that her words may cause offence or discomfort. Again, that's A.S for you.

One gentleman came up to us in his wheel chair and smiled in greeting. My friend started to talk about how she was 'insanely jealous' that her friends got to visit war camps on college trips. Already alarm bells were ringing in my mind as it's not something to be jealous of. Also, such a topic is such a sensitive thing to discuss with no warning. The gentleman's demeanour changed almost instantly. Suddenly his smile faded and he seemed to stiffen with discomfort. I could see that she was merely making conversation about the topic of common interest and something she knew about. She managed to process all this complex information and decipher something that *could* be appropriate to say. She went on to say that it would have been 'so sweet to take a crazy selfie photo of me and all the ghosts' I can't even describe my shock and appalled reaction to what she had said. A 'selfie' photo with the ghosts! Oh my, the sheer dreadfulness of such words! In the horror and disrespectfulness of what she had just said I nearly choked on my water. At this point he had paled and was staring daggers in extreme discomfort at my friend, who was completely oblivious. She was laughing and kept saying

"Laugh out loud, I love ghosts and to hear their ghostly stories!"

Once she had finished laughing, suddenly more serious in her tone, she went on to say

"I learnt all about the war by watching T.V., I learnt that there was a lot of suffering in the war. Imagine how the ghosts at the concentration camp could have told me about their suffering? I could have got ghostly stories and a ghostly selfie... I'm gutted I could not go"

Now I don't know about you, but I personally think that is incredibly disrespectful to say about hearing the suffering of ghosts, and taking a photo... It's horrendous for sure. She did say it in all innocence, merely making conversation about the common interest, and I had to keep reminding myself of this. I understand it is not her fault, but others without an understanding of the difficulties would have probably have reacted really badly to such a conversation. I understand she would never dream of causing upset. I feel it just proves that just because she had the ability to start a conversation about the topic matter does not mean she could determine what topics, or words, would be suitable. I believe she did very well to get far enough to maintaining a conversation, even though it was unsuitable.

At this point, I realised I needed to say something to the gentleman, in the form of an apology and to explain why my friend had spoken in such a way.

"I am so incredibly sorry... we both have a disability."

He paused, giving me a momentary benefit of a doubt, and I jumped at the chance to explain.

"It was completely unintentional to cause upset...We both have disabilities that make it incredibly hard to talk, communicate appropriately or understand language, and read facial expressions or body language. It does mean we can't always tell if we are upsetting people and it also means that we don't often know what topics are wrong to discuss... "

My friend looked at me in absolute horror, the realisation that she upset him sinking in at that point, judging by the way her eyes had widened in shock with

emotional turbulence, and her cheeks were colouring, as she bit her lip trying
to avoid crying. He looked from her to me, noticed my friends apparent upset
at hurting him, and with the realisation it really was unintentional. He relaxed
his grip on the wheel chair, his white knuckles, returned to their usual colour.
I took a deep breath and started the only way I knew how, with an explanation
of our disabilities.

What I have found is that you get turned away from some speech and language
therapist if you can talk clearly, answer and ask questions and read well. This
has meant that both my friend and I have had little support from speech and
language therapist because we both got turned away, due to us both being able
to 'talk'. Clearly we both need the support because despite the ability to talk
well, neither of us can communicate in an appropriate (or any manner) at all.
Please let us try and change this, it is absolutely vital that those in need get the
therapy needed to ascertain the rules of language and communicating. Please
remember next time you speak to someone with A.S.D (even if you also have
this disability) that if they upset you by saying something out of context or
just insensitive or wrong, it is likely to be unintentional.

Understanding your own spoken language
The thing with not understanding other people's spoken language does mean that you don't understand your own spoken language either.

It's not that I don't think before I speak, in fact I spend a great deal of time trying to work out what to say, in order to make sure that what I am saying is appropriate, sensitive and not rude. This is because I know of the stereotypes of Asperger's, and wish not to be a typical empathyless, insensitive selfish robot, that the media has negatively and wrongly stereotypes us to be (I believe with support, we are not all like this, we just need help and understanding).

Another problem is that I'm not very good at processing information; it takes me a while to both process and understand what has been said. Most people merely take a few seconds to understand general spoken language, and then respond appropriately with little difficulty in doing so. Well, it takes me at least ten seconds longer to process such information, if I understand it at all. This is a long time when you are standing in awkward silence with someone, while apparently having a conversation. Such slow processing speed does mean that while I'm talking to someone, and listening to them give me information, it takes me while to process what they said, try to understand it and then work out the necessary things to say, and then pluck up the courage to continue the conversation. Of course, I do not always understand what has been said, which often leads to longer gaps of processing times, the silence growing longer and more awkward by the second.

This makes communication difficult because often people think I do not care for the conversation to go further, as I have remained silent for too long consequently they make the judgement that I am rude, lose interest and move on, often never to attempt to talk to me again. If the person I am talking to knows of my difficulties they generally treat me with much more compassion and allow me time to think, thank goodness.

Communication and language is one of the biggest difficulties I have due to my Asperger's. When I was a young child it was particularly complex for me to communicate my needs and thoughts. Just because I can speak does not mean I can express myself the way I need to. Likewise, I might be able to hear and listen but this does not mean I can understand what is being said.

Example 1

A classic example of me not being able to communicate correctly is when I was a child with my favourite toy aged 3-4. I used to play with a bubble wand which had a clean ladies handkerchief threaded through the loop. I played with this toy all day, every day. I called this toy, 'Church'. My family could never understand why I would play with this 'toy', rather than my real toys, and more confusingly … why I called it 'Church'. They used to ask me why I called the bubble wand 'Church', but I was never able to respond. It was not until at least 3 years later, when 'Church' came up in a conversation; I was able to explain what it was and why I called it 'Church'. I told them that the bubble wand was a bride and the handkerchief was her veil. However, because I did not know how to communicate properly I just said the word 'Church' because that's where I had seen a bride get married (I had got the bubble wand and the handkerchief from a wedding I had been to). At that point my family laughed because they realised that the connection I had made with the bubble wand and a church made perfect sense.

This is just one example of how my Asperger's affected my communication and language. I knew what I wanted to say, I just found it hard to get the words out, so that other people could understand me.

Example 2
This is an example of how I do not understand what I hear and how I take things literally.

I was with my friend in the school playground (not the special needs school), she was feeling ill. My friend asked me "Joely, do I look pale to you? I feel poorly"

At the time, I had no idea what the word 'pale' meant. So, because I didn't know what it meant, it was logical for me to say "no." Well, it was logical to me at the time anyway. Later she said again "Joely do I look pale now?" I asked her what she meant and she said "do I look white?" I looked at her face; she did not look 'white' certainly not white like a piece of paper which is what I had perceived white to be. I told her that "You don't look white like paper so you can't be pale". I now realise what she was talking about. She wanted to find out if she looked pale because she was feeling ill. Had I understood this rather than interpreting the question literally I would have been able to respond correctly, because I now know that she was actually pale. I feel like a fool now because unfortunately that friend was prone to fainting, so I probably did not help her. I'm still sorry about that – you know who you are.

Example 3

Once I was in a geography lesson, and it was utter chaos. Effectively the whole class was being noisy, selfish and immature (apart from me and a select few – unlike many others I was there to actually learn and not be selfish and prevent others from learning). The teacher had been struggling to keep control of the class and she had been trying to get her point across for about 5 minutes. After a while the class started to quieten down, but at this point the teacher shouted

"Just be quiet."

It would have been understandable for her to shout this had she shouted it when they were noisy. I now think she had been building up to shout it when the class was really noisy but did not get a chance as she was not heard over the volume. So, when there was a moment of quiet she shouted so that everyone would hear her. However she actually shouted "Just be quiet." when it WAS quieter- which seemed ridiculous to me. It was quiet and therefore she should not have shouted it at all. I responded really quietly to my support worker

"I don't understand – they are being really quiet now"

This was a true statement, to me at that moment when she said it; the whole class was at an acceptable noise volume which was a far cry from the chaotic volume of noise that was erupting from the student's mouths moments before. Then my teacher looked at me, red in the face, and exploded in rage...

"That includes you Joely Colmer. Detention for the whole class. You have Joely to thank"

I was so shocked. I got really upset actually, I remember feeling so embarrassed and horrified that I had a detention. Not only did I have a detention-but the rest of the class now had a detention too.

Common Sense

Have you ever felt rather silly because you got something wrong that seemed rather obvious to others but to you it made no sense? Well let me tell you friends, you are not the only one. My goodness, the amount of times I have had a conversation with a friend where I have got something wrong and they laugh kindly and say

"How can you not know that? It's common sense."

I hinder to admit that it offends me a bit when people say such things to me. It makes me feel so stupid. I very much dislike it. Surely, if it were common sense, I would have known this already? But no, I did not know it already so don't tell me it is common sense.

However, I have something to tell you; hopefully this will make you feel better. Common sense is rather odd. The 'common' person has common sense, yes? Supposedly so; well the common person does not have A.S.D, because statistics say that less people have Asperger's/Autism then those without. Therefore the common person has a completely different common sense than we do.

Let me give you two examples, which to this day still very much annoys me.

Example 1
I was in a science exam once for my GCSE. In one question in the exam paper, there were two pictures of cows.

The question asked this: "Which cow would the Farmer use for meat and muscle?"

Cow A

Cow B

Sounds so simple, yes? What answer would you give? I expect you think it's simple, exactly what I thought (despite the fact that you may believe that cows should not be used for this purpose). However, it turns out that even though I thought the answer was blindingly obvious… I got the answer wrong. Yes wrong… and through no fault of my own, purely because I see things differently and because my understanding of things are different. Consequently I failed the practice paper for GCSE Science exam – I was one point away from passing this exam but no, amongst other examples of misleading literal language used in the paper, this question also tripped me up and I failed.

So the burning question. Why did I get the most obvious question wrong? I'll tell you…

When I was in the exam, I looked at the picture of cow A and thought to myself: 'this cow looks fairly fat', I looked at the picture of cow B and thought to myself 'Well, this cow looks positively ill, it looks almost anorexic; I can see his rib cage. It's far too skinny – a farmer could not get any meat off that.' Due to cow B looking so skinny I chose cow A as my answer. To me it made perfect sense – How can a farmer possibly get any meat off the other starved, ill looking cow?

I turned the page very confident and certain I had got it right, because it was common sense. Asperger's literal common sense, might I add.

After the exam we were going through the answer sheet. It eventually came to this particular question and the teacher said

> "Well this is an obvious and easy one. Everyone should have got this
> right, although one person didn't"

The teacher glanced at me at that point, I had no idea I had got the question wrong at that moment so I just smiled in a very confident manner.

> "The answer of course is cow B, because cow B has more muscle than
> cow A, therefore it would have been more use to the farmer"

When the teacher said that, I sat there in so much shock and annoyance that my mouth literally dropped open in surprise. Once I had recovered my composure, I had asked my friend who was sitting next to me

"How can the answer possibly be cow B? Look at it, it looks anorexic, you can see its rib cage and bones, there is nothing on it."

My friend looked at me rather confused and amused and said

"Well no, it is obvious, isn't it? Cow B has muscle on it. Look at it, you can see that. It's common sense, Joely."

I shook my head in disbelief; my friend had completely missed my point. So because I see and understand things differently and because my perception was diverse from others I failed that exam… great. (That was sarcasm, friends, it really was not great).

Example 2
At the age of 20, I took a mock Maths exam (it was very easy; I got all but one of the questions correct). The one question I got wrong was because of the wording.

The questions were about a sale in a shop and you buying a mobile phone. In the previous question it had stated that you have chosen a mobile phone that you had bought. So the question that tripped me up, asked me:

"Choose an instrument to measure your mobile phone with"

You may read this and think, ok – the answer is a ruler or a tape measure (the answer is indeed a ruler – I would have known this if it had been worded differently).

I asked my mum,

'What do you think I did in response to such a question?'

She responded that she thought that I listed a musical instrument of some sort or an instrument that measured mobile sounds (kinetic/ signal waves or moving energy sounds). As brilliantly literal as this is, I regret to say that is not what I did. What I actually did was the following –

I took a ruler and measured my mobile phone, literally. I physically took out my mobile phone (in an exam. I could have been expelled!) and drew an exactly proportionate and accurately measured diagram of my mobile phone into the exam paper. I did that because that is what I read that I had to do, I understood the question in the wrong way, and it was not common sense to know not to take my phone out in an exam. Cringe.

I chose an instrument (a ruler, as asked, so in this respect I was right) to measure my mobile phone....

I had done exactly as asked, I just didn't realise they meant the pretend phone I had bought in the previous Maths question about buying a phone. I thought the exam board wanted to find out if we could measure effectively and as they did not provide an image of a phone in the paper to measure, nor did they offer a dummy phone to measure, and they did refer to 'your phone'... so the answer seemed simple... and I measured my own. Luckily, I did not get caught because I would have been chucked out for 'cheating'. Obviously, I now realise the question really wanted you to give an answer of a particular object you would use to measure (a ruler) not for you to literally measure the object using that measuring device. Why didn't the question simply ask that, eh?

It was very embarrassing when my teacher was marking the exam and then called out to me, asking

"Joely, if I asked you to measure this big encyclopaedia book, what would you use, a spoon, a 15 cm ruler, a foot long ruler or a metre ruler?"

I responded without even thinking with

"A foot long ruler"

(It was a very big book, and a smaller ruler would have resulted in moving the ruler multiple times while measuring, which could give it an inaccurate measurement) When she asked me this question I knew the answer, it was obvious. If the question in the test had been worded in this way I also would have been able to answer correctly. I explained this to my teacher, she just smiled at me and apologised for the predicament and said she understood my answer to such a silly question, but regrettably, had to fail me. Sadly due to this stupid wording in the exam paper, I failed the exam paper because I used my phone even though it is strictly forbidden, despite only getting one question wrong and all the other ninety nine questions right. Rather typical. I still can't believe it. I retook a similar exam and got all but three questions correct (yes again those three were worded strangely, so I liked to think I could have aced the exam if it was worded properly. I still passed with flying colours the second time round, so it's not all doom and gloom) At the beginning of the class my teacher had told me that all the exam papers were changing so they should be easier to understand for people with additional needs. So much for that. So it was assumed that the learner would know that when answering such a question it was common sense not to literally carry out the question asked. In important exam papers like this, such assumptions about common sense, should not apply and certainly not affect the learner's grade, because everyone has different common sense due to their disabilities and upbringing. I failed many exams purely because of the wording of exam papers that were not friendly to someone who understands and perceives things differently to others, such exam papers are not really fair, so failing, has rarely been my fault.

Rules and Making Assumptions

People with Asperger's are very good at following instructions, providing those instructions are very specific and understood. In this way we can understand spoken language if it is spoken or listed in a way we can understand. Our daily routines are a sequence of rules that we follow. When this sequence is broken or interrupted we have problems with coping. Even with the best intentions to set out a specific set of rules, all the planning can sometimes be subject to change.

Today I did something very silly. We were at home and my mum was about to leave the house and she gave me some very specific rules to follow while she was out. She told me:

> "A lady from Parcels R Us* will pop round at some point today. If she pops in while I am out, I need you to answer the door, say hello, take the parcel and sign for the parcel she will be holding. I also need you to give her these two parcels and get a receipt for them".

Parcels R Us is a made up company.

So yeah, brilliant I have rules to follow – that is really good; in hind sight it should all be fine. But it wasn't. You see while my mum was out, there was a knock on the door and a lady was standing there, holding a parcel and a receipt. She greets me, and then I signed for the parcel and she gives me the parcel. She then points over to my two parcels on the cabinet and asks if they were for her. Everything happened so quickly and everything matched the rules laid out to me so I said "yes" they were. I handed the lady the two parcels and then took the two receipts. Just like I was told too.

Sounds like I did the right thing. You are right, I did the right thing, but to the wrong company! The delivery lady was from a different company, Packages R Us*.

again Packages R Us is also a made up company name.

It also makes me wonder, as the lady from Packages R Us, who I accidently gave the two parcels to, must also have assumed that I had given her the right parcels as well. She did not check the labelling on the parcels either, she just assumed. Never assume my friends, sometimes it is best all round if you ask questions.

My mum set out a specific set of rules to follow, and even though I followed these rules, it still went wrong. This was no fault of my mum's or my own. We cannot predict and plan for every eventuality in the future, so things like this are bound to happen. People without Asperger's would be able to adapt to the change in rules, but for me, I couldn't and didn't realise I had to.

Following instructions and making connections

The other day I was under a car helping my partner replace the welded differential with an LSD (limited slip differential) instead. I'm rather a tomboy, as I find cars lots of fun and I love getting all grubby helping out with the car. Anyway, whenever I help with the car, my partner is always very careful how he words his instructions so that I can understand what he means and do the job to the best of my ability. He understands me well and it is wonderful. Such an understanding has come with time and I love him for his patience and effort in understanding me and my difficulties. This time though, my partner was very good at explaining in good, specific language what I had to do, but made an assumption that I would automatically make a connection, that he had foreseen as obvious. However, as a part of helping out I made one little mistake, which really, if you think about it, was not really a mistake at all, as all I had done was exactly what he had asked me to do.

I had to guide a bolt through a hole, so that the LSD would stay in place. My partner specifically asked me to guide "this bolt through that hole" and he even pointed very specifically at which hole, while instructing me upon the smaller matters like when and how to do this task. So I did the job and it was all fine. When the LSD was in place, we noticed it was wobbly, and that something was wrong with the car, so we checked the differential and it turns out there were two holes I was meant to guide the bolts into. My partner had assumed I would have seen the second hole (which was close to the first hole) and automatically known what I had to do. So he didn't instruct upon this eventuality the first time, he thought it was obvious and therefore needed no instructions.

As it was, I did not make this connection and failed to automatically guide it through the second hole. Can any of you guess why I did not make the connection? Upon seeing the second hole, many people would make the connection and do such a thing automatically especially as they would have already known what to do. It is a tricky concept but I shall try and explain. Basically, I had been specifically instructed upon one way, and those with Asperger's tend to follow instructions literally and very specifically. Therefore I did just that. I have no choice but to follow instructions literally it's just how my brain works. Additionally, I can't look for these extra connections because I'm already concentrating on following the instructions exactly, which literally leaves no room in my thinking process for new stimuli or information – making new connections. So I would not be looking or concentrating on any new possibilities or connections that would need to be made, due to concentrating on the specific instructions. I had seen the second hole, but was too busy following the literal instructions to make the connection that I would have to do the second hole too. Also, to make matters more complex, even if I were confident that I knew how to do something better than the instructions I was meant to follow, I still can't improvise and do something the way I know best. This is because improvising and doing the way I know to be better, would mean not following their instruction's exactly, not listening to 'truth' of how to do certain things. It just feels untrue or wrong to not listen to instructions exactly and improvise and do something my own way.

Summary

I hope that clears up any confusion. Just to clarify; instruction's have to be clear, specific, literal and every eventuality planned for, with every step (even the tiny steps that would seem obvious) also clarified and instructed upon. Never assume that someone on the Autistic spectrum will automatically make a connection to do something unless you have distinctly instructed them to do it. I once burnt beans in a sauce pan because the person failed to tell me that I had to stir the beans as well, it was not obvious to me to stir, I just thought if it were necessary, they would tell me to do it as they know how to cook, and I don't. Look at it this way, if you're showing me how to do something, it would probably mean that I don't know how to do that thing, so I will listen and follow every instruction literally, without trying to make any connections of what I also have to do next. Never assume I (or others with A.S.D) will make a connection and do something automatically if there are already instructions to follow, because I most certainly will not. I imagine it is a similar case for others with my disability too.

Me, Myself and Everybody Else

My Views on My Disability

I love my disability and what it has allowed me to achieve and I really love life. I don't think it should be perceived as a negative thing. I believe that having a disability like mine is a blessing, perhaps a blessing in disguise for those who don't understand. The people I know with disabilities, I have to say, are the most honest and wonderfully kind people. They are not trying to be, they are just naturally that way.

It is fair enough to say it was difficult for me and my family as I grew up with such a disability, but that does not mean it is a bad thing, not at all. When I was a child people always used to say, 'oh poor you, you have that Autism thing. Poor you, life must be really hard for you and your family.' That used to upset and infuriate me, despite the upset being unintentional. I was on prayer chains at my local church and they would pray for me to 'get better'. It was all kind and considerate of course. However, in doing that, they unwittingly made it appear that they perceive my disability to be a bad thing and that I needed all the help I can get to 'get better'. People's perceptions of my disabilities are one of the many things that make my life very difficult. If people don't understand me they make sure I know about it, they judge me, discriminate against me or get annoyed with me when I do not know what they meant. This means that peoples attitude and behaviour towards me has a ripple consequence of how my disability affects me in daily life.

What I'm trying to say is that disability is not a bad thing, it is a wonderful thing. I absolutely love my life, there's not one thing I would change. Seriously it's brilliant. I thank my stars every day that I am so fortunate, for my fabulously understanding friends and family, also above all, for my happiness. My happiness has been given to me hand in hand with my disability and the unique ability that comes with having a disability that allows one to understand

and accept differences in people. This understanding of differences in people inspire some of my dreams, to help individuals and create an understanding among people about life with disability. I have achieved my dreams. I am happy.

Most of the time I hardly notice my disability at all, I mean it's clear to those professionals and most people around me, but to me it is just me and my life. You see I don't know any different, I don't live someone else's life so I have no idea how much easier life for those without a disability would be.

I would like to give you two examples – one of somebody not realising I have a disability and the other of somebody judging me.

Example 1 – A hidden disability
I was at a big event in my town centre, advertising the Disability Youth Group. I was talking to this one chap from the general public explaining about the voluntary youth group, I work with, and what it's about. I had been told by my tutors at the youth group to tell people the 'basics' about what we do and who we are. So, he walks up to me clearly interested as he held out his hand to receive a flier and magazine I was holding. I smile brightly, as I do with everyone, ready to meet and greet him. I started my sentence with the word "Basically". Before I had said another word, the chap rolled his eyes and

then started telling me about how insignificant the word 'basically' is – as it does not mean anything at all and there is no need to use such a word, blah blah blah. He rambled on about that for ages it must have been his pet hate, because boy! could he talk about it. So, I listened and smiled and nodded every now again in agreement with him and eventually he paused. I, by then felt the bubble of understanding and knowledge of what to do and say diminish as his words droned on. So after a while and a few awkward silences I start to stutter out various syllables in an attempt to start talking again. The change in what was expected of me had completely thrown me and suddenly I could not work out how to act or even what to say. It was very unpleasant and made me feel a fool, all I could think was to start with 'basically' because I had been specifically instructed to tell the general public the basics of our group. Eventually I started telling him about the voluntary group I was working with. During my explanation (in which I mentioned my own disability) I noticed his face flush a red colour in his cheeks, which for me, was rather alarming. Suddenly, he asks me

"****. You have a disability?"

I nodded and told him a vague sentence about my disability and he gasped and apologised to me for teasing and being rude, for using the word "basically", because he has no idea that I had a disability.

This is one example of many, where people have made an assumption about me. I would like to think that this gentleman would have communicated with me more appropriately, by not going on a tangent about the technicalities of the word 'basically', had he of known about my disability. You should not judge someone on face value.

Example 2 – Loneliness and literalism
As a child, I never understood what it meant to be a loner and have no friends; much less did I know that I was a loner, too.

This memory goes back to my childhood, I was probably aged 6-9 years old. I stood at my favourite spot in the school playground alone, every day, oblivious to the noise, commotion and general chaos of a busy playground. I would stand there, every day, always alone. All the other children would play team building games but no one ever invited me and I never joined in. Teachers would look over and I would smile, but they never thought I wanted to join in (probably because I would smile at them every time they looked at me). The other children would laugh, play and squeal with delight every time the ball got thrown in their direction. All the while I stood alone, friendless and endlessly waiting to go inside again. I would talk to my thumbs, (Muk and Mukka), and sing to myself to keep me occupied. I would stand in my favourite spot and gaze through the rugged bushes and look out at the cars that would drive by, counting their passengers. I used to play a little game called "Speedo" (named because of my sister's swimming costumes) where I would attempt to count the ratio of red cars to blue cars in my eye line before the cars drove away.

Something strange happened, a couple (man and lady) who had been walking on the pavement outside my school, looked over at me as they waited for the traffic lights to turn. I remember smiling excitedly at them because I loved it when the green man replaced the red man on the traffic cue. The female made a weird face as she looked at me and said something along the lines of

"What an odd ball that little girl is".

Her comment confused me, what is an odd ball? Why am I an odd ball? Did such an odd ball have spots or stripes or zig-zagged patterns? What makes a ball odd? Is it simply that the ball is different?

Despite the knowledge of me not being a ball, I looked down at myself, almost as if to check. 'No', I had thought to myself, 'I am not a ball… So why had the pretty lady called me an odd ball?'

Ok, so I had been very young, I did not understand these things. She had obviously just made the judgement that because I was standing in a special needs playground, alone and smiling a lot, I was odd. Hey, maybe I was odd, but it is not fair, or nice, for an outsider to make a judgement like that.

The point of all that is to sum up Asperger's – My disability:

1. **Sometimes people don't realise I have a disability**, other times I am judged because of it.
2. **When things / routines are changed from what I anticipated, I freak out** and lose control of any sense of what I should be doing or how I

should be behaving. I will momentarily forget most of what I have been previously taught and will really struggle to cope. This is called having a lack of social imagination.

3. **I can't understand people**; I can't read their facial expressions or body language at all. However, to help make it easier I have researched all of this a lot so I am better equipped to handle these things. Well, so I say...

4. **I don't realise if someone is making fun of me**, or laughing at me or with me. A mystery I am yet to unfold.

5. **When I know what is expected of me I know what to do** and how to act in various scenarios.

6. **Effectively everyone assumes I don't have a disability and would sometimes treat me like I am stupid because of that.** Not that I always notice this. Sometimes others can bully me and will assume I am stupid or really dumb, because they don't understand.

7. **I am a very smiley person and always greet someone with a smile. I am quite confident and try my best to be social**, even though this is quite difficult for me. Such things did not come naturally, I was taught on a daily basis how to smile, greet and socialise with somebody by my amazing family, without this I would be none the wiser.

8. **Sometimes my conversations with people come to a complete standstill after a few sentences** as I have no idea of what else to say and it takes me too long to work something out before the other person becomes bored and walks off to talk to someone else. I find that polite questions are good and taking an interest in the person you are talking to is also good.

As far as conversations are concerned I am still terrible at this art form. Making sure I don't overload a person with information about myself can be quite difficult, because if someone asks me "How are you?" I shall tell them at length (as they asked). Likewise, if I see a friend I have not seen in a few years, and they ask me "so what do you do nowadays?" My answer is always longwinded, and can be judged as rude or self-obsessed, because I happen to do a lot day by day. So as they asked, (they should want to know the answer) I tell them my honest answer, which is something as follows

"I try to volunteer every week with various youth disability projects. I work every day in the Nursery as an assistant manager. I write and do art and illustrations for my book I am publishing. I do various sports, such as swimming, running and cycling, so I can train for my challenges to raise money for charity and volunteering abroad projects for next year. I complete modules and courses for University or College. I do projects and fundraising for my voluntary work abroad. I write my speeches and teaching presentations as I am a public speaker and teaching presentation leader about diversity and life with a disability, I volunteer with health champion work; I do this every day alongside everything else. In a nutshell, that is what I do nowadays.... What do you do nowadays?"

I have loads of different projects I do day to day and I am aware that people get bored and perceive you to be rude if you talk about yourself and what you do, for too long. Yet, when you genuinely do a lot of things of great importance to you, I fail to see which parts I am meant to miss out. I tell them everything as each is no less important than the other, there is no information I could leave out due to unimportance. People are generally uninterested in hearing the full story, but I am just answering the question as they asked. There just happens to be no short answer. If they asked, they should be interested in my honest answer. Instead, emotions and personalities make them feel jealous, bored or judge me to be rude.

As a child I would not know how to answer because there was so much I had done. I got out of bed, cleaned my teeth (50 times up, 50 times down, 50 times round), got dressed, walked to school, had numeracy, had literacy, had a break time and a snack. I got called a name that I don't understand. I had science blah blah blah. What bits am I supposed to say? I have since learnt that when people ask

"How are you?"

Or

"What have you been doing today?"

They don't really want to know all the details; they just want me to answer with a few words saying that 'I am fine' and that I 'have had a good day'. Consequently, the answer one gives is probably not even true because I am answering the question as the person asking wants me to answer. Talk about confusing!

If a person was specific and asked about a particular lesson then I won't go into detail of all that I have done. My family soon learnt to ask specific questions such as

"What did you do at school, in numeracy today?"

this is a question I could answer and give a lot of detail and so on. If they asked

"What's been happening with you, Joely?"

Usually there is so much going on with me, usually all of it is really important and of an interest to me and other people so usually I tell the person everything, it is hardly something I can help. However, people then think I am self centred because I talk about myself a lot, whereas I am most certainly not selfish, I am simply answering their question.

My Mum's View on My Disability

My mother has always said that living in the Asperger's world is far better than living in her Neuro-Typical world. This is because Asperger's allows the individual with the disability to see the world as it actually is, those with A.S understand language very literally.

My mum and I firmly believe that the Asperger's world is simpler. This is because Aspie's are all honest, Aspie's say what they mean and don't try to deliberately lie or confuse people. Aspies don't deceive anyone and don't try to, Aspie's are always honest, determined, play by the rules and are very hard-working. Surely that is the better world. Quite frankly the other world is very deceitful with all the lies, sarcasm and talking in riddles, no one says what they mean anymore, people just assume that everyone should agree and understand their way of thinking. People say things like

"That was sick."

And expect everyone to understand they meant awesome and not literally sick.

My other favourite is when people say things like

"Sling your Hook."

Expecting others to understand what they mean. (Apparently it means go away, like when you sling a hook when fishing, you sling it away from you). Other favourites of general literal language include 'over the moon', 'cheap as chips' and 'on it like a car bonnet'. My mum thinks my disability is beautiful and comes with much clarity.

My Difficulties at School – as Told by My Family

I have gone through all my old folders and come across this little gem. This is a piece written by my wonderful sister at one school review when I was roughly 14 years old (embarrassing). The bits in bold are what was written about me, the bits that are not bold are my comments now.

She repeats what I'm saying in conversation even though she often has no idea what I'm talking about. – This is still true… I believe it is called 'parroting back' information in order to be right – a fear of being wrong maybe? I believe this was meant, so repeating words was my way of making conversation. The skill of conversation is still a work in progress.

She is over compulsive about cleaning. She will clean her teeth 3 times before school. Still true. **And wash her face and hands several times.** Yup. **Even though she does not shower in the mornings she spends 45 minutes in the bathroom.** Now I shower in the mornings and evening too. This is because I used to shower in the evening to save time in the mornings. This is also because I am very bad at organising myself and my time, so I could have egg timers and alarms telling me how long I have left before I need to get out the bathroom but that in no way helps me organise the time and what I actually do in that time.

She still has to be told to wear a coat even though she could be looking out the window at the rain. I'm not sure why this is – I think I used to forget because of other distractions and such. I have never been good at making connections. I feel very stupid in this way, because, generally, it is such an obvious thing- seeing the rain and realising you need a coat before you go out – but this rarely happened to me. Maybe this is because of my disability, or maybe it's just me.

When we walk around the shops she follows right behind me, standing on my heels. She only looks at the things I look at. She does not know how to shop. This is very true, I used to do that a lot, not sure why. I think because possibly there was nothing of interest to look at (certainly not anything worth looking at because I would not get it anyway) and I think I used to follow them about in shops to please whoever I was with to show I was interested in them – I think this was something I had learnt to do. Also, I had very little confidence and understanding of what was expected of me, the prospect of walking off to look at things by myself, scared me a little and I daren't venture off by myself. This is because of my confusion of any situation, – how would I interact with a stranger in a unexpected situation? Am I even allowed to go off by myself? I guess that it became a routine, which never really ceased until my family told me that I could go and look at something by myself in a shop if I wished to, so long as they could see me, and they knew where I was (and I knew where they were). My confidence and zero life skills made me ill equipped to cope with anything new, or out of the ordinary.

When she was looking at a red top in a shop, because it was twisted she couldn't work out how to put it on, I had to dress her. That's embarrassing.

I did have quite a difficulty with negotiating my limbs to the right places, when dressing myself, particularly with tricky clothes like that and my brain could not always keep up with what the necessary action was to take in order to successfully dress myself. (Remember I was 14 when this was written) Although it was a particularly twisted top with several arm / neck etc holes and longs pieces of material getting in the way everywhere – my goodness, it was confusing just looking at it. I probably would have similar problems now just not to that degree. I still have difficulty now, doing up button's and zips, even suitably adjusting clothing that is inside out.

In a shoe shop a young male shop attendant was talking to Joely (he was not talking – he was flirting, I did not notice this as I never did, but my sister and mum later pointed this out to me. I was shocked too) **while helping her with her shoes. It was all going fine until she asked me "which shoe goes on which foot?" The boy looked very shocked, and didn't come back: someone else came to serve us.** They were a confusing pair of shoes those, the outer soles looked exactly the same as the other side so I could not determine confidently which shoe went on my right foot and with no buckles or Velcro for clues it was tricky to determine. I had a guess but back then had little confidence in trying something in fear of making a mistake. Even now, some shoes come with complexities, as if they go on both my left and right feet.

Joely can't wrap presents. She can't fold the paper or use sticky tape. This transfers into her school work, because her work sheets come home very messy and often screwed up and ripped (an attempt of folding). This is still very true. My fine motor skills are poor, likewise so is my spatial awareness.

I took her swimming but I had to tell her 5 times to get her swimming costume and towel. She didn't understand that she needed these things to go swimming. I sometimes don't make the connection between what needs to be done and what is going to happen. I won't always know what is necessary for me to do in order to go out somewhere new.

Joely has to leave for school in the morning at the same time every day – 8.40am. But still I have to remind her of this, and that she needs to look at the clock so she knows what time it is. Even if I remind her what

time she has to leave, she won't be ready on time as she forgets to look at the clock. Even so, she has little concept of how fast the minutes tick by and what job would be suitable to do in what amount of time. This is very true. I'm still like this, often though when I am trying to rush and get things done quickly the pressure makes me go slower. Unintentionally, I do things more slowly because every little thing will go wrong, dropping things, catching them and dropping them again, not being able to hold things, falling over etc and I will end up very agitated and itchy everywhere – Bizzare I tell you)

At the start of a television programme Joely will ask what is happening, but we have to tell her that we don't know what is happening because we have watched the same amount as her. Not sure why this is... everything is very hard to follow and often you don't know if they have watched more of the story line before that particular programme episode etc came on. I don't actually know, because I still do it.

She has to be surrounded by soft things. Still true, I carry unused soft tissues in my pockets for when I feel anxious or if I need them...

She addresses her family as 'people'. This is still true, but it's more now because it has become a little family joke and I do it more to be funny now. Its either 'people' or 'persons', back then it was easier to refer to them as a group rather than listing their names, and they are people, so....there you go... 'people' appears to be the logical conclusion to come to- So people it is :)

Joely was sniffing so I passed her a tissue; she then said "how do you know I need a tissue?" As I can't understand body language I forget that other people can.

Joely panics when the phone rings. If she needs to make a call to anyone, we have to plan out the conversation for her... if it does not follow and something the person says surprises her, she will panic on the phone and not know what to say. Still true... Not sure why but talking on the phone scares me, it's a big deal and it still really throws me if a phone conversation goes unexpectedly or if I have to leave a message on their voice mail.

If I ask Joely to get knives and forks for dinner, she won't know for sure how many to get, even though she knows there are 5 people for dinner every night. I am scared of making a mistake and like to ask.

If she is in an unfamiliar place (a friend's house or school) she will not use their toilet even if she is in pain. Still true, even though I am quite aware that everyone has to do it, I find it mortifyingly embarrassing so try to avoid it.

Joely's pet rabbit of 10 years died, she had no emotions/feelings towards this. I am not sure why this is, but it is somewhat true. For a further explanation please read my section called 'Robotic emotions – death.'

Joely does not like hugs, rather than seeing it as a sign of affection she thinks it's just being squeezed and hates the experience. I believe this is because I did not see what all the fuss was about, you hug someone they could smell of sweat / cigarettes, mould, dirt, too much perfume and other gross mixtures. Gee, they could have horrid feeling clothing on and make you feel all itchy and uncomfortable, making you wish you could throw all their clothes off and run away. Goodness, they could squeeze too hard and prevent you from breathing… So uncomfortable and hardly comforting. Back then what was there to like? I love hugs now though.

I have done a lot of school projects with Joely, I will always have to provide the utensils. I would tell her what to write and where to write it. When I have asked Joely about what homework she has, and why she does not understand what to do (despite covering it all that day in class) she will say that she does not like to ask and if she does, the teacher will repeat and not explain. If a teacher asks her if she needs help, Joely says no, because usually such a question is asked when Joely is writing. So the answer to the question at that precise moment in time is 'no' because she does not need help with writing, but she needs help with what she is writing. This is very true, the timing of questions asked is so important, yet it is such a little thing but makes all the difference. I have written a whole section about this topic. Please refer to 'Too School for Cool – Advice for Teaching Assistants'.

That's the end of the review. It's quite interesting isn't it, all these problems I used to have and some problems I still have. Other problems I have been taught over time to deal with so I have a better understanding now.

As you can see my views compared to other people's views are very different, especially when it comes to school life.

My Difficulties in Daily Life – Explained by Me

This part of the book may sound very negative, but it is all true. I am very used to writing and being very positive about my disability. This is purely because I love my disability because of all the wisdom it has taught me about myself and others. However, I fear that in all my positivity it has decreased people's understanding of how difficult life really is with my disability, for me and for everyone who has to help care for me. I might be 22 years old, but the reality is that I still need daily, hourly support and care by my family.

For this reason, I would like to explain how Asperger's really does affect every aspect of daily life. I'm hoping this shows all the complexities I have day to day, that most other people would not know about, including my family. Such hardships are things that I think most people without disabilities take for granted. I have made a list, because I rather like lists, and have provided explanations with each list. I hope some of you come away from reading this section with fresh enlightenment and understanding of the true difficult extent of our daily hardships. Below is my first list.

Getting up and getting dressed

1. I don't like getting up because I am incredibly tired all day, every day
2. I need encouragement to get up – purely because I fall straight back to sleep – without even meaning to. I sleep through alarms and find it excessively difficult to wake up and stay awake, due to dizziness / shutdowns.
3. I go back to bed during the day, every day to take 3 hour naps (I have no choice – falling asleep while working is very unprofessional)
4. I have to do things in a certain order in the morning otherwise I can't leave the house or do any tasks in the correct manner
5. I need help to choose clothes because I choose unsuitable clothes for the weather. For instance I still wear summer dresses in the winter or don't wear coats. Or I wear 3 coats, 4 pairs of leggings, denim trousers, 2 vests, long sleeve tops while out in public, and carry loads of spare clothes out of fear I will get too cold, it's either one extreme or the other
6. I need help to dress myself because I find it hard to do up buttons/zips/ tie up laces, turn items of clothing in the right way and negotiate where my limbs need to go. This may sound normal, but I reckon it takes it least 15 seconds longer to do these fiddly jobs than the average person. I'm all fingers (that don't work) and no thumbs

Explanation of list:

I am usually emotionally, physically and mentally drained from everyday life, due to my Asperger's and Hypercalceamia and Hyperparathyoidism. This means when my alarms go off in the morning I sleep straight through and won't wake up. It also means that I have to have sleeps during the day, every day, due to being constantly in pain and over tired. I am too shattered to keep myself awake. I don't like walking around my house like a zombie, so shattered I can hardly walk or see straight (literally, when I am over tired I began to see double and my eyes go dizzy and hurt). If I don't have a nap in the day the simplest of tasks will became mayhem with intricacy, if not impossible. I am not very good at choosing appropriate clothes for the weather, mum helps me with this. This is because I have a very specific routine; my every day routine does not allow for weather changes and so does not include a coat. I still have grave difficulty with tying my shoe laces, buttons and zips.

Being in the house during the day

1. I go back to bed in the day
2. I have no motivation to do new things

3. I can't concentrate on anything

4. I don't like to open the door to people, it scares me as I am bad at any kind of social protocol

5. I don't like answering the telephone

6. I have to do things in order, or else I can't complete anything or go out anywhere

7. I like to do one activity the whole time – I get 'addicted' to one routine or activity and find it difficult to try anything new

Explanation of list:

I get stressed every time the telephone starts ringing, I never know what to say, I can't hear or follow what the person is saying and often relay messages wrong to other people (often because I understood the message wrongly or did not hear properly). When the doorbell goes I try not to answer it, as it is a change in routine and I won't know what to expect from the stranger at my door, what to say to them or how to beat address a problem should one arise. I don't have much motivation to leave the house or change my routine because the sheer thought of travelling and doing things alone scares me because I always need so much help with my life skills and independence. The outside world scares me, even when I'm with people that understand me. I don't make connections very well between knowing I have spare time and jobs that need doing. If my mum did not work from home to look after me and encourage me to do things, I would not do anything at all, I would be quite happy reading or writing a book, drawing and exercising all day, every day. When I start doing one activity, I tend to do that activity constantly, to the point of it being ridiculously obsessive or frustrating. I am not very good with splitting my attention. If I have to multitask, all tasks will be completed with terrible quality as I can't focus my attention on all the relevant details to get the jobs done properly.

Any attempt at cooking a meal

1. I can only 'cook' convenience food

2. I can't get more than one thing ready at the same time

3. I don't cook things properly, I don't really know how to, even with instructions

4. I burn things – and myself

5. I can't plan what to eat

6. I forget to check things are fresh

7. I cannot follow a recipe
8. I have coordination problems and can't use a knife – I stab or cut myself
9. I can't use an oven/hob/microwave

Explanation of list:
I can't follow recipes. Even the instructions on a microwavable meal are too complex for me to make sense of. I am not very good at multi tasking, for instance getting the dishes out ready to eat on while I need to prepare food that is going in the microwave. I burn foods while cooking because it takes so much time to do jobs such as taking a dish out of the cabinet that I don't check in time that the food is not burning. I even burn beans. While being shown how to cook beans on toast; no one told me I had to stir them while they were in the saucepan, so I took their instructions literally. No one should assume I know what to do next, because usually I am following instructions word for word because I *don't know* what to do. I have problems following instructions because I don't understand the language used (pound, ounces, gas mark 6,) and a lot of the time I take instructions literally. One instruction told me to measure a pound of margarine, I had no idea what a 'pound' meant, let alone how to measure it. I got a pound coin and 'measured' a pound of margarine. The result was disastrous and my food made me really ill for a long time afterwards. I don't like using kitchen equipment, particularly the gas cooker. This makes using it hard and I try to avoid lighting anything because fire terrifies me. Also, I never know how much gas I need, how do you know how much gas is coming out because it changes. I can't even make tea or coffee, although I am practising daily. I can't measure the right ratio of milk : water. I forget to turn the kettle on, spill the water everywhere and burn myself. I have poor fine motor skills always. I practise things daily but the improvements are slow. I have just come to terms that some things I will always find very difficult, my fine motor skills, amongst others, are one of them. Using a peeler I find difficult as I tend to peel off tiny scrapes at a time and it takes me about three minutes to do each item of food, were as most people would have finished peeling the whole lot of vegetables by the time I had finished doing one or two. I could say it's down to practise, but to be brutally honest this is one thing where it is not. I will always find this very difficult and all improvements are slow and little each time. It is still best to keep practising though. Sharp knifes frighten me so I don't tend to pick them up to use them at all.

Talking and listening to others
1. I avoid people
2. I can't concentrate on what people say
3. I can't speak up for myself
4. I tell people what I think they want to hear
5. I take things literally ALL the time (literally)
6. I misunderstand the things people say ALL the time
7. I can't explain things properly to people, I certainly write better than I talk
8. I find it hard to start a conversation
9. I find it hard to end a conversation
10. I find it hard to maintain a conversation
11. I don't know what to talk to people about
12. I forget things I have been told
13. I get frustrated when people misunderstand me
14. I find it impossible to talk to those who have no interest in talking to me
15. I don't understand peoples' facial expressions or body language
16. When I am stressed or overloaded, I don't always hear what people are saying, because of the back ground distractions and noise

Explanation of list:
I avoid people because I find them impossible to understand. I can't read body, facial language or spoken language. I take everything literally and can't understand sarcasm or riddles. I can't maintain a conversation because my processing speed is much slower than other peoples. It takes me at least ten seconds longer to process information than it does other people. If I'm having a conversation and someone has finished speaking, if I want to respond, I have to do the following before I can speak –

1. Work out what I think they meant (ten seconds give or take)
2. Double check to make sure I have not taken anything literally or misunderstood what the person had said (ten seconds give or take)
3. What is appropriate to say (fifteen seconds give or take)
4. How I should word what I am going to say to best ensure I don't cause any offence (fifteen seconds give or take)
5. Find the confidence to say it (limitless)

By the time I have done all of the above the conversation has moved on and someone else has already interjected and changed the conversation completely.

I know that everybody else does this, but for me it takes a lot longer due to my lack of understanding, confidence, concentration and distractions. This also means that I can go for long periods without speaking because I spend so long processing all the information. Most people think I am shy, I am, but the main problem lies with simply not being allowed the time to enter my thoughts into the conversation. Similarly I don't know how to start conversations. I know to be polite, smile and listen, but even with my amazing siblings I find it hard to keep a conversation going because I just don't know what to say and what questions to ask. I am so horrified of making a mistake and upsetting someone that it takes me ages to think of anything appropriate to say. I normally start conversations by saying 'are you ok?' Sometimes, as a child, regardless of their response, I usually responded with 'good' because I was ill equipped to understand how to handle sadness and negative emotions in people. Nowadays, I do try to empathise with them feel better and compliment them, but the conversation would end soon after. I do tend to forget things people have said to me because there is so much more information for me to remember, because I notice more than others. I have a memory like a sponge. A sponge that holds lots of irrelevant information – such as colours/ patterns and sensory issues. These are what takes up most of my concentration. So my sponge like memory holds all the irrelevant information but drips out all the relevant information, such as what I have been told. The sheer volume and constant amount of sensory issues I go through every minute of every day is higher than relevant information I have been told. So I forget easily, the same goes for completing tasks and instructions. It particularly annoys me when people then get annoyed at me for not understanding what they meant. Even people that know me well do this sometimes. I also find it impossible to talk to people if they have no interest in talking to me. Some people who don't understand me or why I do certain things, (of course I may have made mistakes too, everyone makes mistakes and I am no saint although I always try my best to be good and considerate) may ignore me, and try to cut off all contact with me. This hurts immensely and I simply can't understand how someone can ignore someone like the way people ignore me. Sometimes it hurts so much that I am fighting back tears when I come across such people, and to try and avoid crying in front of them and letting them see how they have upset me, I simply can't talk to them. Even if I could think of something suitable to say, for instance "hi", the words dry up in my mouth in an attempt not to cry. I have this thing with not letting anyone see me upset, only those close to me. Even when I was being bullied when I was 6 years old and I got slapped round the face a few times by a teenager, I still did not cry because I could not bear the thought of that teenager thinking they had won, that they could treat me that way and succeed in making me unhappy. It has got to the stage, that if I have things to do that require a two hour routine to get me in an emotionally and mentally capable state for completing tasks (for instance meeting friends, going to the shops, volunteering or meetings) I have to avoid such people so that I don't get myself so upset that I can't complete the necessary tasks. Not to mention the panic attacks and the intense fear that grips at my heart when I am faced with that situation, it terrifies me, it really does. I have cancelled things many times because I become too emotional to cope with doing any tasks at all, usually because I got ignored by such people. I just don't understand why people could ignore others, if I were walking in the streets and I came across my abusers. I would not ignore them, and some of them have been close to killing me. Hatred does not boil up much more than the intense emotion I feel when I think of my abusers, so there is definitely a reason why I could ignore them... I just can't do it for some reason. I always have to try and make things better by saying something or at the very least smiling. If my bullies passed me in the street I would still

nod, smile politely and walk away in acknowledgment. Even if I then walked away to cry with fear and have flashbacks and panic attacks for the rest of the day, I still could not ignore them, not only because it won't make the situation better, but I simply can't be that mean, that inconsiderate, I can't stoop to that level and be like them. So for those that ignore me, out of politeness and an attempt to make things better, I will try and say hello, but that is as far as it goes because I know I have to try not to be rude but I simply can't talk any more than that (can't, not wont). This is only because I find it difficult enough talking to people who want to talk to me, I still have to face all the usual challenges without trying to process how to make a particular unfair situation better. Usually I can't talk to people I love dearly for long because I find it so difficult to understand, process and formulate a suitable response, it really is exhausting, and that is even when I am comfortable, happy and at ease. Put me in a situation where someone is glaring at me, stony faced and intent on ignoring me as we pass by, I simply can't say any more than 'hello', and even then I get so nervous and scared that I say it so quietly that people have said they did not hear me at all, and had assumed I was ignoring them, even though that would never be the case. So for those who are happy to be rude, ignore or not be interested in talking to me, I just clam up. I literally can't talk to people who treat me this way because it provides too much new information for my brain to cope with, so much so that the processing speeds slow down to an impossible conversation compatibility rate and I simply can't cope. I avoid talking to people because of my lack of understanding of how to cope with their changeability and I am scared that they will see how vulnerable this makes me. People have taken advantage of me and my friendship in the past by using my vulnerability and disability as a tool of power to bully, emotionally torment or tease me and have consequently made me feel quite small and horrifically scared. I don't want to talk to people in case this happens again, I have been too scared to make new friends for fear of trapping myself in such a nightmarish situation again. This, amongst many other problems, is mostly why I live my life in my house every day.

Wellbeing during the day
1. I always feel in pain, usually all over my body
2. I always have stomach cramps, migraines, chest pains, back aches, eye aches, muscle pain, cramps, and ear aches
3. I am always so plagued with fatigue that I often have influenza type symptoms most days, so I always feel ill
4. I get cramping and shooting chest pains that radiates to my left arm and up my neck/ collar bone, every day
5. I feel dizzy most days usually due to sensory stimuli overloads
6. I get panic attacks
7. I get flash backs
8. I get anxiety attacks

Explanation of list:
I always feel ill, this means that I can't usually tell if I am ill with an actual illness or if my body is just being its usual painful self. Consequently this means I don't organise to see doctors because I simply feel that terrible all the time – there is only some many times you can go to the doctor with the same daily symptoms. I get chest pains every day but mostly at night. When I get the searing cramping pain in my chest / collar bone / neck / arm it usually means that if I don't take my medication within ten minutes of it beginning I will be in absolute agony from the same chest pains a few days after (to the point of needing to go to the hospital with liquid morphine, countless tests and x-rays, drips etc). Such chest pains can start from nothing but a tiny niggle of discomfort and then increase to full blown eight / nine out of ten pain within two minutes. Most nights I rate the pain seven out of ten, or on a good night it is only five out of ten. Ten here mean's being in so much continuous agony that I am at A&E in hospital on morphine an undergoing various tests for most of the night.

Due to PTSD (Post Traumatic Stress Disorder) I get anxiety attacks, panic attacks and flashbacks of various things that have happened to me in my past. All of which are very different. A flashback is when something traumatic has happened to you, and the memory of the event(s) are too big and painful to cope with for one to remember entirely. This means that the brain's natural process to make the memories less painful to remember is to shut down your memory of the actual event, so that the only memory you get of these traumatic events come in the form of flashbacks, until you learn to cope with the distressing memories. (Usually a flashback is like little scraps of memory – like watching a film or being in a dream were you can't remember certain details of how things happened, how you got there, who you were with and other minor details) The difference between panic attacks and flashbacks is that a flashback is entirely real, has happened, you get all the same feelings and emotions you felt when the initial incident happened and you feel utterly hopeless. A panic attack is panicking about things that could happen and feeling physically ill. I don't like to go into too much detail here, so I will only say that when this (flashback) happens to me it is truly horrific, all my usual pains and discomforts or problems are enhanced and made worse in a huge way. This is because when in a flashback I can't see anything but the things that happened to me all those years ago in that particular flashback (I have many different flashbacks all of different things / events). While in a flashback, I can't hear anything as I can only hear what happened to me back then and I can hardly move because the pain I felt back then physically disables me from being able to move in reality. It is appalling to the point of being in cruel hysterics in the middle of the street fighting off someone who, in reality to the naked eye, is not even there. This happened to me countless times but one time stands out in my memory because of the kindness of a passerby to help me. It happened when I was walking by myself to college. I was quite happily walking when suddenly out of nowhere I was reminded of a traumatic event that I had kept buried deep in my past. So the flashback started. I came back from the flashback to find myself peering through my arms with bleary eyes at two dogs that were sniffing at my face and feet. I was curled up on the floor in the middle of the pavement, my arms wrapped around my head and my knees held tight to my chest. My knuckles were white, and my whole body was tense, shaking and felt like it was on fire for all the pain I was in. An old lady was crouched by my feet and was peering at me holding the dogs lead loosely to the ground, an expression of confusion, questioning and anxiety on her face. She supported me to ring a cab to take me home, waited with me and even paid for my fare home. Needles to say I had no choice but to go straight home again and

I couldn't attend college for three months due to similar things happening each day. My tutors were very understanding and allowed me to work from home (which is very rare indeed) providing I showed proof of my work. I still achieved great grades by studying at home. People don't understand the true extent of the cruelty of living in a world overshadowed by flashbacks and panic attacks, purely because it does not happen to them. People don't understand that such unspeakable memories, haunt you and can make life a living hell by making even the simplest of daily tasks (made much harder already by my disability) even more difficult to deal with. This effects daily life, even now when I am feeling better within my mental state. I am slowly but surely getting better though, I see light at the end of the tunnel.

Coping with paper work and bills / banking
1. I don't open my post
2. I don't respond to my post
3. I don't understand anything I read in my post or payment bills
4. I need help to fill in forms
5. I am unable to reply to letters – don't really know how to
6. I need help to pay bills
7. I am unable to budget
8. I don't understand the consequences of spending money
9. I find it hard to manage my finances
10. I have no idea how banking works

Explanation of list:
I don't have a clue about any of this or what any of it means. I will open my post if it is addressed to me, but I don't understand what the letter means because it is usually complexities to do with banking. I give my post to my mum to sort out because I would not know where to start. I only respond to post if my mum does it for me or helps me. I don't understand language and layout used in bank letters. Also Maths is my worse subject and understanding numbers on a piece of paper just does not make sense to me. I can read the numbers fine, that's not the problem; I just don't understand what relevance the numbers have and how it affects me. This is why my disability allowance is paid into a joint account with my mum, where we both have to sign to put money onto my card where I can access it. We only transfer small amounts over to my card as and when I need it. This system works really well for me because I only have what I need and do not need to worry about larger sums of money.

If I did not have my mum's help I would not have a clue of how to manage my finances, pay bills, budget and keep my money safe.

Social life and hobbies

1. I can get obsessive about my interests and forget to do other important things I need to do
2. I need help to go out socially
3. I need help to make friends
4. I find it hard to tell if someone is my friend
5. I would like to go out more
6. I have to cancel social meetings with friends because a routine has gone wrong or because I am in too much pain/overloaded/flashback/panicky to cope with social scenarios
7. I find it hard to work out when I am drifting apart from a friend
8. I don't know how to make things better between me and a drifting friend
9. I find it easier to spend time on my own
10. I feel very isolated

Explanation of list:

I have a small group of friends but I am not very good at organising myself to contact them to go out and see them and need a lot of encouragement to do so. This is not because I don't want to spend time with them (I love spending time with my friends, they're all brilliant) but I find it difficult to organise myself. This includes contacting them, organising suitable time and places to meet them and actually leaving the house to meet them. Leaving the house is the hard part… I get very stressed in advance of meeting my friends because this is a change in my usual routine and many things could go wrong. I am always worried about how to handle situations that could occur for example being able to respond suitably to best help my friend's in any new

crisis. The routine of preparing myself to go out of the house is very stressful. As you know I find leaving the house difficult at the best of times. If I have to meet my friends somewhere new, it makes the process even more difficult. If I do manage to arrange to meet them my routine can't be disturbed at all, otherwise I will end up feeling too ill and in pain to be up to seeing anyone at all. I have very little social imagination due to my Asperger's, so I need help getting from A to B safely.

I have had friends in the past that bullied me and had taken advantage of me and now I don't try to meet new people in case I get in that situation again. I do spend most my time on my own and I do feel isolated because of this. I need a lot of help to prepare myself and organise myself to go out socially, otherwise I would not be able to go out at all. I often have to cancel meetings with my friends, which is something I detest about myself. I have to do this because I can't cope with new situations due to my disabilities and mental health. I often don't see my friends for weeks at a time and I terribly miss them. I just can't work out how to make things better, I arrange a meeting, but then, sometimes I have to cancel because my disability or mental health is playing up again, I become too ill, and this is a reality that happens more times than not. The problem is combined between my disability – my Asperger's, my mental health – my PTSD and my anxiety issues. My friends keeping in contact with me often relies on them understanding the difficulties I face. Simply because I can't read people well enough to realise there is a problem, especially as they try to hide the problems to make me feel better, bless them. I would love to be able to see my friends it least thrice a week, I just find things so complex, that seeing them as much as I would like does not often happen. Regrettably, I can't tell when a friend feels like we are drifting apart. I try to make an effort to stay in contact, but my memory is atrocious and I often think I have written messages to my friends, but haven't at all. Likewise, I forget about meetings and miss appointments…. Sorry to all my wonderful friends that has understood me enough to stick by me… I love you all for your continuous support and friendship. I will always try to make an effort; I just hope my disability allows me to.

Leaving the house
1. I have to be encouraged to leave the house
2. I worry for days in advance if I have to leave the house
3. I get very anxious before I leave the house
4. I need to be prepared for any changes in routine, including leaving the house
5. I don't sleep the night before (or a few nights before) I have to leave the house
6. My social imagination is a nightmare
7. I feel sick, dizzy and become in a lot of pain before I leave the house
8. I have to have someone with me if I leave the house
9. I have to do things in a certain order before I can leave the house
10. If I do things in the wrong order before I leave the house I have to start again, this makes my punctuality terrible sometimes
11. I have to check and re-check things before I leave the house

Explanation of list:
I never leave the house without somebody with me, usually my mum. This is due to pain and possible changes in routine, panic attacks, anxiety, due to my Asperger's and PTSD. Even if I have to go to my corner shop (fifty metres from my house) my mum has to explain every little detail and give me a list of what I need to do and buy. Such a list would include, in great detail:

1. Which particular shop I was going to, if it was a new shop she would include a small map of landmarks so I don't get lost with arrows pointing me in the right directions
2. Where to find listed items in the shop
3. A reminder to buy the cheapest best quality brand
4. How much each item costs
5. How much money I have to spend
6. How much change I should get
7. A list of what to say if I can't find the item and have to ask where it is

If she does not do this, I usually lose the money, buy the wrong thing or get short changed.

Due to my Asperger's I am a very vulnerable person when I am out of the safety of my home. When I have to leave the house I become so stressed that

I start to get major stomach cramps, this upsets my routine because I have to change everything to take medication. When my routine has changed, I have to start from the beginning and my mum will have to organise me, remind me of what to do, (go to the toilet, take a coat, tablets and shoes). I have these difficulties to this extent every time I have to go out anywhere. I honestly feel like a two year old with all of these problems, yet I can't seem to help or improve any of these things with ease or speed.

Coping with places I don't know
1. I need to be prepared in advance to be able to go anywhere new
2. I get anxious when I go somewhere I don't know
3. New places make me feel ill / angry / frightened
4. I am not safe in new places
5. I get lost in new places
6. I don't know how to ask for help when I get lost in unfamiliar places
7. I need to have someone with me when I go to new places
8. I have to go home if I am without the things I need
9. I get very anxious in noisy places
10. I get very anxious in places where there are lots of people

Explanation of list:
If I am going somewhere new my mum has to give me a prep talk in advance. She has to explain every tiny detail about what needs to be done so I can cope with going to the new place., this is because my social imagination in terrible. This includes:

1. Where I am going (a little map of land marks for when I get there to show me the best way of getting there if I have to walk)
2. How I am getting there
3. Money- how much I have, how much I can spend and what to spend it on, even what money I should spend on what (pounds for bus fare notes for train etc)
4. What to say
5. Where to sit on a bus
6. Where to stand to get off the bus
7. Where to get off the bus
8. Where I am going
9. How I am going to get there

10. Changes that may happen
11. What to do if this happens
12. Who to go to for help

Even with all this planning I still feel very ill when travelling, with symptoms of influenza and panic attacks. My mum makes sure I have credit and battery on my phone because otherwise I would forget and not remember to check. This is why I try to avoid going to new places.

If I go somewhere new, I will be really stressed because it is out of my routine, I suffer with aches pains, tummy cramps for at least a few days before the dreaded day out, but also for the rest of the week. This makes every task in daily life even more troublesome than it usually is (and such tasks are usually very challenging for me as it is). My PTSD gives me flashbacks when out in public, this makes me anxious and I try to avoid new places for this reason – people don't understand me and I feel like I should be in a straight jacket a lot of the time.

Coping with people I do not know
1. I get anxious / frightened around people I do not know
2. I cannot talk to people I do not know
3. I misunderstand the intentions of other people I don't know

Explanation of list:
I avoid all people, people I do and do not know. People scare me, I used to get bullied in a past relationship (friends / peers) and so I have a big fear of talking to new people or even being near them. Also, I don't understand people, and often don't realise if they are trying to take advantage of me, which usually- they are. People scare me because of how I used to be treated. I will always be kind, compassionate, loyal, honest and caring towards those I know and do not know, I always smile and I am always polite. I never judge someone in a bad way let alone discriminate against them. So even though I can't trust other people, I am always nice to them because I would be a horrid person if I wasn't, I don't see justification in treating others badly or being rude to other people just because you are having a bad day and I promise myself every day I will not treat others badly because otherwise I would be stooping as low as the people that hurt me. My kindness can often be mistaken and this makes me vulnerable.

Sleep

1. I need reassurance to calm me to go to sleep
2. I have nightmares
3. I have panic attacks
4. I have flashbacks
5. I get up and pace around
6. I find it hard to sleep when there is noise
7. I need blackout curtains to sleep

Explanation of list:

I fall asleep easily the first time, but usually when I am feeling particularly ill that day (which is usually every day), I will wake up multiple times that night from nightmares that turn into flashbacks. I often wake up and I am still having a flashback which means I can't fall asleep again. Then I get panic attacks and I start to feel ill and in pain. I have to start my bed time routine again because my bed won't be comfortable enough for me to sleep. These flashbacks are horrid because they are real; I wake up thinking it is still happening. I need reassurance to get back to sleep because I am usually very scared.

When I was younger sleep was a huge issue, and I would wake many, many times a night but not be able to get back to sleep, my quality of sleep was terrible. Now I wake up multiple times a night from pain and nightmares but fall asleep within an hour or two. I usually wake up every night to the feeling of someone touching me, tickling me and it scares me a great deal due to my past experiences.

So all of the above is a list of all of my main difficulties I face in day to day life. I hope I have piqued some of your interest and I hope you have a better understanding of the daily predicaments I find myself in, that others don't face at all.

This whole section was very hard for me to write as I am usually very positive about my disability. I focus so much of my time on improving myself and helping others that I sometimes forget just how difficult daily life is for me and others around me. Even though in my list of difficulties I have written many times that 'I can't do this' or 'I can't do that' I am constantly trying to do those things to make life easier for me and my family. Although I find these things difficult, I want to be able to do them. I will not give up on trying, because even though improvements are slow, they do happen. I am very lucky to have an amazing and supportive family who help and encourage me every step of the way. Without my family I would probably spend my whole life secluded in my bedroom. I would be isolated from other people and I would not be experiencing life to the full let alone achieving and living my dreams. It really helps knowing that my family won't give up on me, so I can't possibly give up on myself. What I am trying to say is that even though it is hard, it really is worth trying to do and improve on these difficult things.

I see my disability as a very positive thing. This is because with my family's constant support I have achieved all of my dreams and lots more. I have got qualifications I previously thought would never happen for me and I have experienced and done things I never thought I could do, things such as representing the country, public speaking and being involved in life changing organisations. I would not have done any of these things if it wasn't for my families support. So despite these problematic areas I have, I refuse to let them upset me, life is good, and I can't help other people change their lives for the better if I can't accept my own life with all of its hardships. I am a firm believer that life is for living, not hiding from.

When I Was Told I Had a Disability

My parents told me I had a disability called Asperger's, when I was 13 years old (I was diagnosed with A.S a year earlier). They said they chose a time during the summer holidays when I would be less stressed about school. They sat me down, gave me a little book for me to read about A.S and explained gently what it meant and how special, lovely and kind I was. I looked at a list of symptoms and characteristics of A.S and found myself laughing, crying aloud in pure relief and happiness. As I read each bullet point on the list of characteristics, I thought 'Yes, this is me; totally me… wow.' and the more I read, the more I smiled and wept with joy at finding out what is different about me. I soon found out that it is not a bad thing to have a disability- it is a beautiful thing.

I was so relieved I can't describe it enough. I had so many questions and I read every book that I could find on the subject. I just wanted to learn more and more and more. Most people I have spoken to have been relieved about finding out they had a disability and telling their friends for similar reasons to me.

When I Told my Friends

The best thing I ever did was tell my friends. When I was ready that is. I'm not going to lie; it was so emotional. We rounded up all of my really close friends at secondary school in the library and explained to them that I had a disability called Asperger's, and what it meant; and they were all fantastic about it. Thankfully my mother was there which was fortunate because I was in tears the whole way through.

It was good because everyone suddenly understood me better and I felt better in myself; I felt like I no longer had to act normal and I could finally be myself. It made my friends treat me better. One friend used to tease me dreadfully about my differences, calling me names, making me feel terrible about being so stupid (I'm not stupid, but when you get bullied in such a way, after a while you believe it). I used to come home every night from school feeling low and horrible about myself because of such teasing. I used to feel stupid and close to worthless. Once my friends knew I had Asperger's, they understood my differences and my disability more, and quite literally the teasing stopped.

It was such a relief because I had been feeling terrible and it felt like once everyone understood that it was not my fault, it just got immensely better. I have never regretted telling my friends, it would have been horrid to be at high school and having to pretend to be normal, especially with all the other pressures going on. I mean, I would have had far too much to cope with in secondary school without stressing out about my disability and being misunderstood too. It was also a relief because I had been worried that it may make things worse. I am still very appreciative to my friends for this. Thank you guys.

Too School for Cool

I shall start with a quick bit of background about the schools I went to –

I went to a special needs school until I was nine years old. That school was fabulous even though I hesitate to admit I remember very little of my time there. The support from all of the helpers that came into contact with me was simply superb and I will be forever grateful and appreciative towards this school for their great help in my development. Without that schools help, I would not be who I am today. Thank you. At the age of nine I started doing dual placement. This meant that I spent four days a week at the special needs school and one day a week at the mainstream primary school. My time at the main stream primary school slowly increased until I was attending full time. By the time I was in Year 6 (about ten years old) I had left the special needs school completely. I then went to an all girls secondary school which was also mainstream. I'm glad I chose to go to an all girl's school because I don't think I could have stood some of the immaturity of some boys at that age. Personally, I doubt I would have learnt a thing with the constant distraction of guys and girls etc. After I left secondary school (at the age fifteen) I went to a mainstream college, but attended the unit that specialised in young people with either a disability or additional learning needs. After a year of the course I decided to leave to go to an Arts University College where for two years (until I was nineteen) when I graduated with three A levels. I have written a separate chapter about what I did after I finished at the Arts University.

"We're all special"
When I was a child I had no idea I was any different to other children, this is because I grew up in a Special Needs School surrounded by other children with disabilities, so it was normal. I really liked it. I was thought to be clever, I had more confidence, and I had friends at my Special Needs School.

I have one memory of my naivety dating back to when I was 8-9 years old.

My best friend and I had been talking about school, (at the time I had been doing dual placement with the Special Needs School and a mainstream school which is where my best friend attended). My best friend had said to me

"I wish I could go to your special needs main school and be with you."

I responded with

"You can, I will ask for you."

My friend looked at me with a funny look which I could not read at the time and said

"I can't though; my mom says that your school is for special children. I'm not special"

I was very confused when she said that, because it had never occurred to me that my special needs school was a school solely for the purpose of educating and helping children with special needs. Plus, I had been told everyone was special. So I responded with

"My mum told me that everyone is special. – So you can come to my school too."

My best friend, bless her, looked at me again with a look of puzzlement. My friend had a hard time explaining to me what special meant in this context. She explained gently that

"Well the kids at your school are different to us normal kids… They look different to us"

(That is a quote- I'm not trying to be offensive and neither was my best friend- she was 8-9 years old at the time. She was very good about it, actually). I responded with

"Everyone looks different to other kids. We are all different looking"

Of course, I took it literally and did not understand what she meant by different. In my eyes yes, everyone is different; I remember thinking that my best friend had blue/green eyes and I have brown eyes, she is pale and I have browner skin. We are different.

I had grown up in a Special Needs School where everybody had a disability of some sort, so this I considered 'normal'. However I left my special needs school and I soon realised that children with disabilities were in the minority. So it turns out that what I thought was normal wasn't, the children without the disabilities were the ones considered 'normal' by the general public. That was the first time I realised that I was actually a bit different from other children. It was rather strange.

Main difficulties at school
First things first, I shall list some of my main difficulties with school and then go into detail about them.

1. Organisation
2. Fatigue
3. Change in Routine
4. Meltdowns
5. Learning Environments
6. Distracted Teachers

7. Patience
8. Exam Anxiety
9. Homework
10. Fitting in

Organisation

At the beginning of each new term Corinna, my lovely sister would spend hours organising me and all of my school work/school bags to make life easier for all. Sadly for me, this never worked for long because each day is different and you are always in need of different things. Over the years many strategies have been suggested, including:

1. Labelled folders
2. Egg timers
3. Do things the night before
4. Having a set visual routine
5. Make sure everything is tidy and in the same place
6. Keep calm and try not to rush
7. Prioritising and making lists for important jobs
8. Writing tasks down
9. Creating specific and realistic goals
10. Try not to do too much in one go

Some of the above were successful and some were not. It has taken me (and my family) many years to work out a system that works for me. The most valuable system for me was writing the tasks down and creating a visual routine. It is vital that my time is effectively organised into routines so that I have enough time to complete each task. This also meant that I would not be rushed and was able to stay calm and focused. Having a tidy and uncluttered work and living space is paramount so that distractions are minimised. This is something that I struggle with because I need a separate routine to tidy. I found that doing things the night before was a big help, it meant that in the morning everything was already prepared and I only had to focus on my morning routine.

Advice to Someone with A.S.D – Organisation
Ask parents / carers / siblings for help and just keep trying new techniques until you find something that works for you. I have tried many different ways to organise myself but the only thing that has really helped was having a visual routine scheduled into my time table. This routine gave me the time I needed to organise myself. This is because if you don't have enough time, you will be pressured and rushed, and your organisation is likely suffer. If you can't organise your time how can you organise anything else?

Fatigue

> "You can't hoot with the owls at night, if you want
> to soar with the eagles in the morning."

Have you ever heard this metaphor? It is a little strange; but once you think about it, it does make perfect sense. It means that you can't stay up late into the night (like owls who stay awake all night) if you want to be up early the next day doing important jobs (like Eagles who wake up early every day to hunt). Resting when it is advisable to rest, (e.g. at 9.30/10pm) to get a good night sleep of eight hours a night, should make life a little easier. Trust me.

Fatigue is a huge aspect of my life and I expect many others too. Sometimes, no matter how good my night's sleep is, I still wake up utterly exhausted. This is because each and every day is entirely exhausting, mentally physically and emotionally due to my disability. This doesn't mean you shouldn't try to get a good night sleep; a good restful night's sleep definitely helps to make each day more bearable, so don't give up.

I was sorting through my bedroom the other day and came across some of my old school planners (basically a diary that tells you your lesson timetables and you homework schedule). It was wonderful reading through these planners. This is because everything I wrote about screams "I have Asperger's syndrome." to me now. This is because I was constantly writing about how I was tired, misunderstood or confused about what I needed to do. Very shortly I will share with you some of my notes from my diary; I found it very amusing, maybe you will too.

School was always very hard work because it was so very tiring. It's hard to explain why. Obviously everyone finds school hard and tiring even without a disability. However having a disability obviously makes every tiny task more complex and it becomes more stressful and tiring. If you have a disability everywhere in school causes complete and utter sensory overload. Schools are not an easy place to go to. My mum used to say that it is like entering a minefield for those on the Autistic spectrum. There are constant sensory overloads and there are regular bursts of sounds, colour and unpleasant sensations. There always seem to be loud noises and there is absolutely loads of stuff to look at all the time. Honestly, I found myself getting heavily distracted during lessons by not only the pictures on the walls but also by the things that other people wouldn't notice (cracks and blue tack smears on walls for instance). In the class room when I was supposed to be learning I was always so distracted by pretty much everything. It did not matter how much I wanted to concentrate I just couldn't. So yes, even when it was quiet, school was a mega sensory overload all the time. I used to dislike it very much. All of these distractions made me really tired. I would get home from school and be absolutely exhausted. Homework was not an option, sleep was the only option.

I am going to show you snippets of diary entries, moulded into one, with a picture of one of the diary entries itself so you can envision the pure chaos that envelops my little world due to fatigue.

This was a page from my first ever secondary school planner; I was roughly eleven – twelve. I have copied my notes word for word but also added in some notes from other diary entries. This was because I was constantly losing my diary so had to make do with writing on random bits of paper. Please note I started writing this diary on my second day at secondary school and it continues on for the first month and has snippets from later on in the same year.

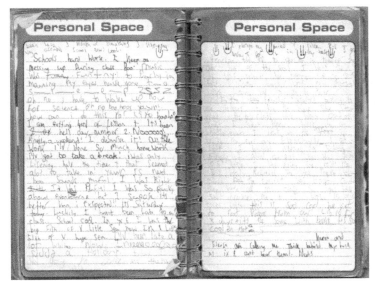

Schools hard work, I keep messing up during class BOO.
Music was fun/ny.
Too early in the morning, my eyes have gone to S – L- E – E –P – . ZZZZZ
Oh no, I have to wake up now for Science. Oh no, Boooo hooo. Yawn.

How can I do this for life?

Boo hoo. I am getting bored of lesson and it's been 'hell' day number two. NOOOOO.
Finally a weekend. I deserve it. All that work and I've done SOOOO much homework I have got to take a break.
I could only listen half the time and that seemed like a lot to take in. Yawn
R.S next, boo sounds awful.
I was right it was awful. These girls were calling me nasty names because I did not know what R.S stood for. Everyone said it was R.S. Not that R.S stood for

'Religious Studies'. My friend *Carol said it was 'Reptile Studies'. I did not know what lesson I was in until I asked my R.S teacher. Everyone laughed and I felt really sick just then. How am I supposed to know that if no one said? Those girls were mean and were laughing at me. They called me spaghetti hair snake.

NOOOO. Those girls were throwing tissue at me because they sat behind me. Gross. I did not cry. Yay.

*Carol laughed at me and told me not to be so gullible, Spaghetti Snake. I don't know what gullible means...... I think it means that there is a snake called gullible somewhere in the world and I remind *Carol of that snake. That must be it; why else would she say that?

She should not have lied about what R.S stood for, people should not lie, it is wrong. So why did she lie to me-it's wrong. How was I supposed to know she would lie to me? Schools not fair and now I'm R – E – A – L – L – Y T – I – R – E – D – . My tummy really hurts and now I feel sick as well. Ewwwwwwwwwwww arg.

I was so panicky about starting Secondary school but I suppose it's better than expected. I have changed my mind I like R.S now because I got a high level 4 in my test. Those girls are silly bullies and immature attention seekers. I ignored them fine and they have stopped now.

Its Saturday today, luckily I have not been late to a class yet. School's cool-NOT...

In year 6 at primary school, I was the big fish in the little sea but now I'm a little fish in the very huge Sea..

Oh no, I have been late to lessons a lot now.

I neeeeedd a holiday, I'm too T – I – R – E –D for proper work and not sleeping... We have a 15 minute break before lunch but that is not enough time to have a nap in. I'm SO tired. NEED SLEEP. Teachers are mean. They don't understand why I fall asleep during class, at least I don't snore ZZZZZZZZZZZZZZZZ *snort.* It's ok though my Doctor once said I could rest during school if I need to by having Fridays off or half days work at home.. Mum said 'Can you please get that in writing, Doctor.' whatever that means.

I got in trouble for yawning in Geography today. BOOO I was tired and it was not fair.

All I did was yawn, and then suddenly this shadow passes over my book and I look up to the monster teacher leaning over me, I'm almost certain I saw a flash of angry red in her eyes- just kidding. Then the silence was ripped apart as she shouted

"That's it, I can't stand this rudeness. Get out of my classroom."

I startled so much with fright because it was nasty and mean.
I tried to say that all I did was yawn and it was not a bad thing to do, I even tried to help the teacher by listing things that were bad, I was very good but she said I should not answer back and was being very cheeky and very rude and that I should get out the classroom before I get in worse trouble. It was horridly unfair.

I had to run to the loos because I was crying and then my teachers assistant *Miss Cool found me and took me to SENCO in LS (learner support) who gave me a bag to breathe into and took me back 12 minutes later when I was calmer. I was so tired my eye lids were heavy like bricks. My eyes were red and puffy and *Carol called me a Spaghetti clown.
Teachers tell us off for eating in the corridors but I get hungry and I need food so I don't fall asleep standing up. *oh no I fell over sleeping standing up. Booo.* BONK..... Oh no, what am I doing on the floor?
Haha

It's ok though I have been here 3 months or something now and I finalllllyyyy know my way around school. Cool. I even helped a girl to class AND I got to my class early. My teacher said I was super kind and gave me a credit. Yay. WHOOP WHOOP.

I still can't believe I asked my R.S teacher what 'R.S' stood for and if it meant Reptile studies. How embarrassing. The whole class did not let it drop (kept teasing me and talking about it) for weeks afterwards. So I imagine you have some questions, many of which I may safely assume have something to do with me being a complete cry baby. Oh yes, I admit defeat. I was a cry baby, I think it was because school was a constant sensory over load and anything that happened outside of the ordinary would tip me over the edge and I would end up feeling:

1. Sick
2. Dizzy
3. In a lot of pain
4. Very tired
5. Very, very emotional. Especially at those unjustified times when I got in trouble and it was not my fault. That is why I cried a lot over ridiculous things

The following is a diary entry about a common misunderstanding of mis-communication and such at school. This particular example really upset me and had me feeling ill and in pain and shaky all day. I finished school so exhausted that I fell asleep on the school bus and nearly missed my stop.

Today I was going to a lesson and my tutor told me to go to see a teacher at the other side of the school. I went there it was about her helping me in C.A.T'S tests. I was not gone long and I rushed back because I don't wanna be late no more. I came back to my form room and my form where lining up to go to their first lesson. Then my form tutor started talking to me about it. By the time she had finished and had stopped talking my whole class had disappeared and were way out of sight. I did not know where to go what so ever, because we had a room change and I got sent away when they were writing it in their books my tutor said it was ok because I could follow them when I got back any way and not to panic.

I was on the verge of crying my eyes out cus I went looking for my tutor form but could not find them. Eventually I got lost I walked around the whole school. My legs got tired because of all that walking around the big school. I could feel blisters in my feet. I even had to go to the loo because I thought I was going to be sick. BOO. Finally I asked a girl I kinda knew who was doing P.E where I was going, she told me and I was relieved I found her because the rest of the corridor was empty because they were all in class already. I got where she directed me and I was 15 minutes late. Teacher told me off and gave me extra hard work than everybody else and I cried because I thought I was in trouble and it was not my fault and she was being mean. *Daphne and *Dorothy are sat behind me calling me thick behind my back, as if I can't hear them. Idiots.

This is a classic example of me getting in trouble for something that I had no control over. The tutor knew I didn't know where to go but still talked to me so I couldn't follow the class. It's these little things that made me over tired, ill and stressed. It was a vicious circle, the more ill and stressed I was the more tired I became and the more tired I was the more stressed and ill I became.

Change in Routines

Chaos and changing classrooms
This is a memory from my main stream primary school.

"Come on every one it is time for R.E. Sam, stop poking your tongue out at me and hurry up – it's time for religious education. Tom, come over here now. Today in R.E, we are learning about Tridents – how exciting."

A teacher had called out over the noisy classroom, supposedly at the end of my Literacy lesson, (don't ask how I remember all of that, it is weird what useless information you remember from childhood). Despite remembering, I had not been listening, simply because the classroom had been noisy before and I was concentrating on my spellings book. As you may know I can only concentrate on one thing at a time. Therefore, when the teacher spoke, I was not listening because of all the other noises in the class room. If the room had been silent or if I was expecting a teacher to speak, I would have been able to hear her and listen to what she was saying. As it was, the teacher had used unspecific language, and was distracted in her talk by other pupils behaviour. Also more importantly, I had no idea I was supposed to listen to something other than the noisy classroom and so I did not follow such vague instructions. Needles to say, while all my friends got up around me to leave for R.E, I remained seated at my table. I could hear chairs scraping, friends teasing, feet clip clopping across the flooring, yet it never occurred to me to stand up and follow them. So I had stayed were I was. The room soon became empty, I looked round. "Good" I had thought to myself, as the easy silence filled the room "I can talk with my thumbs now". (Whenever I got lonely as a child, I always talked to my thumbs and make them bow to each other in greeting and in goodbye. I named my thumbs Muk and Mukka – don't ask why). Up came my thumbs, the one on my right (Muk) bowed first

"How do you do, Mukka?"

And the left one bowed

"How do you do again, Muk?"

So my thumbs and I started chatting.

"I don't know how to spell 'Dalmatians'"

I remember saying to my left thumb.

"It's ok, I can help".

I had made my right thumb say. Is it not strange? I used to do this all the time, but only when alone. My right thumb, Muk, would help me with my spelling because she was always 'right.' while my left thumb would interject with doubt and negativity. I'm quite aware of how crazy this may sound.

Suddenly there was a loud noise in a different class room, something was crashing and people were shouting. Oh how I had panicked – 'I can't finish my game without saying goodbye to my thumbs' I fretted. Even now, if I can't finish a routine, it really stresses me out and I get all panicky and shaky. I had hastily bowed one thumb and the other thumb in goodbye, and ran to the other side of the room (away from the entrance to the classroom – I was frightened). I hid under a table, knees tucked to my chest with my hands clasped over my ears. I did this because I had been stressed and uncomfortable in lesson and was enjoying the silence. In the silence that I craved, the banging from the other room had scared me. Almost as soon as I had ducked down under a table, a teacher walked in,

"Joely"

The teacher had barked (not literally you understand) When she saw me

"Jolly well pick yourself up this instant"

Oh how I had become confused. I remember thinking, why does the teacher want me to be jolly? Like a clown? I always took things literally, and so I had smiled a big grin to be jolly- simply following the instructions, kind of. I was not deliberately being cheeky although it may have seemed it to the teacher at the time. My 'jolly' smile seemed to infuriate the teacher more. She then growled at me:

"Joely, you pick yourself up, this instant."

I then thought 'pick myself up?' in my bewilderment, a thought drifted into my mind about picking myself as I do on the monkey bars on the playground at home. Who can guess what I did? I still can't believe it looking back, what a funny sight that must have been. As I was sitting by a table, on the floor, I grabbed hold of the table and literally picked myself up. My feet were off the ground and I was kind of hanging from the underside of the table. As I hung there, I was watching her, waiting to be told I could get down, smiling like a clown, as I had been instructed to. I did notice a rather strange look pass across my teacher's face but I had no idea what that look meant. The teacher who had calmed down a bit more by then, nicely asked me to carefully stand up and follow her. It would seem she finally realised I took it literally and was doing exactly as she had said. Oh what an embarrassment! I don't recall being at that school for long, I believe I was still doing dual placement with my old special needs school, so this incident happened at the beginning of my dual placement – which means everything, the routine and classrooms, was still all new, scary and full of change. I was still young, in a new environment, and easily confused by literal language. Nowadays, I still get confused with change and literal language, but not to such a degree. Even though the R.E lesson had been scheduled; I did not know I had to go anywhere new, and so it was a change to me. I never had any idea what I was doing at that school, I have memories of wandering around not knowing what lesson I was in or where I was supposed to be – therefore everything was a change and every little task was a mammoth chore of complexities.

The following is another example of my reaction to change in my routine. I can look back at it now and laugh but at the time it was very frightening and made me feel so very ill, sick, dizzy and in a lot of pain. In this particular memory I was at secondary school (embarrassingly I was about 14 years old) and instead of my usual timetabled classes everything had changed and we were having an Enterprise Day instead. I would like to tell you what an Enterprise Day is, but to this day I still don't know as no one ever thought to tell me. It might have something to do with team building exercises... I'm not sure. What I do know is that I was mixed with girls from other classes whom I had never met before (I have no idea why putting me with strangers was considered a good idea – it had proved disastrous), and I was in a classroom I had never been in before with teachers I had also never met. All of these changes in routine were an absolute nightmare for me, and this is what happened. I have decided to write this as script of the general events as they unfolded, I don't know why.

Mum: "Where is she?"
Teacher: "Lost. I don't know where she went."
Mum: "What...why? Has there been a change in routine?"
Teacher: "Yes... It is Enterprise day, all classes are split into different groups looking at entrepreneur work. They all have to do a production of their finished pieces this afternoon, which is another reason why we must find Joely."
It clicks

Mum: "Did you tell Joely there would be a change in routine? Is she with people or friends that she knows? Does the teacher she is with know she has Asperger's? Was Joely prepared for any of this?"

Teacher: "No… I doubt it. I apologise for the inconvenience but I'm afraid there are more pressing issues at hand as we are worried your daughter may have gone off the school premises"

Mum: "Why not? Ok, well, she'll be here somewhere. Joely would not have left the school grounds, because that is a change in routine in itself and she would not know where to go and how to get home. We need to check all the girls' toilets, the library, learner support room and the playing fields. She will be here somewhere."

At this point my mum starts to look for me outside while my teacher searched inside the school. While my mum was searching for me on the playing fields, she noticed a little head peeping out from behind a bush, it was me. I was hiding in a bush because I was so freaked out at being found by teachers and made to complete the Enterprise day. Not only that, but at the end of the last morning lesson I got told our groups had to show our work in a team presentation to the rest of the year. All of this scared me because nobody explained what I was supposed to be doing. I had no idea about the presentation, no idea what was expected of me and what the work was even about- nothing made sense. So when my mother found me I was confused, upset, distressed and panicking hiding in a bush- apparently I was peeping up looking around like a little Meer cat, haha.

I feel the whole situation could have been avoided or at least improved with some simple advanced planning. I should have been briefed before about the Enterprise Day not too far in advance so I did not stress myself over it but not too late either so I could prepare and familiarise myself with the day's events. I also should have been placed with classmates I knew and teachers who were aware of my disability. I am still shocked that higher authorities did not consider my disability in any of their planning for the Enterprise Day. Instead of this being a day of learning for me, it turned into a steep learning curve for them. I think it's a shame that something had to go so drastically wrong for my teachers to realise the depths of my disability.

Overloads and Frozen Defence Shutdown Mode

"Joely, I know you find drawing very therapeutic in times of stress; but I would appreciate it if you could try to listen to me now."

Science teacher speaking to me, I was aged thirteen, in year eight at mainstream secondary school.

There I was in the middle of a science lesson, completely absorbed in my drawing; I had been concentrating hard on keeping a sensory meltdown and the rising sense of panic at bay, by drawing my picture. Vaguely I noticed my teacher kindly speak to me. I looked up sheepishly, to see all my class mates looking at me and sniggering. At that point a mean class mate threw a screwed up bit of paper at my head, which read 'you stupid and you aren't even good at drawing *****'. Instantly I felt ashamed, and of course, stupid. It was horrid; I could feel myself go red in the face, tears prickling at my eyelids at the harsh words written on paper in scruffy handwriting. My heart began pumping fast, my head started to spin and the familiar feeling of pain and sickness in my tummy began once again. The sensory overload was fast becoming a meltdown, I needed help right now.

I put my pen down, breathing heavily with anxiety. With my eyes straining and hurting, I looked at the blurry outline of my teacher, dizziness taking over, my eyes wet with tears. My teacher had then told the nasty pupil off for being mean to me, and had sent her out to see pastoral head of house as a warning of bad behaviour. As his form came into focus a bit more, I saw that he was now looking at me, kindly smiling and expectantly waiting. Avoiding the hot glare of the bully as she pushed past me out the classroom, I looked at my teacher and relaxed a little, smiling in thanks, ready to listen and the meltdown subsided a little. I smiled at my teacher for sticking up for me, but most importantly, I smiled because of his understanding of why it was so necessary for me to draw. You see, the teacher is right, drawing is therapeutic in times of stress; sometimes it's the only way I could keep myself from crying out and having a complete meltdown. You see, instead of screeching or rocking me backwards and forwards, as I used to, I was fortunate in that I learnt to cope with rising meltdowns, with the help of my family and support workers. My techniques were simply to draw erratic and non arty patterns that expressed my whirling emotions, breathing heavily, closing my eyes tight shut, and whispering to myself utter nonsense to distract myself while tapping a regular rhythm with my fingers and feet, either that or I would run out of class to a toilet, to hide and cry.

For the remainder of the science lesson, I tried desperately hard to fight my urge to draw and concentrate instead on what he was saying. Unfortunately, it was no use; despite being a fantastic teacher who understood and taught me well, the scientific language he was using made no sense and I soon felt the need to fight a meltdown once again. I was already fighting sensory overloads, my school uniform was stiff, and much too itchy (even with labels cut out) the science department was always smelly from scientific experiments and I had to move seats and the board now had a distressingly bright light blinding against it. All that brought on an overload, but trying to concentrate on the science as well, well that's precisely what started the meltdown. It's SO stressful not understanding everything around you. So I started drawing more patterns in my book.

I am thankful for my science teacher's understanding. This is because many others did not. They instead would get frustrated, or maybe even angry at me; sometimes confiscating my book until the end of lesson (which resulted in a meltdown and me crying endlessly with a teaching assistant). It was a vicious circle, the more stressed I got in lessons; the more misunderstood I was and the more I drew. Yet the more I drew, the more misunderstood and stressed I became because no one understood why it was necessary for me ease the stress by drawing. It was much like this every lesson. I would get my sketch book out and illustrate the entire page, every lesson, every day, for about three years; filling endless books with my patterned designs of illustrations. It was the only way I could cope.

I used to get meltdowns rather a lot as a child, and then as I grew older I became more able to cope. If my previous techniques failed to work I would isolate myself in a safe, silent and bare environment of soft things for five minutes while I cried I had calmed down. I react differently now, I no longer sit screaming on the floor or rock backwards and forwards trying to block all my senses with one sense. Now sensory overloads often lead straight to meltdowns, this is because as an adult, there is a lot of things to think about at any one time, and these little things of normal adult life are always very complicated and stressful for anyone, let alone those with A.S or Autism.

Learning Environments

Learning environments were difficult at school. Everything was a distraction, there are masses of visual distractions literally everywhere, as schools like to show their students work. In my tutor class room (facing the whiteboard), I would be distracted by everything but also the tiny detail no one else notices as much,

1. The same seven blue tack smears
2. The same twenty eight cracks by the radiator
3. The same six make up smudges on my desk (plus the eleven on the desk to my right)
4. The same forty eight chequered floor tiles
5. The very same thread that had been caught in the blinds by the window and therefore constantly fluttered in the breeze (that was there when I first started)
6. The same smiley face imprinted onto my chair, plus seven initials, and fve statements declaring true love '4eva'. Even the bad spelling in the graffiti distracted me during lesson time

All of that and more distracted me by during every tutor session for a few years, I'm sure. All of this, might I add, is within two metres of each other (apart from the floor-tiles, those spread out along the front). This learning environment was rarely successful, although I was incredibly hard-working and always tried my best (I was a goody two shoes) I found it too difficult to cope with a lot of the time, and was unable to concentrate during lessons.

I would now like to give you a brief outline of how to improve the learning environment for someone on the Autistic spectrum.

Learning environments for me (and possibly others too) are usually better when:

1. **There are fewer pupils in a class.** Less pupils means less noise and fewer people to look at, this as a whole equals decreased distractions.
2. **One to one support.** For those that may need it.
3. **Positive teacher role modelling.** It helps to have a teacher who will help you understand things in a variety of ways.

4. **Keep lessons as interesting as possible.** Using specialised topics or things that interests the class. Create projects that the class want to take part in.

5. **Desks and chairs are always in the same place.** Once you get used to working a certain way it is hard to cope with the transition of looking at the board from a different angle. This is because the lighting changes, reflections will be slightly different, shadows will be in different places and the glare from sunlight may also make it hard to read and do your own work. It is also nice to sit with people you feel comfortable with, so that if you need to, you can ask for their support. Teachers would sometimes like to mix different students together, which for most people was fine. However if I was sitting next to somebody I did not know I would find it so distressing that I would not be able to complete my work at all.

6. **Set timetable.** I would generally take longer to process work and learn than the rest of my classmates. This put a lot of pressure on me to keep up with the class and meant that my work would suffer. Some of my teachers realised this and while I would do the same work as the other pupils, I was allowed a longer time scale to complete it. Some teachers would write special instructions for me to follow in my books, which I found really useful.

7. **Achievable targets.** I found it useful when my teachers set me goals that I could work towards, either during the lesson or over a course of several lessons.

8. **Contact S.E.N.C.O (Special Educational Needs Coordinator).** You may be entitled to a range of support and help but unless you find out what support you're entitled to, you may not automatically receive it. For instance, I was unable to attend a homework club because I could not get home afterwards. During one of my annual reviews, it was mentioned that some travel costs for this type of expense could be covered. At this point, my mother and sister jumped at the opportunity to get the funding agreed so I could access the much needed homework club and get a taxi home afterwards. If this had not been mentioned we would never have known that this type of funding was available to help.

9. **Double check everything.** Every year a review took place with my mum, sister, key workers from my school and representatives from the educational needs local council. During this meeting my learning entitlements and support for the following year would be agreed. Then my mother would receive the written annual statement which included everything that was

agreed from the meeting. Quite often things that had been agreed during the review would be missing. This meant that my mum would have to check everything and send it back if any mistakes had been made, to be re – written to insure I received the correct and agreed entitlements. It was always a long and difficult process for my mum, but it was definitely worth it.

An example of what these meetings achieved was for me to take my GCSE's in a separate room from all the other pupils; I had a prompter (to remind me of the time), time out and extra time. If I had to sit my exams in the main hall with the other children, it would have been a disaster because I would have failed all of my exams instead of getting the good grades that I did. This is why I am very thankful for my mum pushing and checking my annual statement to get this finally agreed.

10. **Time out.** This can be applied for both exams and day to day lessons. As I have said, of the sensory overloads and distractions that occur in a school can be exhausting. Once you become this tired, learning and concentrating is impossible. To avoid getting into this state it is important to be given the opportunity to take a short break (5 minutes) from the lesson or exam. I found it very useful to be able to go to a quiet place like the learner support room or the library to 'chill'. This allowed me to gather my thoughts and regain my concentration so I would be ready to return to the class and start learning again. I understand that this is not always going to be possible but even something as simple as standing outside the classroom door in the quiet corridor proves to be really helpful. I would often ask the teacher for a toilet break, when really I just needed some peace to prevent my head from exploding. (Not literally).

11. **Relevant teacher training.** While I was sometimes given one to one support with teacher assistants, it was very clear that not all knew much about my disability. They were therefore unable to aid me in my learning because those with disabilities on the Autistic spectrum have different learning requirements to children with Dyslexia, for example. One general approach will not suit all. This is why I feel that all teachers and teaching assistants should be given relevant training tailored to the individual needs of the children they will be teaching.

12. **Tidy classroom.** There should be less visual distractions to muddle up and confuse tired brains. I know this is not going to happen but if the learning environment was completely bare, plain (possibly painted pale blue to aid calm and soothing thoughts) and almost clinical, people on the

Autistic spectrum would learn much quicker and find the whole school experience much easier. As this is completely unrealistic, it would be helpful if the visual displays could be minimised, desk clutter removed or tidied away and the classroom as a whole to be clean, and well kept.

13. **Traffic light system.** This is an easy way for students on the Autistic spectrum to communicate with the teacher. The student would have three pieces of coloured paper (one red, one yellow, one green) attached to the inside of their learner books. If the pupil did not understand something, required additional help, or needed to respond to a question the teacher had asked ("do you understand?") the pupil could hold up the relevant coloured paper.

Red: I need help.

Yellow: I am not sure if I need help at this moment but please ask me again later.

Green: I am fine.

Pupils on the Autistic spectrum will often find it difficult to communicate if they need help. I was told time and time again to 'just ask for help' if I needed it, but could I ever do this? No. I never asked for help – even when I was desperately struggling in a panic, I just could not bring myself to ask. It was like I had no choice.

I think the traffic light system could work quite well because it is more discreet, you get a definite answer and the pupil does not feel embarrassed. This would only work if the whole class were to adopt this. If the traffic light system was only applied to those who needed it (pupils on the Autistic spectrum etc) it would defeat the purpose because that child would feel singled out and uncomfortable.

The traffic lights would need to be pre-scheduled into the lesson so that the child knows to expect the question and has time to prepare for an answer. This is because if the question was asked unexpectedly a child on the Autistic spectrum would panic and would be unable to process the question quick enough to give an accurate answer.

14. **Teachers that can positively control negative behaviour.** I had one lesson in which I was supposed to be learning but the behaviour of others prevented me. The teacher had no control over the pupils outrageous behaviour. The teacher was just too kind for his or her own good. This meant that the class room was in constant chaos, so much so, the chairs were thrown about, there were fights, verbal abuse and pupils would storm out of the classroom at regular intervals. As much as I loved this particular

class and I got good grades, I could not improve and do as well as I could have done.

I know this is an extreme example of poor behaviour in a classroom (all my other classes were nothing like this by the way), but if the teacher had been better at controlling the class, everyone would have benefited and I would have found it much easier to concentrate, learn and improve.

15. **S.E.N.C.O Homework clubs.** Homework clubs provide assistance to those in need of help with homework or school work projects. Usually the learning environment during these homework clubs is better because, the students have chosen to be there, which means they won't deliberately cause disturbances but will instead be getting on with their own work. This makes the classroom calm and quiet. Also, if homework is misunderstood, helpers in homework clubs can find out what you have to do.

If I did not have homework club, I would not be able to do any homework at all. Even though my family always tried to help with my homework, if I arrived home without the relevant work or information they could not assist me. The homework club at school was invaluable because the teachers could answer any questions, speak to the teacher that assigned that homework and ask them any questions or obtain missing paperwork. For me, this happened a lot and the wonderful teacher at homework club spend a lot of time and effort chasing down my paperwork.

In reality there is not much we can do to change learning environments because it involves redesigning a whole school and re-educating the teachers. So, it is sadly up to you as the student to make the most of the learning environment you have. So no misbehaving, people just try to concentrate on your work.

Here is a list of some strange things that happen to me when I'm trying to work and can not concentrate:

1. **I start to get itchy.** I get so itchy I am forced to scratch.
2. **My temperature changes** which affects my sensory overloads badly.
3. **Pains.** I spend most of my life in pain because I spend most of my time in sensory overload, and this is very stressful on my body. Whether it is tummy, back, head, eye, skin, muscle, chest pain or exhaustion pain, I would say about 95% of the time I am suffering with one or more pains.

4. **Distraction.** I get distracted by anything and everything. I will start to count lines in wallpaper and then realise that my mind has wandered. Then I would distract myself by thinking about how ridiculously distracted I must have been to have been counting lines in wall paper in the first place. This happens a lot.

5. **Surges.** I get rushes of energy which go through my head when I am concentrating but unable to work out a solution to a problem, or when I am panicking or anxious about something, like driving in a car. These surges as I call them (I have no idea what this sort of thing is officially called) make me momentarily startle and shake my head quickly and vigorously from side to side. It is something I have no control over and it's very bizarre and increasingly distracting because I can feel it building up and then after the shake it just disappears.

6. **Blurry vision.** My vision goes blurry and objects or things momentarily go in and out of focus and sometimes I see double. It's odd, because I have perfect vision (20 / 20 as they say) yet when I read words sometimes the letters move around on different lines which makes it hard to read. I am a good reader so it is usually when I am concentrating, tired, ill or in pain that this happens.

7. **My handwriting becomes terrible.** I start to write upside down and back to front when I am concentrating too hard.- Seriously, if I am in an exam and I am really concentrating and writing quickly, letters would become increasingly difficult to write the right way, how bizarre is that? These are examples of numbers and letters that I commonly use either upside down or back to front, for example, 2, 3, 4, 5, 7, 9, C, E, U, T and P.

Distracted Teachers

I feel bad for saying it but there is one thing I stand for and that is honesty. I don't want to appear rude or unappreciative but this is something I believe may be able to help you people so I shall continue in the vague hope that I am not about to get myself in trouble. I do apologise in advance for any offence I may have caused, I know that the teacher tried and it must have been hard work.

My Maths teacher used to get annoyed with me and the whole class when we had no idea what he/she was going on about. The teacher was forever getting distracted; and would start talking about their weekend in an attempt to get us focused. Yet the conversation would steer so far away from anything at all related to maths that we all had very little memory of what was said before it got to that stage. For example, one conversation went along the lines of this;

"Then we went to the market to buy some bread because the dog had eaten it all. How much did the dog eat? I can't quite recall…. Maybe a few slices of white bread, not brown because my partner despises brown bread. Anyway, who knows what is the fraction of bread he ate in proportion to the whole loaf? Anyone? No... Ok, it was 4/15. What was it we were talking about again? Oh, yes fractions – that was it… So the dog ate three, no sorry, four slices of white bread. How big was the entire loaf? Anyone? Jessica?.. You don't know... do any of you?.. No, of course not, silly me... Ok, there were fifteen slices in the whole loaf, and the greedy little mite ate four slices and all of my special butter which I was not best pleased about – Yes *Sarah it was such a nuisance," *(A pupil asked her/him a question and he/she got distracted at this point, continued-)*

"That dog is quite a pain, my partner is fond of the dog though so I am obliged to keep it. Anyway, the dog ate, well I can't quite remember now… I believe I have gone and forgotten the story to do with my dog eating a small fraction of bread to butter. Well folks, if I tell you about when my cat was foraging through the bin last week you might get an idea of how this fractions business works....."

...And on it went, in case you couldn't follow that rambling as much as me, I thought you would like to know that it didn't make much more sense when the teacher had finished either.

Not helpful when the teacher distracts themselves when talking, how are we supposed to keep up if they can't keep up with their own motor mouth?

Teachers and Patience

I would like to tell you a little more about my Maths class.

My teacher was used to educating grade 'A' students and was instead teaching the bottom set for Maths. This should not be a problem of course except he was in charge of teaching all of us who found Maths difficult; in my class there were pupils with additional needs who required extra support (like me). Such support was rarely offered from our teacher, who used to get annoyed with us for not understanding the methods or mathematics. The problem was that the teacher would explain the mathematics at a higher level than we could understand. It was like he had forgotten that we didn't understand the basics of Maths let alone anything more complicated. Also, the teacher clearly had patience issues. He would only have to explain something twice before his face was turning angry and red, beads of sweat appeared on his brow line and veins were pulsing in his forehead. With his lack of patience and our confusion a vicious circle occurred, from which no one could break free. The teacher would always be saying –

"I can't comprehend how none of you understand this; it is basic, basic, easy stuff."

"You should all know this by now- I have been through this with you close to a 100 times."

"Why don't any of you understand?"

His frustration was nothing compared to the students frustration at being misunderstood, helpless and clearly thought of as stupid. If only he had tried to teach us a different way and had more patience, things might have been different for everyone involved.

Exam Anxiety

I don't get stressed about exams because I know I will always try to do my best and that's all I can do. I have brilliant support from my family. I know that they will not be disappointed if I get a 'bad' grade because they know that I have given 100%. However, I have noticed that before an exam I experience lots of physical symptoms, such as head, tummy and back pain. I don't know why this is but I have become used to it.

If you were to ask my mum if I got stressed about exams, her answer would be completely different. She would say that I definitely do get stressed. Apparently, I am unable to organise myself (even worse than usual). Under pressure it takes me 10 times longer to do basic tasks, such as organising myself to get ready in the morning. This usually meant that I would be running late for the school bus. My mum realised that putting more pressure on me to hurry up was counterproductive because under too much stress I can't cope and end up shutting myself in my bedroom, sometimes unable to go to school.

I always thought that if you were stressed or anxious about an exam it would be because you were being pressured by yourself or by other people to do well. Consequently, because I never had that type of pressure, I assumed I was not stressed. I now realise that stress or anxiety can come in many forms and the fact that I was unable to carry out basic tasks before an exam is a form of stress. One of the many traits of Asperger's syndrome is difficulty with reading emotions in people, for instance, happiness or sadness. I assumed that this meant in other people, but I believe it also means difficulty in reading emotions in yourself. I was unable to realise that I was stressed because I could not read the signs of stress in myself. Luckily, the people around me were able to read these signs and helped me through it.

As I briefly mentioned, before an exam I would experience physical symptoms such as head, tummy and back pains. This affected me severely at school during exams. In lessons I could complete the work and do it to a high standard (if taught properly), yet when exam time came along everything went wrong and I would fail-because my body would be stressed, I would be in a lot of pain and very, very tired and mostly likely going into some sort of sensory overload.

I feel that the whole 'exam' procedure is unfair to some people, people with Asperger's syndrome or to anyone who struggles with exams. Just because you are unable to answer a set of questions at a particular time, doesn't mean that you don't know the answer. A lot of very clever people much prefer to be assessed through practical examination or course work. When I was at school exams were the only option, but now pupils are getting more choice about what they study and how they are assessed. Even though I did quite well at school and got some very good grades (in my specialist subjects), I think I could have done much better if I had the choice to not sit exams and complete course work instead. This is because it would have taken away the exam stress and I would have been able to complete the course in my own time relatively stress free.

So, what can I do about it?

I'm not sure of the answer, If I'm honest there is little I do that you probably don't already know.

1. **I eat and drink well for the week before the exam,** you know, five fruit and vegetables a day, one treat of some sort to help relax me every couple of days and five litres of water a day
2. **I try to make sure I sleep well each night** (early nights – no chocolate, fizzy drinks/caffeine/additives and junk food, no T.V or computer screens etc)
3. **I try to relax** myself by reading and writing stories
4. **I used to do Yoga** – very relaxing and brilliant for mental strength because it teaches you a lot about relaxation and breathing exercises
5. **Exercise,** if at all possible, even if it's just a quick jog round the block or something. Walk up the stairs if possible, don't go in the elevator that sort of thing. I used to exercise a lot. Go swimming, do work outs at home, do Yoga, go to the Gym or go for a run or something. Also doing exercise in the evening tires you out so you are more likely to have a better quality night sleep
6. **I worked out which type of revision works for me.** There are many different types of revision styles, including reading over your work notes, writing your work out again, quizzing yourself. I find it stresses me out too much, so I try not to worry about it. I allocate one subject per day and do a manageable amount of revision on that subject (this subject of course has to be in relation to one of the exams you will be taking, I just want to check you won't pick a random subject to revise).
7. **It is ok to fail,** regardless of what people say. It is ok to get not so good grades, because I can re-take exams like this later on in life where chances are the learning environment will be better for me anyway
8. **I try my best**
9. **I give myself plenty of time** in the morning to get up and ready so I am not leaving rushed and stressed

---

Advice to Teachers – Exam Room Change

If there will be any change in routine (e.g. room change for the exam) then you must let the student know beforehand, otherwise it would freak them out and all concentration could be lost from the stress of finding the new room before the exam has even started (trust me, this happened to me a lot).

Unfair testing

One of the many difficulties people with Asperger's have is the inability to process new information; especially the ability to put irrelevant noises and sights into categories of importance verses unimportance. Sensory overloads are quite common, because those with A.S see and hear everything all the time, which is mentally, emotionally and physically exhausting.

This means while those without A.S can tune out all the noises and distractions as they are able to realise what is important and shut out the rest. As it is, people with A.S can only concentrate on the distractions, (the irrelevant noises and the sights) because their brains find it difficult to process information into back ground noises and sights, so while it is fair for others to be seated in a big hall filled with lots of noises and sights, it is not fair for those with A.S.

Something needs to change, not only are the exams worded in a way that is impossible to understand for those with Autistic and other disabilities, but we are expected to complete exams using the knowledge we can remember on the day (I have passed many exams with flying colours one day, and then failed the same exam the next day due to stress – it's a big problem) and sit in a hall with hundreds of other students and face the hideous noise and visual distractions as well.

My friend with Autism was trying to describe what it is like to take an exam in a hall with lots of other students. I think what she said really sums up, for Auties and Aspies, how it is.

"Imagine sitting in an exam with someone screaming in your ear, banging the table, tickling you and pulling your hair. You would not be able to concentrate on the exam like that, would you? Well, that is what it is like for me when I take an exam in a hall full of other students."

To further explain what it is like for me in a large exam hall, I shall write a list of the sounds and distractions that prevent me from giving my full attention:

1. Teachers pacing, squeaky shoes and squeaky floor, tap tap squeak creak (this is a constant noise as teachers are always pacing) – I have become good at knowing which teacher is walking up behind me from listening to their shoes).
2. My own heart pumping in my ears

3. Tick, tock, tick, tock. (The clocks ticking and echoes)
4. Girls flicking their hair
5. The rhythmic taps of students/teachers feet and pens
6. The sound of girls chewing on the end of their pens – ewww
7. Rustling of pencil cases, zips and so on
8. Squeak of old chairs every time a student decides to move an inch (given there are hundreds of students this is a constant noise)
9. Material of school uniform making scratchy noises
10. Sighs, coughs and sneezes all of which zap me straight from concentration back down to nothing
11. The tables creaking and wobbling about, banging on the floor because they are all old and have uneven legs, so the whole table wobbles every time a student releases and creates pressure (so annoying)
12. The buzz of all the lights high up on the ceiling
13. The weather outside
14. The curtain flowing in the breeze by the windows, the tap as the end of the cord hits the window (this used to drive me up the wall on a windy day)
15. Paper ruffling and turning
16. The scratch of pens as students furiously write down their answers
17. The school bell every sixty five minutes between lessons
18. The ping of elastic bands when the annoying few fling them around the exam hall
19. The crunch of students jaws as their jaw locks when they chew gum.
20. Now and again you can hear the squelch as students stick their finished chewing gum under the table

Trust me; there are a lot more noises I could list.

All of these noises and distractions occur because of the volume of people in such a large space. Not only that, but I have no choice but to listen to all of these things as my brain can't back stream the irrelevant noises. How am I supposed to concentrate on an exam in such unfair and unjustified conditions? So much for fair testing! If I was in a much smaller room with less students, or even better, in a room alone, the amount of noise and distractions would decrease. This obviously makes it much easier and practical for me to concentrate on the exam.

Sort it out schools and exams boards; how is this possibly fair testing?

Homework

Not handing in homework, for whatever reason usually ends up in a detention. I really tried to do homework, yet there were quite a few occasions when I could not complete it. Homework was difficult because:

1. **I never knew or understood what I was supposed to do.** Even if I had written down an explanation of what I had to do, it would never make sense hours later when I read through it. This is because after writing down the homework, I have since been concentrating on seemingly millions of other things which mean my memory and understanding has since diminished. Even if I copied homework down from the last lesson of the day, I still then have to concentrate on other things before I got home and looked in my homework book. For example, socialising, getting ready to leave school, making sure I had all my stuff, finding my bus, preparing what I had to say to the driver and how much money I should give or how much change I should receive, catching the bus, getting off at the right stop and walking home. For many these are things that don't require much attention or thought but for me I have to spend time really thinking about what to do because otherwise I can't operate as effectively as I should. Maybe you can now envision why it is hard to remember explanations used in class once I get home, which makes completing homework complex.

2. **I lost everything.** Apparently this was not my fault, there was simply too much going on and to think about all the time for me to keep track of all my belongings and work. This meant I would often get home without an essential item of work making it impossible to complete my home work even if I had the energy to do so.

3. **Someone would steal my homework from me.** Some of my 'friends' would ask to borrow my homework. As they used the word 'borrow' I would say yes because I assumed it meant that I would get it back. Unfortunately this was rarely the case and it took me a while to realise this. This is also a good example of how people with Asperger's syndrome are easily taken advantage of, even by their own friends.

4. **I did not always have time to write the homework down in my journal.** The end of the lesson is the time when the teacher usually tells you what the homework is and tells you to write it down. This is happening while the bell is ringing, chairs are scraping, pupils are chatting and just leaving for the next class- most other pupils can decipher quickly what to write

down but those of us who have difficulty concentrating in such chaos find it hard, especially when pressured with no time.

5. **I would be extremely exhausted** by the time I got back from school. So much so that there was little more I could do than sleep, sleep was unavoidable. I would be so tired that completing simple pieces of homework would become a huge issue. It is so much more difficult to concentrate when you have had a whole day of exhausting sensory overloads and meltdowns. Once I completed a mock exam during my Maths class at school. I found it easy and got all the answers correct, passed with flying colours. But, when I got home that day and had to complete the same mock exam for homework; I found it nearly impossible because none of the questions made sense and I became easily confused. Needles to say, I failed that second exam paper and got it least 70 % of the questions that I had previously got right, wrong. This is due to over exhaustion and not being able to concentrate properly after a long days work. This happens frequently, in exams and lessons. Just because I can't pass an exam (due to stress and fatigue difficulty), does not mean I don't know the answers.

This leads me on to my next point; I had continuous help with all this from my parents, siblings, teachers/SENCO and I attended homework clubs every week. I don't think I could function daily if my mum was not constantly reminding me to check my homework book. If I did not have the great support of my wonderful family sitting with me every night trying to sort all my homework out with me, nothing would have got done.

Fitting in

This section is directed at parents, rather than at people with A.S.D.

I think that I was somewhat saved from bullying at my secondary school because of my sisters help with what I wore. I am very fortunate in the fact that I have lots of beautiful and lovely clothes. My sister apparently once told my mum that

> "Joely needs to look more 'normal'. Joely must fit in at secondary school or else the other girls will eat her alive."

Or something to that effect, but the concept is still right. Although 'eaten alive' here means the other girls would really bully and tease me for it. It was down to my sister and mum for understanding the need and making sure that I have such fabulous clothes and always look good. I went through secondary school with decent clothes, they were not designer clothes nor expensive. My clothes were just nice, flattering and made me feel confident that I looked nice. I would feel happy on mufti days at school because I knew I had decent clothes to wear.

I am forever grateful to my sister for that because those clothes made me fit in with the other girls at my school. Girls would compliment me on my outfit not tease me because I looked 'gross' on mufti day. I can't stress how very important it is.

There is absolutely nothing wrong with being an outsider, but being an outsider and being bullied for it does some horrid things. It crushes your development, self image and confidence. I had enough to deal with, with my disability, sensory overloads and general day to day confusion. Not having to worry about my clothes and what other girls thought really made a difference and helped me cope with teenage life. I strongly believe that I would not have achieved so much if I had not had the confidence I gained from clothes. It makes a huge difference, and if you only do it to gain confidence then that is good enough.

I must stress that these clothes that look good, don't have to be expensive. If you find a decent charity shop you could find some quality high street brands for less than half the price. Shop when the sales are on, and make sure you buy what your child actually wants. Trust me, there is no use in buying something that you think would look nice if your child does not like or want it. This is because:

1. It's a waste of money, time and effort (whereas the time, money and effort could have been spent on something you are both happy with. If you can't find anything you both agree on the first time don't buy anything at all and save the money for when you can shop another time)
2. The child will never wear it anyway

The majority of my clothes were actually hand-me-downs from my older sister. I had no problems wearing hand-me-downs, because my sister was always super stylish.

I completely understand if you are reading this thinking

> 'I have far more problems than to think about fashion.'

I don't blame you as I completely agree. I also think there is more to life than naively following fashion trends- I can't stand fashion. None of our clothes were fashionable or 'on trend', but they just looked nice and suited us. It has very little to do with vanity as well; wearing nice clothes, and being comfortable in your clothes, and your own skin, simply give the tools needed to become more confident in other areas of life. I believe that confidence, self belief and self image is very important to finding true happiness and holistically developing into a strong and confident adult. If doing something as simple as wearing nicer clothes can make children's journey through school a little easier, than I say you should go for it.

Of course on the other hand, if your child is perfectly happy wearing the clothes they wear then don't try and pressure them to change. This is all about your child's happiness after all.

Peer Pressure

'Social pressure by members of one's peer group to take a certain action, adopt certain values, or otherwise conform in order to be accepted'

Taken from www.dictionary.com

The above quote makes it seem as if peer pressure is something people do to become accepted. While this is true, most people experience negative peer pressure from those around them and negative peer pressure can be harmful to any ones health and emotional well being.

Common types of peer pressure include:

1. Drinking alcohol
2. Taking drugs
3. Smoking
4. Humiliating others
5. Bullying others

Although I have not succumbed to peer pressure it is still there, although I mostly experienced it when I was a lot younger. I believe it is an unfortunate part of growing up. You regularly see it in teen movies, where the 'cool' kids bully the new kid in a form of an initiation into a certain group of 'friends'. I have used '' marks as the people applying the peer pressure certainly are not cool, nor are they the new kids friend.

In my teenage years there was a lot of pressure to do everything, including drinking alcohol, skive school, smoke cigarettes and participate in generally stupid/dangerous activities. The thing is, I never gave in because I did not feel the need to conform myself to suit other people's expectations. One of the main reasons I stood my ground is because my family have always taught me that people who pressure you to do something you feel uncomfortable with, are not your true friends and that you should only do what you are 100% happy with. I was brought up with a clear sense of what is right and wrong, I also knew that i should never have to change myself to suit other people.

Peer pressure to drink alcohol
Do you want to know the secret for the best hangover cure? Here it is…

Don't drink a lot of alcohol.

That is the best hangover cure and preventive you will ever need. Better still, if you don't want a hangover, then don't drink alcohol at all.

In all honesty, I am a party animal; I go out clubbing and stay up to ridiculous hours of the morning and stumble into my house, utterly exhausted, (yet always sober) usually when 'normal' people are on their way to go to work. I'm a right crazy fool, eh?

This usually paints the picture that I drink an obscene amount of alcohol and get drunk, because that is the party hard-core clubbers life style in the society that we live in. It's ok though folks; I'm not like that, I drink maybe two alcoholic drinks and then I am on water and orange juice for the rest of the night (it's much more fun, I always have a natural buzz). I prefer to be safe and know I am not being taken advantage of. I tell the numerously annoyingly flirty guys that I don't drink; the response that never fails to shock and disappoint. I tell all of my friends and despite the occasional raised eye brows, I get complete and utter respect for it. Water and Orange juice for me, please.

Advice to Someone with Asperger's
Don't change yourself to fit in. Please don't ever feel the need to change yourself to suits others; chances are, if people don't like you for who you are, they are not worth knowing at all. It is sad, but none the less true.
If peers are pressuring you to change yourself, to dress a certain style, act a certain way, do certain things that you are not 100% comfortable with, you should talk to a trustworthy grown up about your feelings, who may help you cope and deal with the situation effectively.

Advice for Teaching Assistants

As a teaching assistant, the one thing you have to remember about an individual with Autistic spectrum disorders is that they are often clever when given the chance to shine. This is especially true with regards to their favourite or specialist topics of interest. Indeed some people with Asperger's are very clever and sometimes even more knowledgeable than their average class mate.

I had many wonderful teacher assistants when I was at school. Some of them were awesome actually. I had some really cool ones that all the students seemed to really warm to. Now the aim of the teacher assistant is to assist the teacher and help the students when they can. However, every student is different. Each person or child learns in their own way, because of this, you cannot use the same teaching style and expect it to work for everyone. This is especially true when teaching people on the Autistic spectrum.

A classic example of how using the same approach for everyone may not work is when a teacher or teaching assistant asks the pupil if they are 'ok'. For somebody who is not on the Autistic spectrum, this is a very simple question but for somebody like myself the question is not specific enough. First of all, the question "Are you ok" is actually a very silly question with a million different responses. For example the pupil may think you are asking about their general health and wellbeing and respond 'yes I am fine'. But because you are asking them whether or not they are 'ok' with the work they are doing, they could have answered the question incorrectly.

Basically, you need to be very specific when speaking to somebody with Asperger's. You need to think about:

1. The timing of when you ask the question
2. How you ask the question
3. How you word the question
4. How many times you ask the question
5. Give the student time to process information
    If you ask the pupil a question straight after the teacher has finished talking, it is unlikely that the pupil would have time to process the information and would be unable to give an accurate answer. For me, I would need roughly two minutes to process the information from the teacher before I would be ready to answer any questions. Obviously the time frame will vary from pupil to pupil
6. Don't answer questions with questions and don't keep asking questions when they have not answered yet.
    Chances are they are still processing part of the first question and will get

very easily confused if you continue to ask. For instance asking "Do you need help?" to the student, then the student does not respond so you ask "are you ok?" These are two different questions and require a lot more time to process/work out what to say and answer. You have been warned!

7. Get to know every individual student and their learning habits. It will make your job, the student's job and the teacher's job a whole lot easier if you do.

A great example of asking the right question and getting the right answer is when my parents recently went on holiday. My parents went away for one week which meant I was home alone for the whole time (I was 20 years old by the way). My brother lives just round the corner so was regularly popping in to check I was ok and my sister who lives ten minutes drive away, was also calling me regularly to check if I needed anything. One day my sister called to check if I had enough food in the house for my lunch and dinner, just to clarify I would not starve. She specifically said

"Do you have enough food in the house for your lunch and dinner for the next two days?"

I responded by saying

"No, I don't have any food in the house at all"

At this point my sister arranged for some food to be brought round to my house. When my parents returned from holiday and were checking with my siblings how the last week had been, my sister mentioned that she had sent some food over because I had said that I did not have any. My mum and dad were shocked because they had left me more than enough money to buy food when needed. My sister's reaction to this was to laugh because she instantly realised that if she had followed up the initial question with

"Do you have enough money to buy food for this week?"

I would have said yes. However, this is not the question my sister had asked. I assumed she knew already, because my theory of mind is a bit weird and I thought she knew what I knew, so I didn't think to tell her I had money to buy food. My sister felt very foolish because after years of experience with understanding me and my difficulties and dealing with me, she felt she should have known to be more specific.

I know this is unrelated to school, but it is a classic example of how you need to be very specific and ask the right questions to find out the information that you want. My teacher assistants would always ask me if I was 'ok' and I would always say 'yes'. Had they asked 'Do you need any help with your school work?' They might have got a completely different response.

Getting to know your pupil is very important because it will really help you to help them learn. Some of my teacher assistants and support workers did this very well but others not so much. It is hardly their fault though. They were just trying to help but got their timing slightly off, that is all. They probably got taught a way that works for the majority of students. I feel timing is vitally important to receive a correct and helpful response from the student.

I would like to give an example of how timing is important.

One time at school, my science teacher was explaining the work we needed to do for that lesson. As soon as my teacher had finished explaining, my teacher's assistant (sitting next to me) asked me if I was ok and if I knew what I needed to do. Even though it was a very specific question the timing was not helpful. I had not been given enough time to process the information from the teacher and work out if I understood or not. I need time to process the information, and the instructions then I can work out if I understand it or not. Before I can answer any question I have to go through the below process:

1. I think I understand, but I have to try to do the work myself first
2. I don't understand, so I need the work explaining again in more detail
3. I do understand and don't need help now, but I might need help later

In this example, because I had not had enough time to work out whether or not I did understand the work, I was unable to accurately answer the question. By the time I had processed the information and realised that I did need help the teacher assistant was helping someone else, and if I'm honest, I was painfully shy and had a fear of asking for help anyway, I was fiercely determined to work it out for myself. This meant that the teacher assistant would have assumed I was ok and would not come back to help me again.

So what do you do? I hear you cry (Hey, I have got super good hearing- I can hear your thoughts). Think of your timing first; give the student a minute to process the instructions, then ask the student a specific question and remember to give the student time to respond. Not only should you give them time to respond, but you should make sure you don't interrupt their thought process. If they are taking a long time to respond, it is simply because our processing speeds are much slower, and each time you interact and distract the student while waiting for an answer, the processing speed will get slower and you'll end up waiting even longer. Even if the student tells you that they are 'ok', remember to go back to them at regular intervals.... I will explain more about this later.

Something else to bear in mind – Don't surprise the student
You'll be shocked at how this can affect the answer so much. If you shock the student, the instant reaction to both avoid trouble and to not look silly is usually to respond with a 'yes' answer. Therefore if you shock a student with a question the response may be incorrect. I know this because my teacher assistants would constantly be popping up from behind me to ask me a question, this means that I can't see them approaching and it usually shocked

me so much that I would jump into the air. My shocked reaction would be "yes I'm fine." and so they would leave me struggling unaware that I needed help. The reason I think I am so jumpy is because when I am concentrating on my work, I have to give it so much of my attention that I become oblivious to my surroundings. So when somebody approaches me it often startles me so much that I can't concentrate on the question they asked, or continue with my work. For this reason, I would prefer that the teacher or teacher assistant would approach me from the front (so I can see them) and for them to first say my name (being shocked from someone saying your name is less to cope with than a question, therefore better) and then wait for me to acknowledge them before asking any questions.

One last thing to also bear in mind... Don't distract their flow of concentration.

If the student is writing down something with intent concentration it is probably best not to distract their flow; even if you need to prompt them about how much time they have left. It is almighty hard to get back of that concentration and thoughts once you have been distracted. I know it goes without saying. Also, if you are sitting next to them, don't distract them by doing anything. I once had an exam with a speech and language therapist who sat opposite me constantly drumming her fingers on the table. It was infuriatingly hard to concentrate and after a while it got too much so I asked her to stop tapping as politely as I could. She stopped and then after about forty seconds, she continued to fiddle with her pen making the light reflect off of the lid and distracted me further. It was such a nuisance. I could barely work out what I was doing after that, my attention and ability to work was shot to pieces. It has such a big affect on me.

I had some really good support workers. They were really brilliant because they got to know me really well. They learnt all of my learning habits and how I liked to work things out and all my little methods. So that combined, we worked together very well with lots of good results. The most obvious example I can come up with is that when I was struggling with a spelling, they would leave me to it. Sounds bizarre, yes it does, but I am very thankful for them for it. This is good because I am good at spelling, confident and more than capable. Therefore every word I could not initially work out how to spell, I would be determined to find a solution by myself, and usually I could succeed. It is something I have always been thankful for. So these teachers assistants were good because they would just let me work it out, whereas the ones who did not know me quite so well would realise I was struggling and instantly tell me how to spell it. It used to infuriate me.

In my opinion you want to help the students but you don't want to block their learning by helping them too much. That is what I think any way. It's striking the right balance that counts.

Summing up

My main advice is to get to know the student you are assisting, get to know their methods how they understand things, how much support they need and when they require the support. Learn when to push the student, learn when to give the student a break. Make sure you get to know the student and that is the best advice I could possibly give you.

Advice for People with Autistic Disorders Regarding Pressure at School

One thing that most people notice with people with Asperger's is that they are either gifted in English or Mathematics. Oh my goodness, let me tell you this, my 'good' topic is certainly NOT Maths. I am terrible at anything mathematical or mental arithmetic. However my good topic is English, my mother says that one of the best things she ever did was teach me how to read because I love it and therefore I read so much. My mother and I would go to the Library and take out 12 books at a time and then return a few days later to do the same again, I could read for England. Anyway, I procrastinate.

We always said we could deal with Maths later in life (I re sat my GCSE Maths when I was 20 and gained a grade B, a thankful enormity compared to the frightful grade F I got when I sat the exam at school). So all of you out there who have a bad subject, don't fret, you have a lifetime ahead of you to learn about that subject. I advise you to make your priority the subjects you are good at; this will build your confidence, self esteem and do you a world of good. Once you have time, confidence and other skills under your belt (what a funny saying that is- as if skills that lack physical content can fit under a belt) you can then worry about the things you were not so good at and try to improve them. I am not saying you ignore the problem, because believe me, I still tried to improve. I attended all of my Maths classes and completed all my work. But, when it came to my GCSE exams, Maths was not a priority. I decided to postpone my mathematical learning for a few years and I'm really glad I went back to it and improved my grades.

My family and I made the choice to focus on my good subjects (such as English and Art) for my GCSE exams so that I could get the best grades possible. If I was pressured to also do well in Maths, I am in no doubt that I would have failed all of my subjects because I wouldn't have been able to cope. Luckily I was able to do the best I could with Maths, but under no pressure. The thing that helped me most with this is my brother. My wonderful brother would help me out with the hardships that Maths entailed in homework and course work. My brother is brilliant at Maths, and he is really good at explaining in a way that I can understand. He is a real bright star, shining light on problems in the depths of my dark confusion. Thank you bro.

Another one of the reasons that we decided not to focus on maths for my GCSE's was because the learning environment and teaching methods used during my Maths class were not suitable for me. If I had one to one lessons with my brother I think I would have passed my GCSE Maths easily. Unfortunately, I had to 'learn' Maths at school with my Maths teacher. Which as you already know, did not go well... Hence my grade F.

Advice for Parents Regarding Exams

While on the subject of advice, I think it is important to outline some of the things that I think are really important to make exams fairer for a person with A.S.D. As I said before, people with A.S.D are very clever, they just need the extra opportunities and support to let them shine.

I advise that students and SENCO should really fight for extra support during exams, such as:

1. A quiet exam room (small with less distractions on the walls and preferably none on floor/tables and chairs)
2. Extra time for students to process information (it's not fair that it take us longer to process everything and still have the same amount of time as everyone else who don't have these problems)
3. An exam room with less students in (less students = less distractions)
4. A reader (someone to read exam questions for you)
5. A prompter (someone to remind you how long to spend on each question, or to prompt you to move on to next question when stuck)
6. All help from staff should be someone the student already knows and likes.
   - If you give a student a helper on the day of the exam whom they have never met, they won't like it, the change will freak them out and you might as well have not had help there at all.
7. Break times /time out helps reduce stress levels (I was allowed break during exams, merely to go to the toilet if in pain or to take a breather to de-stress and I found such breaks enormously helpful)
8. Check everything you are entitled to on your statement (if you have one) and make sure you get it all.

This is where your SENCO worker can really shine. If they can sort these problems out then you have got a winner. My idea of a winning SENCO is a brilliant worker who understands your needs.

This is an example of why the above is necessary
I realise a lot of people without disabilities get exam anxiety but when you have a disability like Asperger's you experience extra distractions. These are so great that they take up all your brain power, energy and thinking. In a normal

exam there would be an average of one hundred people in one hall, and while everyone is 'silent' (not talking), there is still a lot of additional noise, as I have previously listed.

In my earlier chapters I briefly touch on the subject of Monotropic (can only think of one thing at any one time) verses Polytropic (can multitask thinking strategies). The above is a classical example of how someone with Asperger's is Monotropic. While people without my disability would hear some of the noises, and will sometimes become distracted by them, they are still able to block out irrelevant noise and vastly focus on the task at hand.

I have given the above advice to parents as I feel it is incredibly important for everyone to be treated fairly. If your child has Asperger's please fight for their rights and what is fair. No matter how clever they are, being in a busy hall is a sure way to fail. Everyone deserves their chance to shine so make sure your child gets what they are entitled to.

Summary

For someone who has Asperger's syndrome, being at school is like being in a mine field. It is extremely over whelming, stressful and full of sensory overloads. But, if given the right support from parents, teachers and friends, it can be a great learning experience and you can achieve some amazing things. Make sure you 'fight for your rights'. It took my mother and sister years to get me the support I needed and deserved, but it was worth it in the end because I came out of school with 8 GCSE's (all but one C grade and above) including an A.... who would have thought?

Seen through the Heart, not the Eyes

I still find relationships a mystery even though I have been told I am good at communicating with people (laughable really). When I was at primary school I was quite the loner. I hate to admit it but I had no friends, in fact I was so bad at socialising and knowing how to act in social situations (school, parties, after school clubs and Brownies etc) that I just didn't know where to start. I think I found it so difficult coping with life and sensory overloads; I did not have a lot of time to think about relationships and socialising. I did however; know that in social situations, I should behave in the following way:

1. Be kind
2. Be caring
3. Be polite
4. Smile
5. Take an interest in the other person

If I found myself in a social conversation the only thing I knew how to say to the question

"How are you?"

Was to respond in the same way

"Ok"

Even if they said "good", "bad" "ill", "tired" or "My auntie just died- but I'm ok, I guess", I would still reply with the same word – "ok". This last example really happened; I had no idea what to say or do as I was very young. I was not very good at expressing sympathy or empathy, so I really didn't know how to re-act. Even though at that age I had experienced the death of relative and. I did feel sorry for her but I did not know if that was something I should say or not, I did not want to risk upsetting the person further by saying stuff out of line. So I merely said "ok...." hardly ideal. I feel terrible now because it is evident that I should have been more supportive.

When you ask somebody how they are, there are millions of different responses that the person could give. For this reason I was unable to prepare answers and because it takes me longer to process information, I am unable to quickly come up with an appropriate response. This is why I would always say "ok". It was the only response I could give to continue the conversation and also end it.

Likewise, if they asked me how I was feeling, I would always reply with

"I'm fine"

Regardless of how I was feeling, as I had little idea of what else to say. I had been taught to say that "I'm fine" because I had heard many other people say they were fine in response to the same question so I assumed it was the right answer and copied those role models. Now I realise that the question is personal, and has a personal answer and requires you to answer from a personal level of understanding. As you can imagine, I found all of this difficult as a child, to be honest I still do now.

After I have given my basic response of "ok" or "I'm fine" the conversation would come to a standstill because I did not know how to continue it. People, who meet me for the first time, think I am very shy because I barely speak to anyone, or they think I'm rude because I don't know how to make conversation with them or respond properly to their talk. My sister has been with her boyfriend for some years, but it was only last summer that I was able to start a conversation with him. It's not that I don't like him; it's just that I have no idea how to start a conversation.

When I was a child with a group of people who were having a group conversation, I would stay completely silent. This is for the following reasons:

1. I was very shy
2. I rarely heard what the people were saying because of my hearing problems
3. When I heard them, I rarely understood their spoken language, because everything is usually a confusing riddle

4. I was too distracted with sensory overloads
5. I very rarely knew what was going on, where I was supposed to be or what I was supposed to be doing, let alone concentrating on conversations
6. I was often distracted by pains from my ears or stomach
7. I also had nothing to say because it took me too long to process the information and form any opinions

As I got older, I slowly developed ways of coping with the sensory overloads during social situations and was able to decipher the English language (even though some of it is still a mystery). I also developed my own opinions and had stories of my own to tell. Now this would be great, if I was actually able to get my words out. As it is, when I am attempting to join in with a group conversation, I still stay very quiet, only managing a few words if I get the chance. This is because:

1. I find it difficult to keep up with many people talking at the same time
2. It takes me a long time to process what has been said
3. If I understand the conversation, it also takes me a while to think of a suitable response
4. Once I have formed my response, I get nervous about what I am about to say, in case I am wrong and have misunderstood the conversation
5. Making sure I give my response at a suitable pause in the conversation. I often interrupt people because I mistake a pause in their talking for the end of their sentence.

All of this takes so long for me to process that the conversation would have almost always moved on without me being able to say anything.

Jelly No Friends'
When I left my special needs school (at which I was very popular- everyone has difficulties there so it is not hard fitting in and never being judged) suddenly I had been transferred to a different mainstream school, where I had very few friends.

One day at my new primary mainstream school when I was in year five (aged about eight), my whole year was gathered together to have a special assembly. We lined up ready to walk into the assembly space when one child was taken out of the queue by a teacher and spent the assembly in a separate room. The special assembly was aimed at us pupils to make friends with the boy who had been taken out. This boy, we all found out, had difficulties with socialising and could not help growing up with no money for good school clothes. It turns out that the poor kid was being bullied a lot and had no friends because he was different to other children. To be honest immature kids (and adults) don't always like what they don't understand and not many children liked him because they did not like his clothes (second hand apparently) and because he smelt a bit funny. I guess growing up in a special needs school had made me very tolerant and understanding. So it hardly bothered me at all- in fact I don't recall ever thinking he was any different to other children. I thought he was normal, like me (hey, I like to think I am normal). During the assembly as the teacher explained his circumstances that he had no friends, I remember feeling so sad. I felt really sorry for the child, because his inability to socialise was being pointed out rather ruthlessly in front of a hundred kids who just look for reasons to bully others. By showcasing all of the boys problems in front of all those children, I thought it would make matters far worse because the bullying would not ease and only get nastier. I already tried to be friends with him by smiling and stuff and I was one of the very few children who offered to be his friend. I felt so sorry for him, I remember thinking 'how horrid that would be to have no friends, he has no friends, and now everyone knows it- how nasty of the teachers'.

I did not understand on the teacher's level that they were trying to help. As much as I felt bad for him not having any friends it never occurred to me that I was actually exactly the same as he was – without any friends.

I did not realise at the time that I was always alone and ignored by everyone, teachers and students. I actually had no friends either.

Indeed, during the same week it was time for assembly again and I was lining up waiting to walk into the assembly space with the other children when I got pulled out and taken to the art area. I had no idea why, I was just happy that I would not have to sit and get bored and achy. So I accepted the art area offer swiftly.

So I was in the art area with my teacher's assistant completely oblivious to what was going on. During which time, the whole year was in assembly being told by teachers about my difficulties. They explained that my disability meant that I had problem making friends. Everyone was being asked to try and be my friend. It horrifies me and when I found out I was so ashamed. The same thing that happened to the poor little boy was happening to me and I had no idea about it.

So, what I thought was so horrid and I felt so sorry for that little boy for having no friends, I was actually in the same situation, I just did not realise it. I had no idea.

I mean, I looked over to the assembly area a few times and saw a few people with their hands in the air, one boy shouted out about someone being stinky and having nasty ears. I did not make the connection and still had no idea they were talking about me.

I had never been so humiliated in that year because after that everyone started teasing me about my ears – apparently my horrendously painful and quite frankly foul smelling ear infections was mentioned as a reason why I found it difficult to make friends. Since then many pupils teased me about it for a long time afterwards.

I did have foul smelling ears, because I used to be partially deaf I was prone to some hideous ear infections, to the extent of my ear drum bursting and a constant stream of foul smelling yellow liquid dripping down my neck and getting my hair all knotty. It is so gross, all those ear infections but that's what you get when you're clinically deaf in that ear for most of your life. Kids don't care about that stuff; it was just another reason for them to bully me.

It is not all bad news though, as much to my good fortune, after a while at that school I became really good friends with two girls. My friendship with them was great, they did not seem to care that I was different and we all lived on the same road, every day after school we would go to our park which was round the corner from all of us. Together we had a fabulous childhood, running around playing Dinosaur games, running from Dinosaurs and creeping through exotic rain forest away from lurking Dinosaurs. Trust me we had the most amazing imaginations. Going through time vortex and travelling through time, rolling down grassy hills, climbing trees, running about, doing monkey bars, swinging on the swings, cycling – everything. It was truly wonderful and just what I needed. Those friendships set me up for life. It made my life easier and also made me practise and understand what it means to be friends, how use to all of the friendship skills in a way that is beneficial for my friendships in later life. Those friends made life bearable they really did, in fact if I was not friends with them my future of making friends would had been severely affected and I would have found it increasingly difficult to make friends. After all, the longer you wait to make friends the harder it becomes.

Throughout my childhood, I never had a big circle of friends; I always had one or two close friends. Despite the hardships of not having many friends and being bullied, the friendships that I did have, were wonderful. Even though I found it difficult to communicate with my good friends, it was still worth trying to make the effort, because the memories I have with them, I'll never forget.

I'm going to write down some tips about how to make friends, but don't put yourself down if you find it difficult to follow these tips, everyone is different and everyone is good at various things. Finding things difficult does not make you silly or stupid.

How to Make Friends

We are at the section where I can bet a few of you flipped straight to this page. So here I go. Making friends can be difficult yes, but it can be done (I'm being serious, have faith in yourself). What you have to remember is that you are no better than anyone else and no one is better than you, we are all equal. Even if you have a disability, even if you have different cultural backgrounds, we are all equal and deserve the same human rights as everybody else. Don't allow people to treat you badly but try to tell someone you trust like a family member or adult (teacher) if you think someone is being mean to you. However, there are some lovely people out there who will be friends and like you for who you are, so there is no need to change yourself or pretend to be something you are not. There are nice people in our big wide world; you just have to meet them. I am no expert on socialising or anything like that, I can't pretend to have all the answers, likewise I can't guarantee any success, all my advice can be effective over a period of time, if it does not work so well now maybe it will work better later on. The first thing you need to understand is where you can meet new people, new friends safely. It is a good idea to start friendships with a person you feel comfortable with; maybe someone you feel is similar to you, such as religion or disability or even a similar hobby that you like. I am going to write a list of possible places that one could meet new friends.

Where you can find friends
There are many places where you can meet new people, and make new friends, here is a list of a few:

1.   School/College/University
2.   Clubs
3.   Youth groups
4.   Volunteering
5.   Work – there is a section later about help with jobs
6.   Places of shared cultural interest, maybe Churches or Mosques

If you attend a school then the trick is to join after school /lunch time clubs that you are interested in. They could be after school clubs or maybe there is a local youth centre. Get some help to go on the internet and check out local things for you to do. Clubs are a great way to meet new people that may have similar interests as you.

I know a lot of people with Asperger's lack confidence and independence but soon you'll be coming on in leaps and bounds (getting better at things) even if you don't feel like you have changed, you are probably doing really well. You just have to try, and if you feel that you have 'failed' just keep trying- sooner or later you'll make friends worth keeping. I know it is easier to stay cooped up in our bedrooms but there is a big wide world out there that we have to take part in and it is better with friends. Life is for living and enjoying not for hiding away from people.

By Joely Colmer.

Make sure you are not rude

I have found that neuro typical people (people without disabilities) find some of the things I do and say rude, even though it is never my intention. This is because I have a lack of sympathy and I am unable to understand or be able to read people's emotions- e.g., when they are upset or anxious about something. So I often don't react in an appropriate manner.

Advice to Somebody with Asperger's – Successful Polite Conversation
Take an interest in what people have to say, even if you couldn't care less about what they have to say. Usually, it is polite and easier in the long run if you just try and take an interest. If you take an interest in other people, they will respect and begin to like you and maybe want to be friends.

Often when I have a conversation, I am distracted with lots of other things going on, this makes it difficult to keep track of what has been said. I can also appear rude, because I am not giving 'normal listening' signals. Sometimes as much as I want to listen to somebody's every word, my surroundings can be a barrier, and prevent me from listening effectively. It is not my fault, but it does mean that people think I am being rude, because I don't respond in the way I should. I have found it helpful to pretend I am listening even when I am really struggling. Even when I can barely grasp what the conversation is about, if I hear one topical word, I will build on that.

Example of me 'parroting' back words
My friend- "He told a funny joke and it was really funny."
Me- "A funny joke? What funny joke was that?"

It usually works very well. I recommend you use a similar technique if you find that you are struggling to hear their every word and still want to appear like you are listening to them.

If you feel you talk too much about yourself and if you feel that people get fed up with you (which, no offence, they probably do) you should give this technique a go to see if it works for you too.

Advice to Somebody with Asperger's — Listening

Smile a little and nod during the conversation, this is good because even if you are struggling to voice your opinions, you can still look like you are interested in the conversation. I usually parrot words back at them (a common trait of Asperger's). and then build on that word by asking questions.

It's rather cheeky but it works.

Advice for People with A.S.D – Making Friends

1. **Smile**

   Smiling is a natural way to make others smile back, if you genuinely seem happy most of the time, people, in theory, should warm to you (sorry, I'm talking in riddles again. I meant people should 'like you'). If you smile at someone with whom you have made acquaintance, then you may even get a little smile back. Beware, if you smile too much, it can be taken as a negative rather than a positive, so don't grin (smile) ALL the time. I have sadly been perceived as a bit odd because I smile too much.

   However, little smiles every now and again are good.

2. **Saying "hi"**

   If you have smiled at somebody and they have smiled back, it is now time to start a conversation no matter how small. A classic example of this is when you walk past each other in the corridor at school. Say "Hi" as you walk past. I advise that you only do this with a person that has already smiled back at you or smiled at you a few times. You do not want to say "Hi" to everybody that passes you, as you may be perceived as odd.

3. **Do make a Compliment** every now and again.

   Most people like to be complimented, so saying something as simple as "I like the T shirt you are wearing" can be an easy way to start a conversation. You could even then say "Where did you get your T shirt from?". Complimenting is best in small doses. It is difficult to get the balance right but it is best to try.

4. **Don't Pretend to be somebody you are not**

   Even if you are scared that no one will like the real you. If they won't, or don't like you, then they definitely don't deserve your friendship. Find someone worth your time. No one is worth your friendship if they make you feel that you have to change yourself to be liked. There are people out there who will genuinely like you for who you are. – Go meet these people, at local youth clubs for instance, make an effort.

5. **Eye Contact** (oh no)
   You dislike it, I know...So do I. Eye contact seems to be the dreaded little thing we all probably hate. Hate is such a strong word because there is no reason to dislike it at all. In fact, it's easy once you get used to it. I know it makes us feel uncomfortable, it makes me feel as if I'm drilling into their minds and searching their souls, but, eye contact is really good and helpful for the following reasons.

   Good points of holding eye contact:

   A. You will have a better chance at understanding their facial expressions and what they say if you do this. This in turn will positively affect a lot of other things during socialising with people
   B. You may eventually learn to tell apart sarcasm from genuine distaste.
   C. If you maintain eye contact it will appear that you are interested in what they have to say (even if you are not interested at all it is good to make it look like you are)
   D. You can tell a lot about the person by their eyes. For example raised eye brows tend to mean that the person is surprised
   E. You will have a better understanding of how to react to what they say and what to reply. You will probably begin to learn the art of conversation
   F. After a while, eye contact becomes natural, it can make people like you more because you are looking at them. If you are trying to make friends you have to make eye contact otherwise the person will feel as uncomfortable as you do.

   Bad points of holding eye contact:

   A. It makes us feel uncomfortable for a while until we get used to it
   B. People have funny eyes/facial features
      Note. Don't point this out if someone does have funny facial features, it is considered rude. If there's something unusual about the person

that can't be changed e.g. a big nose (even though I personally can't see the problem with big noses) don't mention it, they won't thank you for it. They may misinterpret what you meant even if you did not mean to be harsh. You have to be very careful.

I have recently read an article, which stated that young people and children with Autistic spectrum disorders avoid eye contact if they are trying to work out a difficult problem. This is to avoid confusion or distractions. Hopefully, the more you practise making eye contact and basic conversation with people you feel comfortable with (family), the easier it will become. I once took an online test to see how well I could read how eyes portray different emotions. I had to look at one hundred sets of eyes, and identify the correct emotion displayed. As I have Asperger's I thought this would be particularly difficult, however when receiving the results, I scored above average and was pleasantly surprised. I even scored much higher than my sister, who does not have Asperger's. I think this is down to the fact that I do make a big effort to make eye contact with people and practise on a regular basis.

Don't punish yourself if making eye contact is difficult at the beginning, remember practise makes perfect. Eye contact can be a bit of a nuisance but in the long run it is most certainly better to try.

6. **Ask Questions**

Ask good questions about the subject the person has been talking about:

A. "What did you do at the weekend?"
B. "What are you going to do this weekend?"
C. "Do you have anything interesting planned?"
D. "How is school/work going"
E. "How are you?"
F. "Can you tell me a bit about your work/college course/school project, please?"

The following are really bad questions, avoid asking questions of a personal nature:

A. "How old are you?"
B. "How much money do you earn?"

C. "How much do you weigh?"

D. "Why does no one like you?"

E. "Why do you have spots?"

F. "Why do you look funny?"

G. "Why does your disability make you look silly when you walk?"

H. "Why does your disability make you stupid?"

I. "Did you know that *10%* of the population thinks that sufferers with anxiety just make up symptoms for benefit support?"

not a real statistic

The last case in point is an example I heard someone with Autism say to a person who had previously said they suffered with anxiety attacks. Uho – you can imagine how that ended? Badly! The kid with Autism was into statistical and factual figures as a specialist topic; he was clearly just making conversation, by talking about a statistic in relation to anxiety. He did not realise how upset the kid with anxiety would become (she ran off crying) because of the content of the offensive fact. People with Asperger's don't often make connections of the effect their words have on other people, especially when their words are merely the truth, or indeed, facts. Why would something true be bad?

The 'bad questions' as listed above, are all examples I have never used (of course, some are terribly rude and mean, not to mention incredibly wrong), but I have heard others use some of these examples in complete innocence, in an attempt at making conversation with peers. However, due to how these questions can be perceived, conversation often fails rather miserably, by upsetting, enraging, or making the person they are talking to feel very uncomfortable.

7. **Avoid Rambling**

I have a tendency to ramble on and on and on and on...and on....and on... until people get really bored with me. You can usually tell someone is getting bored when they become restless, when they break eye contact and look away and try and change the topic. They may become fidgety by playing with their hands/fingers touching their face more than normal and changing standing/sitting position.

If they are smiling at you and nodding usually it means they are interested or being polite. If they want to change the topic then it's usually best that you let them. It is quite possible that if you have been talking for a while or telling a story you find interesting they may become slightly restless if they also have something to say but can't say it because you are talking so much.

8. Topics

I find it so difficult to actually talk to people sometimes; especially when I'm in a group. It's almost like I have things to say but someone gets there before me and before I know it the whole conversation has moved on and I won't get a chance to say anything at all. I don't always mind this to be honest with you, I quite enjoy just over seeing conversations and not actually taking part unless I have a valid thing to say.

So do you have a specialist topic of conversation? A specialist obsession or favourite thing you like to do that seems to be all consuming in its brilliance?

I bet you do.

The thing you need to do is make sure you talk equally in topics (if they have relevance to one another), so you can talk about what you want but make sure you give the other person a chance to talk as well. This might sound difficult but once you get used to it can become very easy indeed, so don't worry – practise makes perfect. Try and distinguish what it is that they may like to talk about.

It is usually a good idea to discuss things that you have in common, for example if you have met at school and are in the same class, you could talk about your class work, or things that happened that day in class.

A. **School/College/University/Work** – If you both attend the same place. If you have met somebody at school, then it would be easier to talk about school as it is the common ground.
B. **The weather** – don't talk about it for too long. People get bored easily. Unless there has been a horrid natural disaster somewhere in the world in which case it may be disrespectful to appear uninterested in world affairs like that.

C. **Television/films** – You can talk about your favourite films good and bad films you have seen, films you want to see.... the list goes on and on.

D. **What you have been doing** – don't talk about this for too long, I'm not saying you have to time yourself but be aware of how long you have been talking.

E. **What they have been doing** – Asking them this simple question makes you appear interested in their life and is an easy way for you to stop talking and to just listen. Most people like to talk about themselves, so asking questions like this is a good starting point.

Once you get to know someone, topics of conversation will become easier.

More topics – current affairs

People with Asperger's are intelligent people, but not everybody wants to hear the complete history of the Ancient Egyptians. Unless you find somebody who has the same interest as you (this is going to be rare in my case) then people could swiftly become bored with your ramblings. Having specialist topics clearly makes you quite clever, because you have spent time and energy researching them. Sadly, it is unlikely that your specialist topic would be a normal topic of conversation for most people. Current affairs, i.e., what's happening in the news and magazines are a popular source of interest in conversations. If you could spend some time researching current affairs (by watching the news on television or reading informative magazines) you will find it easier to follow and join in on other peoples conversations. The knowledge you have about current affairs, can also be a very good way to start conversations with people. You may sound educated and interested in the world's affairs which are quite important to many people's hearts.

Summary

Making friends can be difficult but having good friends is wonderful and well worth the complexities. Once you have made a friend, all the things you find difficult (keeping eye contact and the art of conversation) will become much easier as you get to know them. I know it is hard, and it may take a while but please try. Good luck, people.

The 'S' Word

This section is aimed at young people (with or without disabilities) and the odd bit of parental advice included.

How many of you have fast tracked to this section I wonder?

Or rather, how many of you shy away from this section and have tried to read this part in private? This, I feel is a very important bit, as if I knew the answer it would give me great insight upon how ready you really are for a mature relationship like this. I know what you are thinking. I'm a freak, no one will like me. It's not true, you are not and don't ever let anyone tell you that you are. If people do tell you that you are a freak, then you must find it in your heart to believe they are wrong because they are. I believe there is no such thing as a 'freak' quite simply because as humans, we are all equal regardless of our race, our cultures, sex, age, beliefs, disabilities and whether we like guys or girls. We are all equal because we are all different. We should embrace our differences; life would be very dull without variety. Just because everybody is different does not mean we are not all equal. If you were to stereotype a 'freak' as someone who is different, however if we are all different and all equal, then surely that makes everybody a freak?!

Being individual is very attractive to the decent people in life. Why should you care if horrid people tell you that you are a 'freak' their opinions should not matter to you, because they are not worth your time. Try your best to distance yourself from people who are mean, say nasty things, or upset you. There are lovely people out there who will think you are attractive inside and out and not think of you as a 'freak'. Stop caring what the mean people think and stop thinking badly of your-self. It is not worth trying so hard to impress people who quite frankly are not worth your attention or thoughts at all. People will like you, so stop fretting.

Now that bit is over with, let us begin...

I believe the most profound beauty is from within and I especially believe girls and guys don't have to be skinny, wear makeup or wear revealing clothes to be beautiful.

How do you gain confidence?

Ignore society's rules and stereotypes (skinny, tall, make up etc) and believe you are beautiful, look in the mirror every day and tell yourself that you are beautiful. If you are a beautiful person by being kind (being a beautiful person by being kind is better than being a physical beauty – trust me), the good people will value kind beauty more. Make sure you compliment yourself each day, try to avoid looking at yourself in the mirror and thinking

"oh no, my hair's a mess, I look fat, I am all spotty again... woe is me'.

The more you believe that you are a beautiful person, the more confident you will become, and the more confident you become will enhance your chance of making relationships.

Its rather odd, that some years ago, when you hit your teenage years, sex was not so important, boyfriends and girlfriends were not important, but nowadays children of 11 years old are looking for boyfriends or girlfriends, talking about their first kiss, whether they should have sex with their crush at a party or not... It quite simply terrifies me how quickly young people are growing up nowadays. It really does horrify me, when I was that age I was still running around the park, rolling down muddy hills and having laughs with my mates. Gee, it was not until a few years ago that I had my first 'crush' on someone... It is strange.

Advice to Parents – Communicating with your Children
I believe that the perspective of sex and lovemaking is taught by surrounding environment, family and peers. If you are parents who are equally as scared of our sex crazed society as I am, maybe it's time to try to support your child, even more than you undoubtedly do already. Try to avoid lecturing or disapproval. The way you act in day to day conversations that shed light on your view points of society will be far more effective than that dreaded

"We need to have a parent to child chat"...

I am not saying you should avoid talking about the importance of safe and loving sex, in fact I have had such a brilliant relationship with my mum that I never felt embarrassed to talk about sex and things with my mum. This is because I know she would not get angry at me or disapprove of my opinions quite simply because they have been formed by my environment and family. Make conversations of this topic sensitive and light that shed light upon your own opinions and what you think about the matters. Children are more likely to listen if they are intrigued by you; if they are interested they won't take offence at your words and may not see it as 'nagging'. If you listen to your child without disapproval or anger, they are more likely to listen and learn from you in return, not all circles are 'vicious circles'.

Making love should be the most wonderful and pure thing in the world. Sex is not about doing it because you feel like you should be, maybe because your partner or peers are pressuring you. No, love making has to be special, beautiful; everything about love making should be unique. Making love should be about wanting to take away your partner's pain, ceasing their struggles and making them feel wonderful; sex should be about making love with one person who you want to spend the rest of your life with (hence the belief in chastity). Love making should be about love, not lust, not doing it for the sake of it, not doing it to fit in, not sexualising yourself or others; just love. Lovemaking is all about the true essence of romantic wonderful, soul enriching love between two people, and nothing else. Love, trust, happiness and selflessness are all the things that bring love together. I do believe, the longer you wait to make love, the better the relationship you may have.

As a child growing up, my family were wonderful in teaching me the dangers of some teenage boys who say anything at all to persuade you to have sex. So many young teenage boys are after sex and don't really care how they get it. Likewise of course, with some girls. Being cautious is crucial for safety and emotional wellbeing.

Are you really ready?

This has to be the most important question that you'll ever face in your teenage years. I can't stress enough how important it is to be truly ready for sex. I recommend you talk to someone about your thoughts and feelings about sex; communication is never a bad thing and more often than not, it helps. Someone who usually understands the importance of sex and is very trustworthy is probably the best person to ask. You can either talk to:

1. A parent or carer
2. A sibling
3. A teacher
4. Your Doctor
5. A friend who you can really trust
6. A youth worker
7. A counsellor
8. The person you are considering sex with – this is very important, because if you feel uncomfortable talking to them about sex then that is a sure sign you are not ready

First things first, chances are if you feel embarrassed about reading this section, then you are probably not ready for any type of serious relationship, let alone making love.

Usually you're in a relationship when you consider sex. If you are not in a relationship but you are still considering sex then I strongly advise that you wait. Advantages of waiting for sex:

1. I think you should be in a very stable relationship
2. I think it is best that you can show and share with your partner absolutely everything
3. You should want to 'make love' not have sex. Making love is about being loving. I will admit it is very hard to explain. If you are in love with no doubts at all then you will probably understand what I mean by making love, in which case you are probably more ready than not

4. You should not consider having sex just because everyone else is having sex.
5. Sex is all about showing that you love someone

If somebody is asking you to do something that you feel uncomfortable with, then obviously you shouldn't do it. The person may not realise, they are pressuring you and may say things like

"If you loved me, you would do it"

However, if they really loved you, they wouldn't pressure you and make you feel guilty by saying these things.

The 'S' word and protection
I can't stress this enough.

You have to use protection and you most definitely have to be prepared.

Protection as you may already know protects you from two things:

1. A sexually transmitted infection or a disease (STI or STD)
2. Unwanted pregnancy

There are many different forms of protection, condoms being the most common, you can buy them in any drug store or pharmacy (Boots or Superdrug). Everybody finds it embarrassing buying condoms, so you are not alone. The people who work in the stores will not laugh or judge you. Please remember, that it is the responsibilities of both of you to be protected, so never rely on the other person to sort out the protection.

Your Doctor or school nurse will be able to give you free advice with regards to protection. Again, you may find it embarrassing to talk to these people but they are professionals and have heard it all before. They will probably respect you more for being honest with them.

There are other forms of protection, for example The Pill. However, to discuss these forms and what is suitable for you, you need to have a chat with your Doctor. Safe sex is the only type of sex you should be having. I can not stress this enough. It is so important, I have stressed it twice.

'S'uality

I know this is a very risky subject to have an opinion about. Especially because across the world there are some very strong views about whether it is right or wrong to be gay and whether it should be accepted within society or not. I just believe that everyone has the right to be happy, understood and not judged, regardless of differences. No one has the right to judge whether it is right or not to be gay or different. To me, saying

"It is wrong to be gay"

is as terrible, narrow minded and horrendously evil as saying…

"It is wrong to be disabled" or "it is wrong to have black/white skin"

It is not wrong to be different from others at all, it is not wrong to be any of these things. Sadly, this is a huge topic for discussion. I imagine a lot of you are reading this and thinking that I am being ridiculous and should be ashamed of my views on equal rights for everyone regardless of differences; Whereas, others may agree with my views. We are all different, and entitled to our own opinions, human rights for everyone, because we are all equal regardless of differences. Although as we have rights to our own personal opinions we must not let our prejudices vent or discriminate against people, because in many cases this is wrong and illegal, and could be considered as 'hate crime'.

I do wonder though, when the human race is beginning an epic journey of understanding differences and making all life more justified, why it is that sexuality is still so hated and feared?

Personally, I think you should try not to be ashamed about sexuality. It is actually very normal for most teenagers to doubt their sexuality at some point in their teenage years. I believe the most recent figure is that 8 out of 10 people admit that at some point in their life, they had being attracted to the same sex, either being gay, bisexual or lesbian, most of which felt uncomfortable with admitting this and 'coming out' as the saying goes.

As society changes to allow people to be honest with themself, as society accepts being gay as part of human nature, the number of people openly admitting to feelings of attraction towards the same sex, will only grow. Don't let anyone tell you it is wrong, if you feel this way about the same sex or think you do, you need to do what makes you feel comfortable. A lot of people can't bear the idea of telling their friends and family that they are attracted towards the same sex due to their families / environmental beliefs that it is wrong.

Sure, I could be upsetting a lot of people here, for which I apologise profoundly and I really do not wish to cause offence or upset, I am sorry for any discomfort I may have caused. You, like I, have the right to your own belief and opinions which have been created from your own cultures, religions, environments and role models from your childhood, we just have to all learn to accept that others think differently. Quite frankly I believe in love being the most incredible thing to happen to a person, love can make one feel amazingly happy, and can change ones emotional and mental wellbeing. Love can also improve one's health (emotional and physical) because it decreases the problem of loneliness. I believe love can make you feel valued, appreciated, cared for, listened too and nurtured which in turn enhances self esteem and positive emotions and how they treat other people and their outlook on life. I therefore believe that everyone deserves to fall in love; as it is so wonderful, everyone deserves to feel all the incredible emotions that love brings and everyone deserves to be happy. We are all equal and I am a strong believer that it does not matter which gender you like, love is love, and you can't help who you fall in love with. A lot of people fall in love with a type of personality, someone loving, caring, kind, funny and someone who makes them feel happy, safe and motivated to live their life to the full. Surely if a person is feeling all of these positive emotions, why would it matter if they fell in love with a male or female? It's up to you to make your decisions and judgements about what you think upon the subject.

Spot the Signs – Abuse in Relationships

Unfortunately, vulnerable people (I hate using that phrase) are more likely to be victims of theft, bullying or abuse. I found this out through my research into one of my voluntary projects, which is called 'The Safe Places Scheme'. This project was designed to make public places in my local town safer for disabled young people by providing safe places to go to, if needed. Due to my research, I feel it is important to make you aware of the various signs of abuse in relationships because sadly abuse, could be inflicted by someone you know and trust.

Signs of Manipulation in a Relationship

1. The person can make you feel upset frequently and make you feel more and more worthless the more you are with them
2. They may try and control money/income how or where to spend it
3. Shout at you. Short temper
4. Sulk when they don't get their own way and if they feel guilty they take it out on you
5. Glare at you
6. Call you nasty hurtful names
7. They will never admit they are wrong, especially if they are. In fact they will make you believe you are wrong by creating some twisted story to make you believe them
8. Blame you for things they have done, such as skiving, drink, drugs, alcohol and stress
9. Threaten or wheedles you to get their own way
10. Flirt outside of the relationship
11. They may try and control who you hang out with/cut you off from your friends/family, socially isolating you
12. They may treat you badly out of guilt, even when they know they are doing it
13. You feel an urge to not discuss problems with them because you feel that they will handle it badly and blame you or make you feel bad/argue
14. No matter how much you try nothing is good enough
15. You feel like you are not listened to and you feel like your opinions and feelings are not valued
16. Physically hurts you, your family/friends or threatens to

Although these are signs of possible manipulation in a relationship, some of these signs are just merely common. Don't forget the perfect relationship does not exist. However, that does not mean you should stand for being treated badly, because there are many people out there who will love you and treat you well and look after you.

If you think you are in an abusive or manipulative relationship you must talk to someone about it, whether it be a friend, parents/carer, support assistant or teacher. Talk to someone you can trust.

Having the right type of relationships can make the difference to you having a lonely life and having an exciting and loving life. I know it is difficult to take the first steps, but it really is worth all of the effort. I currently have a wonderful boyfriend who I am very much in love with. It may have taken a lot of years to get to this point, and believe me, there was some hardships along the way, but I wouldn't change it for the world. I love life.

Mate Crime

Who here has a best friend? A friend who makes you laugh until your belly aches? A friend who laughs with you? A friend who says they will stand up to those bullies? A friend who understands your highs and lows?

What about a friend who says a lot of these things, but doesn't do any of it? What about a friend who is slowly isolating you, using their knowledge of your highs and lows to control or manipulate you? A friend, who laughs at you, disguised as laughing with you... and is actually bullying you? Wait, what? Friends don't bully...Do they?

This, is the sad reality of so called 'Mate Crime'.

Most of us have heard of a Hate Crime; which is where someone actively bullies or abuses someone because of their diversity (disability, age, gender, sexuality, race, religion etc). Mate Crime is the grooming of vulnerable and disabled people by those who pretend to be friends, using someone's disability against them, and targeting the,m because of their disabilities, before exploiting the vulnerable; financially, physically or sexually. Just like Hate Crime, Mate Crime is an offence; abuse that is punishable by the law.

These so called mates can manipulate their disabled friends for pin numbers, taking money or personal possessions. They feign friendship, but are not kind or particularly accepting of their disabled friend's differences; making their disabled friend feel insecure about their diversities. They subtly isolate with back handed compliments, making the disabled person the butt of every joke regardless of the disabled person's feelings. They know what to say to make the disabled friend feel guilty for not bending to their every desire; often leaving the disabled friend trying to do just that, in desperation to not lose their 'friendship'. They take their insecurities or their anxieties out on their disabled friend, and have a speciality with using the disabled friends disability, and lack of understanding against them. They are experts at taking advantage and manipulating the disabled friend to make them do things they are not comfortable with. Whilst simultaneously making their disabled friend believe that due to their disability, they really don't deserve any better, seeing as they are "Too 'difficult' and 'selfish' for 'normal' people to deal with all the time". Ultimately they are experts at making the disabled person think that they are actually really lucky to have them as friends, because no one else would 'put up with them'. In these ways, I believe that Mate Crime has a few similarities to gaslighting.

For instance, even when I was being bullied by those I trusted, I never realized it until years later.

It slowly corrodes at your sense of self worth until there is no turning back; and you are left weak, defenceless, lonely and terribly confused with how you feel so hurt and bad all the time. Years later I can see I was depressed. I would think to myself;

I have friends now, finally! So why do I feel so... Alone?

Speaking from experience there is nothing harder than finally realizing the truth; that year's of friendship was tainted with bullying from Mate Crime. It is much harder to report than bullying because these people who are abusing you are your friends; people you trust, people you would never wish any harm onto, people who you thought you could not live without... People you love. It's a horror that boils your blood with hurt and distrust. It claws at your heart, tearing apart everything you thought you understood about relationships and yourself. It corrodes at your self-belief, and your faith in the human race.

What if they were right? What if I really did deserve their abuse? What if it IS my disability?

Advice
If you have been affected by bullying, or Mate/Hate Crime then please remember that there are many people, and professionals (Police, GP's,

Charities, Councillors, Therapists, School, Work, University) who can help; please seek their support and please report it.

Never forget, that there is always room to make a difference, and that is what we can all do. Remove the poisonous people from your life by reporting them and leave those haters behind, because you do deserve better. Take courage from support networks / charity, seek therapy and help from family and true friends. No matter the ordeals that have made you feel worthless, no matter the hardships you have had to endure, have hope in yourself and your future.

We must try and help build that understanding of healthy relationships, and a support network for vulnerable people to escape bullies, to prevent future tragedy. Keep inspiring yourself, keep up that motivation to make a difference and achieve your life goals. If you feel strongly about any issue, like bullying or Mate / Hate Crime, then remember this; whenever there is a struggle, or chains that try to hold you back, there is always room for improvement, a voice to be heard, a calling and an opportunity for change. Become that change.

Mate Crime : Volunteering

Once upon a time, I could never envisage myself as an accomplished communicator, as someone who could rise above the bullies, and use my Autism disability to my advantage; but then my life changed. I changed; all because I started volunteering. I have written a little story to describe the moment I finally realised that the friendship I experienced was actually wrong for me. That I had been a victim, not a friend; that I had to let go of the bullies, and move forward with my life.

"It's raining. Droplets splatter uncomfortably onto her face as she stumbles down the hill. Tears mingle together as the judgemental accusations echo around her tired and frazzled brain. Footsteps pound on the wet path behind her and someone is calling her name. The girl begins to shake as anxiety takes control; oh no! Not again... The person has caught up now, holding up their hand and waving for her to stop walking. The girl stumbles to a halt, breathing fast. What now? She can not cope with this right now, please just let her go... "Oi! Your disability is SO frustrating; I can understand why you need some sense beaten into you sometimes. After all I have done to help you... I tried to help; but you don't deserve help when your being like this..." Say's her friend with a shrug and a shaking of their head.

The girl stiffens, suddenly afraid, eyes taking in every detail of the wet pavement beneath her feet. Her legs started to quake, heart hammering in her chest. How can she say such a horrific thing? Surely that is not what real friends do? The girl wonders, through gasping breaths. Here it comes; the sickness, the uncontrollable horror as depression rages through her blood, shaking her making her feel worthless. She resists the urge to scratch. To yank. To pull at her hair. She can't cope.

"You're selfish enough to throw it back in my face, with accusations that you are not smart enough to understand. Look, it's not my fault you are never going to amount to anything; you should be thanking us! You're so stupid that you would be lost without us" shouts the friend, fire burning in their eyes, as they spit the words out like acid on their tongue.

The words sting, stabbing her in the heart. Suddenly the sickness rose, distasting her mouth, her surroundings swirling around her, and a little quote running through her mind from an article she read recently... she couldn't get it off her mind. As she stood there, shaking, shivering, arms hugging close as she rocked back and fourth, the quote was all she could think about...

"Friends do not hurt each other, they make you feel safe, not alone. Friends help and support you and make you feel better, not worse. Friends will apologise for wrong doings, not manipulate you. Friends will try to recover bridges, not make you feel guilty. If your friend is just pretending, and makes you feel negative or disheartened or like you need to prove yourself to be in their company, then they are not good enough for you, because you deserve better. Leave those pretenders, and trust that you will find better friends who deserve your friendship, elsewhere"

The quote spun around her head, until all she could see was the bold italic print, indented into her vision. The girls friend was still screaming out accusations, hatred simmering as she pointed out every hardship that girl had, and couldn't control, as a result of her disability. The girl shut her eyes, "why is my friend making me feel bad for my disability, for things I can not control... is she really a friend?" In a final moment of gut wrenching horror, and screeching white noise, her friends words became a blur of abuse. The girl couldn't hear her, nor, did she care. She couldn't focus, this quote just seemed too important right now. Suddenly her breath came short, and shooting pain pierced through her, as the realisation came crashing through to reality. This was not friendship, it never was. It was abuse. It was lies. All lies. She had to get away, before it was too late. The girl charges on and pushes past her friend, now a stranger. Running as fast as her legs can carry her, her saviour, a simple brick building, looms ahead of her. She's home.

Laughter can be heard over the bubble of excited chatter. She opens the door and steps inside breathing a sigh of relief and is immediately met with the smell of toast. With terrible self destructive thoughts roaring through her tired mind, the girl wipes the tears from her eyes and looks at the floor, ashamed. She didn't feel ready to say "hello" yet; the emotional pain was still too raw.

"Hi, super star!" Someone grinned, as they flounce up to her high fiving her with excited clumsy hands. She laughs despite the negative wash that had bathed her with sorrow. The muscles that had been so tense before begin to relax. She inhales again as a smile replaces the sad grimace on her face. She walks in, relaxed, laughing, joining her real friends. This is her home, right here; with the support from these wonderful like minded volunteers, who have become close friends, real deserving friends. She was so relieved to be a part of such a beautiful little close knit community now. No longer was she bullied for her differences, but celebrated; no longer an alien as an outcast of society, but a worthwhile member... she now had hope and opportunities to enable her to strive for a better future.

It's all ok. She's safe. She's supported. She's with her family again... She's home."

You want to know something? That was me. Although the story is mostly a fake, the emotions behind it are true; I was that lonely and afraid little girl, struggling with relationship breakdowns on her journey to one of her first voluntary sessions.

At the beginning of my voluntary journey I was depressed, lonely and afraid for the future. A victim of bullying and abuse made my Post Traumatic Stress Disorder a nightmare to deal with. I was drifting into the darkness, not certain I would make it out the other side (sorry, that's a story for another time). When I was referred to start volunteering with a youth disability action group called the Chatterboxes, I had no idea just how much those inspiring people would enlighten me, uncover hidden skills, and just how much I would learn.

I honestly had no idea how happy I would become.

Volunteering with a wide variety of projects has completely changed my life for the better, enabling me to adore my disability and achieve my dreams! The chatterbox sessions are utterly precious because the staff are amazing; support that is showered upon us all simply drenches us in self belief, confidence and life skills. I suddenly found myself with the rare opportunity to learn my independence, socialise, participate in team work exercises and able to amount to my full potential, while surrounded by a team of like minded people who were all motivated to help make change while having fantastic fun with their friends.

From the very first session I adored it... I turned up for the first event clutching a note pad, a nervous smile and a broken heart. And slowly but surely those wonderful people mended the gaping holes within my heart, and filled it with the glorious sensation of making a difference. I loved it; the relaxed and fun atmosphere, being surrounded by like minded disabled people who understood, accepted and celebrated our differences. On that first day I left the session with pages of ideas, compliments swirling through my brain and cheeks that ached from so much laughter. I left with my head held high, that much more confident and happy; I had already decided that volunteering was the path I should take. Within a month I was happy. A changed person; And so I threw myself into volunteering...
and the rest, as they say, is history.

Emotionless Robots

It has been said that people with Autistic spectrum disorders don't always show much emotion, even when someone close to them has died (friend or family). The same has been said about me. It makes me sound so heartless, so cold, so... cruel. Consequently, this is judgment I don't take kindly too. One reason for such a judgment is that people with A.S have trouble reading emotions and picking up on social cues. This means it can appear that those with A.S don't notice, nor care, when others are upset. Misreading someone's emotion is highly likely to result in inappropriate reactions. This is true of anyone with or without Autistic Disorders.

To try and make this a bit clearer, I shall tell you the story of my pet rabbit. When I was about 14 years old, my loved pet rabbit of 8 years died... and it did not appear to bother me. I did not seem to cry, or talk about missing my rabbit, nor did I appear shaken or changed in my behavior at all. This makes me sound cruel, emotionless and careless. However, in a way, because I was aware my poor rabbit was unwell and probably dying, the months before my Peter Rabbit had died, I had gone into the garden most days to spend time with him. I would spend a long time in his hutch, stroking him, crying at the thought of losing my one friend who I can talk too about everything, without judgment. I mourned his departure before he died because I knew the end was near. After he died it was almost as if it was unnecessary to further mourn him as he knew that I would mourn him and he knew that I loved him. Logically (for a child with Asperger's, or perhaps, just me) I thought that because he knew I loved him and had already mourned him, it would be best for me and my school work to move on. Somehow, a switch called 'turn off mourning' was turned off in my brain, and I swiftly moved on without appearing to care. I wish to explain how I mourned as a child as I feel it is important to show that we all mourn in different ways.

When I was a child I used to have a wild imagination. Through my imaginative play I mourned, developed and learnt. My hallway is quite large so I used to pretend it was an interior ancient Roman garden, this is because most ancient Roman gardens would have a tree planted within their interior garden. It was believed that this tree represented loss of souls to those dear to us. At stressful times, I would visit this imaginary Roman garden often and pray to the house Gods for the safe keeping of my loved ones souls. In a way this was my coping strategy for tough times with death. When alone and unseen, I would be stood in the center of my hall way gazing in awe at an invisible tree and stroking its fragile branches, smelling the delicate scents of the flowers. Each flower was believed to represent a lost soul, I would pray to the gods of the house for the safe resting place of our long gone souls. My family always thought I was not upset when death claimed our loved ones, although I must admit I did not show it as it felt unreal, and in some parts the reasons behind my lack of emotions is indescribable. Maybe, I just hadn't made the connection between the word 'dead' or 'death' and realized that it meant that no one will ever see the dead person ever again... they were gone... from our physical lives... but never from our hearts. However, it always upset me somewhere deeper, somewhere unseen. Alternatively, my love of Egyptology often took over and

I used to pray to Egyptian gods of the underworld and passing, Anubis and Ammit in the Duat (Duat = Underworld). I used to wish that my loved ones soul would be able to continue their voyage towards Osiris and immortality and remain well rested. (Anubis- Ancient Egyptian god of the afterlife, half man, half dog. Ammit- A female demon that devours souls and had the form of all three of the largest man eating creatures in Egypt – Crocodile, Hyppo and Lion). I used to pray to the two of them (Anubis and Ammit) to have mercy upon the souls taken from us. I used to wish to them to weigh our loved ones hearts with care against the light Ostriches feather (Feather of truth – Goddess Ma'at). This is a favorite scene I would draw in Hieroglyphics as a child, as seen below, it is not copied from anywhere, I just merely wrote with hieroglyphics and drew it all myself, describing the story my way. Although admittedly if you translate it, I doubt it makes much, if any, sense at all.

I am uncertain if my family knows about this or not. The atmosphere when I used to act out such a mourning ceremony would become peaceful, yet I could always feel a cold aura of sadness engulfing me like the wind of a hurricane. Egyptian Gods and Roman antics… That is how I mourned as a child, through history and play. The best way for a child to express their negative emotions and feelings is through therapeutic play, a specialist interest, music, dance, toy phones, role play and puppets etc. That is exactly how I mourned and coped with the difficulties that came with death of a loved one. So even though I appeared to have no emotional response to death, I had a complex coping strategy as a way of mourning.

Funny mourning story

This story is rather irrelevant, however it is a funny memory I have of mourning, which I thought you may find interesting.

One time during a pretend play mourning ceremony, I accidently stabbed myself in the hand. I was an older child, possibly 9 or 10, and it was early morning and I had been standing on my bed playing out the mourning scene with my special Egyptian statues that were on a shelf above my bed. This is because I had just woken from a nasty nightmare about a loved one who had horridly passed and needed reassurance from the Egyptian gods. Suddenly, as I was standing on my bed, acting out this ceremony with the Egyptian statues, for some reason, I lost my footing and I fell over. I tumbled off my bed and landed on the floor with a big thump. It was only then that I noticed a little stinging sensation in my right hand. I look down, and to my shock I saw that I had managed to impale my hand on one of my statue's (Anubis) long, tall pointy ears. I must have done it as I fell. I don't remember it hurting much, and wasn't tearful – I thought it was funny. (I never noticed pain – I was always quite stoic, when I shattered my Elbow into a million pieces when I was 8, I didn't even cry or make any fuss at all). I had to hold the statue that was stabbed into my hand, with my other hand, to ensure it did not pull my wound any further apart or do more damage (yuk). So in the early morning rays, I walked into my parent's bedroom, normal as you like with this statue sticking out my hand. As I stood in front of them, they were both still asleep, so I thought to myself, 'I should wake them up by explaining what happened'. So I did.

> "Mum, dad, wake up. I stabbed myself… Look."

I said as I stood in front of their sleeping faces. What words to wake up to. I have hardly seen them move so fast in my life. Apparently, the accident and emergency nurse said that I was very lucky not to lose full use of my hand because the statue's ear had stabbed less than 1cm away from a vital nerve ending that could have prevented me from using of my hand for the rest of my life.

Copying misunderstood emotions

I could be wrong; but I suspect that due to my Asperger's disabling me from reading negative emotions in other people, I simply can't understand the emotions in myself, either. This is why I feel that people might look at those of us with Asperger's and wonder why we seem so cold and uncaring when it comes to death of a close one. As a young child, you learn many things you can do, so that you can carry with you into adult life. Such skills include socialization, fine motor skills, gross motor skills and even how to cope and understand failings and negative emotions in yourself and other people. Obviously, if you are a child with Asperger's where primary difficulties are within all of these areas, it will take longer to learn these skills. Many adults with Asperger's may still struggle with such difficulties that most children without a disability mastered in their early years.

Somebody with Asperger's will learn various coping techniques to deal with difficult or emotional situations. "Parroting" back, is a classic example of how someone with A.S reacts to a situation they do not understand. It can be defined as "repeat or imitate, especially without understanding". This is extremely common in children without A.S.D, up until the age of about six years old. Most children will grow out of this "parroting" phase when they learn a better way to articulate. Unfortunately those with A.S take much longer to grow out of this stage (if ever at all). I am still learning how to communicate without parroting.

As a child, I simply copied what I thought I saw in other people. An example of this is when my granddad died. I reacted and portrayed very little emotion, because that is how much I had seen and understood others behave. As a child I didn't realize reactions to such things should be from a personal level of understanding.

Children with A.S may not seem like they care when death grips their loved ones. It may appear that they have not shed a tear or changed in grief at all. They may seem like emotionless robots, even. However, they are likely to be upset, but numb. It is possible that they have already mourned those who have died before it happened so logically it is not necessary to do it again. Due to a lack of understanding that other people have minds, if someone with A.S has finished mourning they will assume everyone else has finished mourning too. Also, they may be copying what they understand in the adults around them. Somebody with A.S may easily misinterpret an emotion in other people, so when they copy what they see, the copied emotion and behavior is inaccurate.

I am not an emotionless robot, of-course I care.

Missing Someone Close to you

When you miss someone, someone who nurtured you and made you feel happy... When time grinds on by and you feel lonely; always remember the value of someone's words. When you miss their smile, the twinkle in their eyes, their embrace or their happily laughing face... it seems that the more you try to picture their face, the more their image, once etched into your memory, begins to fade away. When you try to listen out for their voice, hoping for words of comfort, their words can be so silent, whispered with great intent, but lost in the white noise of our minds. Someone's words that mean so much, are what we miss most about them, their chatter and little quirks, the way they spoke and how their words made us feel.

In times like this, when you are sad and missing someone dear to you, picture the words they might say to you, and embrace them with all that they are worth.

"I love you"

Watch the letters spell out the words in front of you. Watch the words as they turn into bubble writing. Fill the letters and words with colour and picture, memories. Gaze out into space and watch the words as they float around you. Find peace within yourself and comfort from the sight the words can bring. "I love you" Allow the words to cuddle your emotions, allow a tear or two before you watch the words dance, their happy memories surrounding you. Reach out your hand, stretch towards the words, and lightly grasp them, feel the weight and meaning of the words between your fingers, and lock them securely in your heart. Know that these words, that mean so much to you, will always be there, locked for safe keeping within your mind and heart. You see, words will always be there in times of need. Someone's body may sadly die, but words, words may never die. You are never alone when you have words because our words represent the very essence of which someone is, who they are and what they believed... words are powerful, so remember to look for the words of loved ones you miss when you are struggling to hear their voice or picture their face. Know that you are never alone; there is support for you, all of you, where ever you may end up.

The Force of the Hurricane

I have been bullied a lot, in different ways, and it's not nice. It feels like the bullying will never end and that you'll never get over it. However, take it from me, I am a survivor of bullying and I am reassuring you that life does get easier and you can get over it and lead a fairly happy and normal life after bullying, (I've led the happiest life), especially if you tell someone you trust that you are being bullied. Half a problem shared, is half a problem solved, ever heard of that one?

Hurricane

To me, hurricanes are like bullies; please bear with me.

A hurricane can rip through entire towns and cities, tearing apart homes and families with the force of its power. A force of nature, at one of its most feared, it can leave entire communities at its mercy; Homes are often left in tatters, ruined, bleak and ghostly; despair hangs numbly in the air as people try to rebuild their lives. Families suffer in silence, physically and emotionally torn apart at the hurricane's ghastly wake. Does the hurricane care for the damage that it causes? No, of course, not, it's a hurricane, and obviously it has no feelings. No, the hurricane simply starts up, from heavy wisps of winds and thunderous storms, to a full blown enchanting terror. A hurricane rises tall, godly, above the land, intimidating, grey masses swirling round, encircling, clouded, dark grey, thundering. The sheer fright, of watching a hurricane, can strike you down; it mesmerises you with the unholy beauty and leaves you standing gobsmacked, too scared to even move or look away. The eye of the storm right in the centre of the chaotic whirling of high speed winds, is where there is most calm, and is claimed to be the safest place to be. Once you are in the eye of the storm, you are left terrified to attempt to free yourself from the hurricane's eye; too scared of being ripped apart by the hurricane's damaging exterior. The eye is claimed to be the safest place to be; yet, the outside is so vicious, uncaring, that you often forget there is a calm interior at all. The hurricane rips apart any object within its path, with a brutal force that controls; no action to be taken, but flee for freedom, for life, or try to wait the hurricane out, at the centre of the storm.

In a metaphor type way, part of me still thinks that my abusers and the people that once bullied me were like hurricanes; brutal, uncaring, destroying entire families, emotionally and mentally, because the effect bullying and abuse has on the victim, impacts vastly on their family, too. Yet, the bullies... they were captivating too enthralling, and when you drew close to the eye of their chaotic bullying storm, it's even harder to rip your gaze from their strong friendly beauty. It draws you in, partly convincing you that they are not bullying you, rather they are just misunderstood, manipulating your judgment of right and what is wrong. Bullies are manipulative, twisting your judgement to think it is safer at the eye of the storm, (with them) than to flee and get away (be without them). The worse type of bullying I believe is from someone you are in some kind of relationship with. This is because that desperation and that cruelty, (knowing they care and are genuinely nice people, but still bully you and make you feel small or treat you unfairly), and that unjustification never really leaves you. You expect to be bullied by someone outside your relationship circle, but to have it done to you by someone you trust, someone you care so dearly for, someone you would never wish any harm onto, someone you're having a relationship with, it literally tears you apart, much like a hurricane does a victim's life. This is why I feel that bullies are similar to a hurricane; they walk around, tormenting, leaving people quaking in their shoes, too scared to react. Bullies that care not for the affect they have on people's lives. Abusers and bullies who harm you in more ways than one, then leave you crying, shrivelled on the floor, so they can pick on their next victim, messing with another family, tearing apart another home. Abusers that are so wicked and dreadful on the outside, but on the inside, you see an air of vulnerability about them, the part of them they don't show anyone; the calm, at the eye of the storm. The only difference, pointedly, is that a bully has a choice; despite appearing to have a heart of stone, a bully does actually have feelings, so why does the bully still not care for the widespread damage they have caused for countless families and people's lives? Why do the bullies and abusers still tear apart people's lives, leaving them desperate to rebuild their lives, engulfed by sadness? Why must such bullies act in this way, when they have feelings, a choice to be nice and do good to the world at their feet? Why must they act like a hurricane, and spread fear amongst people, when there is a calm eye, choices, feelings, at the centre of the storm?

The answer to these questions is mostly unknown. Bullying stems from the environment, from upbringing, their own experiences; indeed, usually they themselves have been bullied and so they bully others too, and so, the cycle continues. Bullying is often a result of low self esteem, an attempt to make the bully feel better about themselves, by being mean, and bringing other people (often people they are jealous of or feel intimidated by) down to their level. I find that it is best not to question, but to accept that there are bullies, and that is just life, you have to learn to deal with it safely. Report it and make sure the bullying has been disciplined fairly (don't sink to their level, by being mean back, or you are just as bad a bully as they are), and move on, for your own sanity and happiness, move on.

The Six Different Types of Bullying

If you think you are being bullied then it is quite a serious issue but you do have to be certain of the facts.

I believe there are 6 different types of bullying:

1. **Physical.** Hitting, kicking, biting, punching spitting, pulling hair etc. Physical bullying can include any physical contact that would hurt or injure a person or intend to hurt them. It can also include a victim being force fed drugs, alcohol and food items.
   This is the most well known type of bullying and can leave the victim with anything from scratches, cuts and bruises to broken bones.

2. **Emotional.** Emotional bullying is usually bullying made to make the victim feel worthless, stupid, nasty, fat, ugly, anything at all. It can also include severe and persistent rejection and ignoring the victim, taunting, harassment, ridiculing, threatening and belittling. Manipulating and scaring the victim enough to make he or she do what the bully wants.

    This type of bullying can cause a child to become nervous, withdrawn, lacking in self confidence or aggressive.

3. **Verbal.** Verbal bullying is usually when the bully is calling names that can cause offence to the victim. Sarcasm, belittling and persistent mocking. This is a type of emotional bullying.

4. **Indirect.** This can mean a bully making up rumours, (perhaps using internet messaging also known as cyber bullying or 'trolling') about a person with the purpose of socially excluding them from a group of friends and making them unliked amongst peers. I call this bullying from afar, the type of bullies who are operating but you don't realise it. For example, you don't always become aware of who made that terrible rumour up about you, do you?

5. **Discriminatory.** Racist, homophobic, hostile or offensive actions towards ethnic minorities and gay, lesbian and bisexual groups. This can include intimidating or threatening behaviour directed at somebody because they are different. People who bully others for being different usually do it because they are scared.

6. **Social isolation.** This type of bullying means that the bully is isolating the victim from a group of friends, this can be through making up rumours and changing the peer groups perception of the child (victim) to something negative.

I would like to give you a few personal examples of bullying and how it can affect people.

I have experienced a lot of verbal bullying, especially during school. This generally included people saying mean things to me that made me feel upset, low or depressed. Most of the time, the bullying I experienced was in the form of sly back handed compliments. A backhanded compliment means that somebody pays you a compliment but implies something nasty at the same time. I think it's quite a clever trick, but very horrid of course. I had a friend who was absolutely lovely but had a habit of doing this. Here's an example –

> "You look kind of nice with that make-up on, but you definitely need make-up"

See that? That comment involves both good and bad points, it is called a backhanded compliment because it is a nasty comment (basically saying the person is ugly, because they 'definitely need make-up') disguised as saying something nice (you look kind of nice with makeup on), but the purpose of the comment is to make the victim feel kind of low.

Looking back, I now realise I was verbally bullied rather a lot. At the time, I could not read the signs and sometimes, despite the upset the nasty words caused, I was oblivious that what was being said to me was with the intention to upset me. Now my communication and social skills have improved (a little bit), I am much more aware of this and will not stand for it. If somebody is saying something to upset you, please do not ignore it; tell a trustworthy adult, teacher, parents or sibling, someone who understands or knows you well. I think it is a good idea to write down a diary of things which have been said to you so you can hand it in to a teacher at school.

I have also experienced a lot of emotional bullying. A common type of emotional bullying is when a group of people or person pressures you or manipulates you to do something you are not comfortable with. A classic example of this is being bullied to try smoking. They might tell you

> "Everybody is doing it, don't be a baby. Smoke this cigarette."

One time, I was with a group of friends who were all smoking, they passed me a cigarette and all told me that I had to smoke it. They even said I was "letting the team down" because I refused. Even though I was a victim of this type of bullying, I never gave in (and still to this day have never held, let alone smoked a cigarette). I can completely understand why somebody would give in to this type of bullying because it is easy and normal to want to fit in and be accepted by your peers. But giving in does not make the bullying go away, or claim you any real friends. I have always believed you should be your own person and should never change who you are to make others happy, but that's just one of the things that makes me unusual.

Understanding That There is Always Someone Willing to Help

This is a little story about finding comfort in a world of pain – a story about when I realised that there is always someone who is willing to help you.

Many years ago, after a particularly nasty spell of physical bullying, I found myself sitting at the foot of my favourite childhood tree in my local park. Curled up with my head down, sobbing into my hands and snivelling into a disgusting wet and torn tissue; I was fearfull and utterly spell bound by the memories corroding my sense of ease. After what seemed like hours of sitting and crying (although it wasn't that long), a faint voice called out to me.

"My dear, what's wrong… My goodness, would you look at that swollen bruise… what happened to you, dear child?"

I was startled, badly shaken, and stood up, swiftly, stumbling to a halt. I looked up in a state of dizziness to find a middle aged lady standing in front of me, holding a half eaten ploughman's baguette that was protruding out of the hastily torn down packaging. Her chin had bits of grated cheese and lettuce, which she hastily wiped away with the sleeve of her clean cardigan which was missing a button. As I looked at her, I noticed that she was wearing blue freshly ironed jogging bottoms, an ironed sports tee shirt and a long flimsy pale pink cardigan with her greying blond hair neatly held into a tight high bun, not a strand of hair out of place; This amused me for a moment as it looked as if she had lied to her husband (or someone) about going for a run around the park, and gone to buy food instead. This tiny thought tickled me in my moment of misery and I suppressed the tiniest of smiles. I looked up cautiously at the lady, who was surveying me with green eyes, carefully lined with blue (who makes that much effort going for a run, I ask you?). Not meeting her gaze I unhesitantly responded to her question ("What happened, dear child?") by saying

"I'm fine, really – nothing's happened."

I laughed shrugging, hoping to comfort her away from asking more painful questions. The woman gazed at me, frowning slightly now, slowly edging closer to me, as if nearing a wild sleeping tiger.

"I'm afraid that you look quite upset my dear child… What are these terrible marks on your face? May I help you, please?"

She asked calmly, quietly, I panicked and noticed I was not convincing her and rushed to aid the situation, as I was scared my bullying would come to light, and I was frightened to upset my abuser.

"I am fine… It's nothing…I walked into a door, because I'm pretty silly like that."

I had said in a loud booming voice that betrayed a few tremors. I shrugged, laughing it off again, she looked at me and made this face and shook her head slowly, clearly not believing the oldest lie in the book. Reaching into her sports bag and she removed a business card from her small faded white leather purse, I noticed the outlines of a blue and white gym membership card in her purse cards sleeve (I know this because I have the same gym membership card to the same place, it's very distinctive).

"Please my dear, I can only imagine how little you trust in people right now…"

She said with concern seeping out of her voice so thickly that even I could tell she was close to tears… But why, I didn't know. She extended her hand, offering me the business card. I looked at the card for a moment, and took it from her hand, sceptically, scared to make any sudden movements. I looked at the card, for just a moment or two, realising she worked for a religious organisation that specialises in providing people in need with shelter and hope, I smiled at her kindness. Whether or not this meant she thought I was homeless, I still don't know (that would be funny; I was dressed up nicely, wearing a nice blouse and knee length skirt with boots, now scuffed and scraped in mud. Sure, I had looked a bit scruffy and muddy from running in a panicked haste through an alley way of protruding scraggly bushes; but before that I had made an effort to look nice… so surely I didn't look homeless?). It was a rather beautiful design on the card really, but I was not concerned with that at the time. I had been lost in thought, in pain and anguish, but mostly hope, by looking at the card. The lady spoke; undeterred by my cynical silence and zapped me back to reality.

"You may find it hard to trust, and that's ok…You must know that there are many helpful individuals who outnumber the wicked few… and you may not trust me, and that's ok, too. I want to reafirm your faith in good people; I am one of the many good people who would help you, if given a chance."

She said in determination, watching me intently. I looked at her now, through my pain, I was still doubtful of her intentions. I gazed at her, searching her green eyes for answers of her true objective; did she really wish to help me? She paused, and gently reached forward to take my hand, probably just in hope to comfort, but I snapped my hand away, as instinct took over, as if to protect.

"Pick yourself up, dust yourself down and try not to think of the bad
people and think of all the good people do instead, try not to let the
wicked few cloud your faith in the good of humanity... Please my dear
child, Let me take you to casualty it least..."

I shook my head, eyes widening at the horror of having to explain to casualty,
wavering more now and she back tracked hastily saying

"Ok, calm down dear child. Now please, if you want any help, the offer
is always there; email me... label the message 'help in the park' and I
will help you in any way in which I can. Please, just let me help you, dear
child... Please?"

I looked at her startled. She was kind, smiling encouragingly at me, and I
finally realised that she was genuinely troubled for me. An almighty surge
of relief swept through my fragile being and the biggest urge to hug her
came raging threw my system. I gripped her business card tight in my hand,
knuckles white, and found tears settle on my eyelids; and before I had even
noticed, I realised that I had been crying silently for a while now. My body
began heaving, quaking with silent tears, and I became so emotional that I
could hardly see straight – but I couldn't let her, or anyone, see me in such
distress; I was too used to hiding my tears to better prevent future prospects
of being beaten again. This is a technique that does not work and you should
certainly tell someone you trust if you are being bullied. With all my might,
I wanted to cry on her shoulder and surrender to the agony of my emotions
and experiences, but I couldn't. I shook my head, my eyes turning wide at the
prospect of having to explain what had happened and I panicked.

"T-Thank you... You're t-too kind, but I, I just can't. I, I... I'm sorry"

I stuttered in gaping breaths. It was all I could do to break apart and run away,
which I realise now, I shouldn't have done. I turned and I sprinted away from
the woman's doubtful and concerned face, as fast as my aching legs could
carry me. I was trying to protect myself, and possibly her for helping me, but I
now realise that I hadn't helped anyone by running away in fear and confusion.

"No, Please... Come back."

I heard her cry from a distance and then again she called out to me

"But I can help you."

She yelled more quietly now, as I was running away. Yet, despite her kindness, I couldn't look back. I reached the corner, and slowed, walking fast. Countless thoughts racing around my mind... "Why did I lie by saying that I walked into a door?" and "why must we hurt one another?" ... But the main thought streaming through my mind was that of the lady's concern ... "Why had this random lady cared enough to try and help me, when someone else cared so little to hurt me in this terrible way?" "Why did she care enough to help?" "Why couldn't I allow her to help me?"

A little bit of faith in the good of humanity had been restored.

There I was, after being beaten up, and being asked the question of 'what happened?" and I used the oldest excuse in the book, by saying "I walked into a door, because I am silly like that." It really is, the oldest excuse in the book, and no one believes it any more, I never used to understand what this saying (oldest excuse in the book) meant. However, once I used it myself in the very same context, I finally understood that sometimes, a little lie is sometimes preferable to cover up the agony of the extensive truth, but that does not mean it is right or helpful.

I took great comfort from the lady's wisdom and kindness, even in my darkest hours I think of that time and draw strength to move forward. You see, the lady is right, even when people do terrible things, there always will be much more good in the world than there is bad, and I always take comfort from that. There is always someone who can and will, help you. I never did email her, but I didn't need to, just looking at her business card and remembering her words, was comfort enough to help me.

Summary
Since those days, I found that it is best not to try to understand the reasons why people hurt each other, because to those with a kind heart, we will never understand. What I learnt that day is that there are always good people, warm hearts with smiling eyes, genuine people who will help you, no matter what state you're in. That lady, volunteering, school and my family's generosity to

others has taught me that there is always someone who will help, there is always someone who cares, there is always light, in a dark situation of gloom. The best things we can do, is gain support from charity, family and friends, and learn to accept that this is just the sad reality. Pondering why life is so unjustified is never going to help; it will only make things worse, likewise living in the unjustifications of the past, can literally drive you insane, like it almost did with me (At least *I don't think I'm insane*, the funny thing is, someone who is insane would say that too). The vicious circle will continue if you contemplate the unjustifications too much, especially more likely if you don't tell a trustworthy adult. One of the reasons I am happy now, is because I admitted the truth of the bullying to my family and my friends and they got me support and the bullying stopped, and has never resumed. Just remember some people are nasty, but most people are lovely, trustworthy and beautiful inside and out. Remember that you are nicer than the nasty people, and that is all that matters. Keep strong, keep smiling, live with no regrets and be happy with, and accept, every aspect of yourself.

Bird Egg

How I overcame the need to question why people hurt others, and the memory of how I realised that I had to stop myself from reliving the unjustifications of the past.

When I was a small child, I went to the park with my best friends every day after primary school. We climbed up the trees in the park and often sat, observing the world around us. We sat up there in the branches, always in the same place every day, and observe the variety of people that walked through the park, watching the wildlife that would pass us, watching the life that stirred all around us in the powerful gusts of wind. We sat in our comfortable spots and watched. People walked passed, unobservant of their surroundings; their hearts seldom skip a beat at the beautiful surroundings. Every day we did this, we saw the same people walk past, a joyous couple, hand in hand, four old ladies walking their dogs, three men and countless families with children.

One day during spring time, my friend and I climbed our tree, and sat there watching the world change in our surroundings. We climbed up high, and to our upmost delight we saw a nest, buried deep within the trees branches and leaves. Just as we had glimpsed it, there was a beating flutter of wings, a stir of cracklings and whistling as the mother bird flew away. The nest stood there, strong, purposely built and beautiful; from within, we could see the tops of eggs; their shells glistening in the sunlight from the rain drops that had come down moments before. Immediately, I stretched towards an egg, curious to touch its shell, intrigued by the colour, texture and the little life that grew slowly within its delicate shell. My friend started in horror as my grubby hand extended towards the eggs.

"No. – Stop."

She cried out, loudly, I looked round at her stricken face (not that I could read her facial expression, it's merely a guess), and I paused, shaken.

"You can't touch the eggs; the mama bird will never come back if she smells us kids, on her babes."

I hadn't known this, and recoiled instantly, dreading the thought that I could be responsible for the little hatchlings being without a mother; they would suffer, horridly for sure. It was a horrendous thought and saddened me to my very core. So that day onwards we sat at a distance, and watched the nest, waiting for the day where we would witness the birds crack open the shell and take their first wobbling steps and flights of adventure. The birds became important to us; nothing else really mattered apart from checking to see if the bird eggs were ok. We became guardians, and prided ourselves on how much we cared, where the rest of the world seemed not to notice that there was beauty everywhere around them, new life, everywhere. Which really, if you think about it like we did as children, new life everywhere, unwitnessed, but still there, it is a truly marvellous thing. We saw the good in everything, in our majestic bubble of happiness and delight; we overlooked the negatives that harvest hungrily on the outskirts of our glee. We even dug up worms and left them in a pile on a branch by the nest to see if the mother bird would use them or not (she didn't, of course). We guarded the eggs and it turned out to be a project that was both precious and delightful.

Weeks later, we walked to our favourite tree, excitable and eager to see our baby eggs that we so cherished. When we arrived at the bottom of our tree, we stood observant, faces upturned, squinting in the streaked sunlight overshadowed by tall, knotted trees. We stood watching from the floor surrounded by sticks, dirt tracks and grass. Rustling, high up above us, in the twigs of the trees, we could see a ginger and black cat, fur sleek, well kept, bold green eyes, a red collar with a tinkle of a bell. The cat was skipping high up in the branches, making the branches shake and send a flurry of leave's tumbling down to the floor, like a beautiful leaf water fall. I watched the leave's fall, overjoyed at how many were falling, and how beautifully they flowed and spun to the ground. I was happily dancing underneath the rain of leaves, oblivious to my friend's growing discomfort. I could not sense the change in (or any) body language at all.

"J – Joely, look..."

My friend had meekly said, her voice high pitched, but barely audible above a whisper, biting her lip in apprehension. I paused and watched her trembling figure, upturned to the branches. My friend ushered me to the base of the tree, I stopped twirling under the leafy waterfall, and followed her as she climbed up the tree. Immediately, we went to see what the cat had disturbed, I soon remembered the eggs and my heart pounded at the thought of the cat being so close. What if something had happened to those tiny little life forms? ... What sort of protectors are we, if something had happened to prevent those baby birds from striving for life?

We climbed, careless of our clumsy actions now, higher into the leafy wonders, and much to our horror; we saw that our nest, that we had fought so hard to protect, now lay in tatters. It had been torn apart, sticks everywhere, a speck of its former glory, the eggs mostly gone... accept one. The lone egg lay there, the shell that once gleamed with pale speckled splendour, was now only slightly cracked with a strange substance seeping out of it. Feathers were everywhere, surrounding the eggs nest; tiny feathers, stuck down, lumpy and insignificant as if they were held down by glue on a painting. My friend tried hard not to cry out in horror as she reached deep in the birds nest to give the bird's egg, a first and last, cuddle. She cradled it, with tears seeping to her eyes, careless that the liquid stained her clothes. This is the first time I saw my best friend cry out in grief, and the sadness affected me also, and she sat there sobbing. I meanwhile, was very upset, but sat next to her watching, in my favourite spot and waited for her to stop crying, and then I cuddled the egg myself. I was used to tears, but not a true sadness from grief of death like that. Suddenly, I was asking myself questions, "why did such a dreadful thing happen?" "Why would a cat, or anything, do something so horrid to harm another living being?" "Why would the cat bully the poor eggs like that?" I thought to myself, the horror of it seeping through to my frazzled brain, making my heart pound like a hammer and my head swirl like a spinning top.

We sat in our usual spot, taking turns to cradle and cuddle the fragile and delicate egg, trying our hardest not to crack the shell any more. This time, as we observed the world, from up high in our leafy wonder, we were grasped by the reality of it; despite the beauty, we saw less glory and more darkness. The trees looked less bright, the splendour was less so. We realised that the world was a scary place and we had been so comfortable in our little bubble that we had not seen it before. I had been entirely captivated, happily watching the leaves fall from the trees, shaken down by wildlife before. The leaves breathed a sigh of life in the soft breeze, and we sat there we watching them fall to the ground, enthralled by the beauty. The leaves had fallen, after being shaken down by wildlife, with an essence of purpose, pirouetting, and dancing in the wind, twirling and gracefully falling to the tune of their very last song. It is strange how much the mood and atmosphere had changed so drastically in so little time. Yet, this time I watched the leaves fall, with an air of desperation... the sad show of leaves falling to the ground, softly, sadly became a tearful and burdening task. Why was everything dying, and falling to its disgrace, around us? We felt burdened to watch them fall to their leafy grave, amongst hundreds of other shrivelled leaves rotten and rid of all of their usual bright colours.

We had buried the bird egg in a little dug grave we had made with handpicked flowers from the cycle track field. My friend put the egg gently and hesitantly in the ground, and I asked

"Why did the cat do that? It's so mean. Why did the cat hurt and bully the eggs like that? It's nasty and mean"

My friend tried to explain to me, that it was just the way things are, creatures do that, its animal instinct, we just have to accept it as a part of nature, and move on. She explained to me, tears sprinkling her red rimmed eyes,

"Some animals ARE mean, and they hurt each other. Mom says you shouldn't try to understand why others are cruel, just accept that cruelty happens and you are the better person. People and animals are mean but mom says there's always someone who can help- Like us, we're helping the mom bird by burying her little egg."

She had said, matter of fact, then following my confused silence she continued, sadder now;

"Some humans are mean too; they hurt each other and make us sad. Humans don't care for nothing if they hurt each other. People do lie and they hurt us. That's just life; you have to accept it and move on, or you won't be happy; mom says that you get used to the worlds cruelty, kiddo."

Summary

I ponder her words to this day; it makes me sad, that at such a young age, my friend was not naive, but somewhat experienced in the ways of the world. As indeed, there are some animals that prey onto others, as part of animal instinct, but where does the instinct come from when humans hurt others? Humans, despite technically being an animal, don't prey onto other humans like that for survival purposes like animals using animal instinct do, so why do they hurt and bully others, if they have no biological excuse?

The answer, is that ultimately, there is no reason that will justify hurting others deliberately; emotionally, mentally or physically. No justification at all, and that is because bullying and hurting others is, and always will be, wrong. Trying to understand the reasoning behind unjust and hurtful behaviour of others will only upset you further. I have discovered that after living with the past unjustifications, for so long and trying to work out the answer to "why do people shamelessly hurt each other so much?" I realised that asking those question does your mental and emotional well being no good at all. It hurt me so much, I got myself in such a state with my mental illnesses; that I realised in asking such questions, I was literally driving myself insane. I now know that it is best not to try to understand, because those who are genuinely caring and nice towards everyone, regardless of anything at all (race, ethnicity, ability, gender, sexuality, age etc), just can't understand, and it will do them no good at all to ask such questions and live in the unjustifications of the past. I realise now, that I don't need to understand why people hurt each other, but only accept that it happens, it's a part of life, and there is always something that can be done to both prevent and help some people from hurting or being hurt. You can get involved with voluntary work, charity work, to help others. It's best to stop asking why? And start creating action plans to make this unavoidable nasty reality better for as many people as you can. It is possible, with support, you just have to try.

Chin up, folk.

Standing up to Bullies

I know it is easy for me to tell you that you should stand up to anybody that is bullying you, but I realise this task is extremely difficult. Nobody should be able to make you feel sad, lonely or depressed; so if you can pluck up the courage to do something about it, then you must. I had my own way of dealing with bullies, this is not something I was taught and not something I recommend, but if I'm honest it did help me through some tricky situations. I used to:

1. Never give a reaction
2. Never cry, no matter how much it hurt
3. Never looked away; I always stared them straight in the eye (this was to assert my authority and to tell them "you will not bully me – Stop")
4. I tried not to show any weakness

"No, you can't hurt me anymore..."

Advice to Anyone being Bullied
1. Tell a trustworthy adult, teacher, or family members who can help you
2. Keep a dated record of what was being done or said to you, for example a bully diary
3. If possible, avoid being with that person or group of people
4. If you do find yourself in their company, try to stay calm, and ignore their bullying as much as possible. Take calming deep breaths and count to 100 in your head (don't count out loud), and count higher, until the anxiety of the bullying subsides a little

Discrimination and Stereotypes

Discrimination is when a person is treated less fairly than another person usually because people have prejudicial thoughts about things or other people, and then act upon those prejudiced thought, treating them differently because of it. I believe that before discrimination happens, you have prejudicial thoughts – because discrimination is acting out your thoughts. For example, one can have a thought (such as an able bodied person looking at a person in a wheelchair and thinking they are 'stupid' despite knowing nothing about them) but that's not discriminatory, it becomes discrimination if the person starts treating the person in the wheelchair differently because of that thought. Discrimination could perhaps be bullying, tormenting, treating the person unfairly, emotional and social negligence or treating them like they are not a part of the society. Prejudicial thoughts often stem from a lack of understanding of differences which can offend and really damage one's self image, confidence and lust for life.

Throughout my life I have faced much discrimination and stereotyping, although I feel that compared to others with disabilities, I have been lucky. When most people meet me for the first time, they assume that I am really shy; it's only when somebody gets to know me that they realise why I am not talking. I do not remember facing any discrimination while I was at my special needs school. The reason I think, is because I was no different to anybody else. It wasn't until I started at mainstream school that I noticed I was being treated differently to the rest of the children. Sometimes this was blatant discrimination or it was more subtle and indirect. I have many examples of this, so I would like to tell you just few.

Example 1

When I was at mainstream secondary school and it came to that time of the year when I had to choose my GCSE subjects I really wanted to take Drama. I was absolutely adamant that I wanted to take Drama because not only did I love it and everything it brought with it, I was actually very good at it. Actually, I was brilliant. Anyway, I was with my parents at the GCSE Option Evening. This was where you and your parents could go round to all the different subject areas and talk to the teachers about what studying that subject at GCSE level would involve. One of the first stands that we visited was the Drama stand. My parents knew how much I loved Drama and wanted to get some information about the subject so they could support me through my GCSE years. Neither myself or my parents were prepared for what the teacher was about to say to us. He told us that I would not be able to study GCSE Drama because of my disability. He thought I might not be able to cope and he may not be able to teach me effectively at a GCSE level. During our previous Drama lessons I had noticed that he clearly found it difficult to deal with me. He always struggled to explain things to me. But, despite this I often got top grades. Just because he found teaching me uncomfortable, doesn't mean that I shouldn't have been given the opportunity to take GCSE Drama if I wanted too. I could almost understand if I had bad grades… but I didn't.

That completely crushed any confidence I had. I very nearly cried, I was at an age where I had a choice and a valid opinion, but my choice and my opinion were taken away from me, so I no longer had that choice. I was upset and confused about why he would say such things when I clearly was so good at Drama (I still believe I would have done really well, performing runs through my whole family- Ballet, Dance, Acting, Sports etc). I was so dismayed that I felt like I was as small as a speck of dirt that had been swept up and disregarded in a bin somewhere.

My mother and father were both furious, although they stayed calm. My father says that my Drama teacher said those things more because he thought that I would not be able to cope with the stress of the course. This is understandable; I can't deny that; however, I strongly believe that even if the Drama teacher had these concerns, he could have handled the situation differently and looked into supporting me to make the course easier by contacting SENCO. I had support for nearly every subject, so I don't see why I couldn't have it for Drama as well. You know what, of course it would have stressed me out that's what GCSE work does, it is intense work; that's the point.

Summary
Consequently I did not take GCSE Drama and I missed the escapism dreadfully. I wish we had contacted SENCO for advice on this, because I am sure they would have provided me (and the teacher) with support. However, getting the support I needed was too difficult and a very long process, we had many other priorities regarding GCSE and support at that point, so we chose not to fight this battle, this time.

Example 2
I was at my mainstream secondary school and was about 14 years old. As I have already mentioned, I really loved performing and Drama while I was at school. During this time, my school were putting on a school production and were calling for auditions to take part in the school play. I was extremely keen and was looking forward to auditioning as I had hoped I would be given a role in the play. To cut a long story short, I spent a lot of time rehearsing and had three auditions in total – most of which went really well. Basically, there was a mix up each time I auditioned. Despite taking part in the three auditions it appeared that none of the teachers had been taking notes on my performance and somehow, did not witness my audition at all. Obviously, I did not realise this at that point.

A few weeks later it was announced who had been successful to take part in the school play. All of the children gathered around the notice board to read from the list of those who had auditioned to see who had been selected to perform in the school play. I was so excited because I thought that I may well have made it as my auditions had all gone really well. This is unlike me to think so good of myself I usually just assume I have not done well to save disappointment and to make my failures easier to cope with, after all, there is nothing like celebrating doing well at something when you least expected it. This time though I really thought I had made it, however, not only was my name not on the list of those who had passed the auditions, my name was not even on the list of those who had auditioned in the first place. I had done three auditions none of which had been judged.

Ridiculous – I was very annoyed and so upset I just cried there and then, people said it was melodramatic but then they realised why and said it was very unfair too because I did so well. Even if, I was not good enough to take part in the school play, I still should have had the equal opportunities to be considered at the auditions, like everybody else.

Summary
It could have been a big misunderstanding and maybe the teachers did genuinely miss my three auditions (although I feel this is unlikely). Looking back at this situation, it seems as if they missed me off the list purposely to make their lives easier, because teaching me at best of times could be difficult. Maybe for an extra curricular activity they did not think it would be worth the added effort… Especially as they could easily find someone who had the same talents as me, but who was 'normal'.

What is stereotyping?
We all absorb stereotypes from influences in our childhood, and from the society we live in. I am a great believer that our childhood and environment is the main maker of what we become later in life. As children we absorb other's opinions and stereotypes because we are too young to form our own and I imagine a lot of us carry such thoughts and opinions with us as we get older. These can influence our own trains of thoughts and make us see things and expect different things. Our childhood environment creates our initial stereotype. That can lead us to make assumptions about what is wrong and what is right. Such assumptions about what children can achieve or how they

ought to behave at certain ages for example, girls wear pink, play with dolls and boys wear blue and play with cars. Also, girls can only be Nurses and boys can only be Doctors. This is called stereotyping. In this particular area, without realising it, we can make assumptions about children's potential for development because a previous stereotype within our minds stemmed from our childhood environment. Stereotypes don't just happen to children, or by children everyone can stereotype and unfortunately most people do, even if they don't realise it.

Example of how I was both stereotyped and discriminated against
At mainstream secondary school we had to book a two week work experience. I chose to do mine in a local Nursery, because I already had lots of experience working with children from working in the nursery (which my mother ran) at home and I knew I was good at it. We contacted one nursery and they said yes – I had a confirmed work placement at a nursery. I spoke on the phone to the nursery who said they were really looking forward to having me work with them as they could really use a hand and knew I had experience with children at home.

However, then the nursery phoned my school and spoke to SENCO to confirm details, who in turn informed the nursery of my disability. The nursery rang me back less than an hour later, saying they could no longer have me for work placement. In the morning they said 'yes' they would love to have me, but by lunch time they had found out about my disability and they said 'no'.

Hmmm, something smells fishy... (Meaning the situation seemed very suspicious).

It feels like they found out about my disability and instantly did not want me, that they made a stereotypical discrimination against my ability to do the job well due to my disability. Are you suspicious yet? We were.

To add to this scenario, when work experience week had finished I found out that another girl in my year had done work placement at the nursery that declined me because they had no space.

Both myself and my mother were extremely annoyed that I had been turned away because of their narrow mindedness. My mother is not only a childminder, but a trainer for other new childminders in the area, so she is extremely well placed to know whether or not I would be suited and capable of the role. Unfortunately we could not prove they had discriminated against me, so there was nothing we could do. It all just seems very strange that I was told they had no places, but they had one for someone else after my rejection.

I have experienced many types of stereotypes, not just because of my disability (like the above example) but also because I am a girl. I know this sort of stereotyping is normal and many girls will face them. However I do not feel this is right. The following are things that people in the past have assumed about me, all of which are completely wrong.

I am a girl so I know nothing about cars, nor do I want to find out (SO wrong)
I am a girl so I know how to cook... (I wish)
I am a girl so I am broody when I see babies (not yet)
I am a girl so I like pink things and cuddly toys (Pink = NOOO)
I am girl so I always want to go shopping to buy shoes and cute pink clothes. (Yawn... What a bore)
I am a girl so I am a bitch/slut/ man eater/blah blah blah...
I am a girl so I am...You get the picture, I am sure.

You may not already know, but I am a huge car fan, some would even call me a bit of a petrol head. I am always trying to learn more to better my understanding of mechanics. I pride myself on not being completely uninterested when people talk about cars. My specialist subject is now gearing more towards car mechanics, whereas before it was Egyptology, history, cell replications and Fairies.

This is a story of being stereotyped and proving them absolutely wrong
Once when I was volunteering at a festival, I had a break from work so I wandered around all the other stalls at the festival. I came across a stall with what looked like a Honda S2000 engine (I was right, of course). My interest was piqued and so I had a close look at all the valves and piston heads within the engine. I do love cars and the mechanics of the workings – it's all so fascinating. There was a group of guys who were in charge of the stall. I am ashamed to say that they did not take too kindly to me taking an interest in the

S2000 engine; as almost immediately some were teasing me and being quite sexist. One of the men approached me and said

> "This here, is a really special car engine because it works differently to usual types Honda makes – Not that you would know the difference in car engines, eh?"

He said not too unkindly. I had responded with a smile, as I had not yet processed his comment to be negative or rude. Two of the other blokes laughed and one, who seemed more unkind, said

> "Look at her mate, she ain't going to have a flaming clue, too much of a pretty dear to get your hands dirty with mechanics aren't you, love?"

I understood that comment as negative, and his comment stung me like a wasp; I couldn't help but roll my eyes. My smile had now frozen, my lips instead curled into a reluctant grimace. I couldn't believe their tones and behaviour towards me. I am a girl, so they were making the very wrong assumption that I don't know anything about car engines. My blood was beginning to boil. Yes, I am considered 'pretty' for some strange reason, I wear nice clothes, whatever. Does it even matter?! What an earth does that have anything to do with my knowledge of such things? They were clearly stereotyping me because I was a 'pretty' girl. What an utterly ridiculous thing.

He then said

> "Do you want to know why this engine is different to others darling? I can explain the process in VERY simple language so your pretty little head can try and understand."

in a sneering tone, with a glint in his eye. Ok, if I was in doubt of the rudeness before, I certainly was not now; there was no doubt that he intended that comment to be rude and hurtful. I looked at him steadily making eye contact, trying hard not to glare and appear rude – how condescending he was being. Despite my efforts at avoiding this, my eyes began to narrow and my gaze hardened. He was clearly expecting me to accept this rubbish that was oozing out of them and accept his offer of an easy explanation. However I would decline because I already knew how the S2000 engine worked anyway, the judgemental cheeky sod.

He wanted to wow me with long words and confusing language in his 'simple' explanation. Maybe he thought it would impress me or make me feel inadequate and inferior... no, not me. I smiled politely at him and said

"No, thank you, I already know how it all works"

in a tone slightly betraying my annoyance. Needles to say the guys all found my words amusing as they soon started to cackle like witches over a cooking brew.

"You're a funny one, you know that? You couldn't possibly get those hands dirty to work a man's load."

And then there was a pause, as the men all shook their head in varying stages of amusement, my heart pounded as the urge to slap them grew stronger. 'Keep calm Joely', I thought to myself, I then reminded myself that slapping them would make me as bad as them, even if they started it'. That is how I kept myself calm in this unjust situation. The man continued grinning toothily at me, and not in a kind way.

"Oh really, go on then pretty one, do tell us how you imagine this complex engine works. Don't worry; we're all here to help correct you when you confuse yourself with pretty shoes."

spluttered the ruder guy in front of me, looking over at the other guys who all nodded in bemused agreement. I felt a shiver run through my spine as I started to feel sick. I couldn't believe their behaviour towards me. Everyone of them was laughing at me, teasing me because I thought I knew what engine it was and how it worked. What's worse- they now wanted me to prove it. I may know how it works, yet I am no expert... Now I had to show I knew how it worked (to a bunch of horrid experts), purely to prove a point – the point being that they should not be judgmental meanies. What is worse, I shouldn't have to prove my intelligence levels at all; why do people judge and discriminate, as it is clearly and horrendously unjustified?

This only frustrated me further because I knew that I had an understanding of the engine and how it works – just like them. I also knew that I should not have to prove my knowledge to such narrow minded idiots. However, they were being so sexist and mean that I felt like I needed to prove them wrong just to wipe the smug grins off of their horrid faces. Proving them wrong would be better than a slap; it would serve as a reminder not to judge. So I did. I proved them wrong.

> "First of all, I don't need to prove my intelligence to you, as it should not be a questionable matter to all of you judgmental 'gentleman'."

I said this trying to sound more confident than I actually was. I became anxious, my legs were shaking and even though I was fairly confident with the ins and outs of how such an engine worked- explaining the process in front of bullies like this made me feel weak. I had little confidence of the matter before, let alone now.

One guy promptly said

> "Prove it you pretty thing, what is this – an engine, is it?"

He said mimicking confusion, scratching his head like some sort of bemused cartoon ape. They all started laughing again and I could feel my cheeks burning red with anger – why do some people feel the need to bully and makes others feel small to make themselves feel powerful? It is utterly horrifying.

I decided not to be angry, and instead prove them entirely wrong. I won't write my explanation here as it would bore you. However at that point I told them exactly what I knew and wiped their smug grins off their sexist faces. I gave them a long detailed explanation of how the engine works (I was right –it was a S2000) wowing them with long words and confusing language that I apparently should not know because I was a girl. I quite literally astonished them. I have to say, watching their mouths drop open, their laughter turn into an uneasy stunned silence as my explanation got more detailed was superb. During my explanation I realised that not only was my explanation right, they were utterly flabbergasted, so I grew in confidence and I even drew a quick demonstration on their white board. I savoured every last bit of it. When I finished I said

> "I have not studied this on a professional level – if at all – so you can forgive me if I was a bit wrong. Your question still remains, did a 'pretty' girl know how the Honda S2000 worked, or not?"

I asked with a sweet smile knowing that the answer was yes, a 'pretty' girl did know how the Honda S2000 engine worked. I knew from their reaction how well I had done. My annoyance for their sexism slowly subsiding and was swiftly being replaced with pure adrenaline and pride to be female (or indeed, just a human) and standing up against judgmental bullies like that.

I am pleased to say that they all nodded, admitting I was right. A few could not meet my gaze, particularly the main mean guy; the others were staring at me with their mouths hanging open. One of them said this, maybe an attempt at an apology

> "Sorry ma'am, I shouldn't of, ummm, you were, well, effectively word perfect for someone who shouldn't know… for someone who is a… who's a… a …"

'For someone who is a girl...' I thought to myself, finishing his sentence in my head. I smiled at him, refusing to sink to their level with anger

> "Thank you kindly gentleman"

I said, emphasising the word 'gentleman' as he deserved it this time for apologising

> "Do me a favour, don't be so stereotypical and sexist next time; you never know who will swing by and prove you completely wrong"

I had said brightly with a big smile. Their astonished gazes fell on mine at that point

> "Goodbye gentleman."

I said vibrantly, as I turned to walk away wearing the biggest smile on my face – I was so proud of myself. Once I had turned around I suddenly realised that there were at least twenty people gathered round who had watched the whole argument. Females with push prams looked at me and nodded with smiles, one teenaged kid with glasses and freckles with blond curls, squeezed my shoulder saying

"Good work"

to me as I walked past. I glowed from the praise and as I walked on, a man nodded at me stating how ****** awesome I had been and another was so impressed he asked for my mobile number which I politely declined as always. I smiled at all of them, feeling like I was on cloud nine, I felt so elated, to realise that so much support from the crowd was in my favour. The looks some of the crowd were giving those judgemental mechanics, my goodness – if looks could kill. I walked back with a big smile- my entire being was shaking from adrenaline and I could hardly even walk properly from the shakes I was experiencing. I sure did show them. They couldn't have been more flabbergasted. Just because I am a girl, does not mean you can judge or discriminate against me. I sure showed them who is boss.

"Pack it in"

This chapter is about the different types of behavior that people with A.S.D may present. Some of the behaviors are traits that I have, while others are common, but not ones I possess. This chapter is made up of personal stories and advice for parents and teachers.

Whirlwind

As a child I was described as a 'whirl wind'. I would run everywhere, or rather sprint everywhere. I would be out walking with my family, and something would catch my eye and I was off. I would get distracted and I would sprint away, without warning. I could enter a room and within minutes the room would be totalled (messy is an understatement). You may be thinking that this is relatively normal, especially for children at certain ages; they learn and develop through tipping toys out all over the floor. However, I am talking extremities here. I was not doing this only at the usual age of two; I was still running off and causing utter havoc everywhere I went until I was nine. Don't forget, as a child I could not hear instructions or understand them, so this made it very difficult for me to stop my 'whirl-wind' antics. As a child, my boundless energy knew no limits and I would run into every room and sprint around in circles. This was a way of releasing my energy to keep me from going crazy with bad behaviour and overloads. My parents soon learnt that it is best I expel my energy outside where I am less likely to break everything. Hence I was always taking family walks, going to lots of places like the beach, the forest, streams, parks, castles, farms and exploring our environment as a family. I didn't understand this at the time, but we all did this because spending quality time together as a family is absolutely paramount to the holistic development of any child.

When speaking to my parents about my whirlwind behaviour, they told me how difficult it was for them to control and cope with me running off. I would literally run in the opposite direction from my family, at every opportunity. I wasn't deliberately escaping, I just got distracted by minor details (like a pretty leaf or something) and would run off to investigate. I would always forget what I was meant to be doing and chase off after what ever had caught my eye. I would delve straight into whatever it was I wanted to look at, a stream, mud, completely oblivious to any dangers or anyone calling my name. If something I wanted to look at was too high for me to reach, I would try to climb. Or I would continue to jump and crash about until I could reach and touch it (and usually accidently break it) until something else had distracted me.

Every two minutes my parents were chasing after me to drag me back to where I was supposed to be. Luckily my older brother and sister were well behaved; otherwise it would have been a complete nightmare for my parents.

This behaviour was not a form of attention seeking; I was not running about and stomping to get my own way or as a form of protest. I had just learnt that when you run around, jump and stomp, not only is it fun and stress relieving, but anything that is too high for you to reach, will likely fall, and you will be able to look at it. I had never made the connection that in doing all this jumping and crashing about, the item may fall and inevitably break. When we were on a family stroll (in a forest perhaps), I would never know why, there was a reason to it. So, because I did not know why we were walking, I would assume I could go off and chase after butterflies and explore of my own accord. Either that or I just did not know how to cope with any of my surroundings or overloads. Running, jumping and leaping around touching everything was the only way I knew how to relieve myself of stress without screaming out.

I believe part of my behaviour as a 'whirlwind' was a preventative for a sensory overload. If I was able to run around, leap and go really crazy, I could shut out some senses and quell my overloads for a bit.

My parents took me out to allow me to expel my energy in a positive manner – through running about, exploring and developing / learning through my senses. They realised it was the best way for me to develop and had far more positives than negatives. For that, I will be forever appreciative. I know that if I had never been allowed out of the house, if I was never allowed to explore or shake off my 'whirlwind' antics, my behaviour would still be very 'whirlwindy' today; I would not be quite so fortunate with my other abilities as a consequence.

Whirlpool
The following is a story I feel I must share, as I feel it sums up my whirlwindy behaviour quite well.

Throughout my sister's childhood and teenage years, she was a brilliant and very keen swimmer. She would train eight times a week, usually twice a day. She competed at the weekends in very important swimming competitions. When I was about six years old, my family went to watch my sister swim at a competition. We all walked into the swimming pool area as spectators for one of the swimming races, while my sister got ready for her race. I had been holding my mum's hand as we stood metres from the side of the pool, watching a race. I looked at the swimming pool and got really excited – I loved swimming. As my mum bent down to put some water proof covers on my shoes, she momentarily let go of my hand, and I tore away from her grasp. Without warning, I sprinted away, and jumped straight into the swimming pool... and landed, smack bang, on a swimmer. As you can imagine, this caused quite a stir, not only for the swimmer I jumped on, but for my parents, the life guards and pretty much everyone else around me. There was a big kerfuffle and the life guards were not best pleased at having to fish me out, especially as I insisted on swimming, and thought it was a game to try and escape the life guards grasp. Under the hot gaze of all judgmental eyes, my family had to take the walk of shame, out of the swimming pool area, while they all tightly grasped my hands. I trudged alongside them, my clothes soaked and my hair dripping wet, grinning from ear to ear, completely oblivious to any commotion I had created. I got quite a telling off, of an understanding nature.

Although, admittedly at the time, I genuinely thought I was there to go swimming, I hadn't realised I needed a costume (or indeed, even to ask permission). Talk about bad connection making. What an embarrassment!

Consequently, in all future swimming events, my parents (and I) had to watch from outside the swimming pool, peering through the crowded windows. This was solely because if I was inside the swimming pool area, I was guaranteed to run and jump straight into the pool again– regardless of anyone swimming, my or anyone else's safety. Obviously this was too great a risk for my parents to take, and we all quietly agreed that supporting my sister from the outside of the swimming pool was far better for everyone involved.

That is what my whirlwind behaviour was like as a child, but my strange behaviours did not stop at six years old. Oh no, not me. As a teenager, I was strange, weird, random and very, very hyper much of the time. Its like I have previously said, it was not unknown for me to start dancing in the street or give a twirl while walking down the road. I still needed to release nervous energy much of the time, so I always behaved in a rather, well, strange, odd, hyper, crazy and random fashion.

Midnight mayhem
I would like to tell you a story that involves my partner in crime (metaphor, I have never committed any crimes, that would be bad and selfish). I feel it is a good example of how I am still, at the age of twenty five, experiencing whirlwind behaviour.

It had been another night of agitated power that helplessly bubbled inside me. I could feel the whirl wind from my childhood begin to grow, and I knew there was no point in fighting it. Although it was long gone 11pm at night, I could not sleep. I was lying in bed, restless, tossing and turning, unable to shut my ears to give my mind some peace. My eyes blinking, wide awake, the streaked darkness from the night distracted me from the silence I much craved. My mind racing as the rain flickered lightly onto my window. Why does something so quiet, sound so loud? Thump Thump Thump… Bloomin' raindrops…

'Oh no, I'll never get any sleep' I thought to myself gloomily as I miserably covered my head with a soft pillow… That is when another more interesting thought filtered through to my tired mind…

'Maybe I should go out exploring somewhere?'

When you're tired, a multitude of things can seem like a good idea. When in reality, they are not necessarily good ideas at all. (I'm full of these silly ideas). Suddenly my heart was buzzing and I felt a jolt of energy run through my body. What a fabulous idea – I shall go out. I should go dancing; I should go running down the street, as fast as my legs can carry me, I should jump about and sing in the rain… I should… Get out of here.

After consulting with my parents and going through all the usual safety check procedures, I text my partner to meet up with me. After an hour's worth of mental preparation (while dancing to music on my roof top) I was still hyper and jittery with energy, I was ready to go out. I walked downstairs to say goodbye to my parents, who were used to me going out randomly at that point. After them fussing over me having enough credit and battery on my phone, who I was with and all sort of other necessities to keep me safe, they gave me some advice and a hug, and let me go with my trusted partner.

So off I went, it was now gone midnight, at 12.38. I met with my partner and we danced in the middle of my street. Smiling and giggling, pretending to be ballroom dancers (we were a bad impression of such elegance, I am sure). A car drove up and an old lady peered at us, in upmost disgust and confusion. In a giggling heap, we finished dancing, and we ran off to our car and drove into the darkness, hood down on the car, wind blowing through my long, untied hair. The night sky kinetically glittering and gliding above us as we drove, I lay back in my seat, head upturned to watch the whirling stars and tree branches, and I sang. Music was blaring and I was laughing and smiling with joy at my terribly out of tune voice. Once arrived at our destination, my energy was still not satisfied, so we ran, and leapt through the town centre and in fits of giggles we had found ourselves at the seafront. It was 1.55 am when my partner and I decided to take a stroll along the beach. The night was clear and dark, the rain had long since stopped and the air was cool. Moonlight was twinkling through the clouds, shining over us in cold beams of light as we cartwheeled, play fought and danced on the soft, cold sand. We danced together, and spun each other round, practised jumps and gave each other piggy backs. In a moment of clarity, (or insanity) I ran into the sea and squealed and jumped about at the ice cold splashes. Surfing the waves and letting the water calm the wildness that was taking over my being. My partner dipped in with me for a short while to keep me company and then waded back to shore, where he busied himself making the car nice and cosy for me once I got out. My clothes soaked and my skin goose pimpled from the cold, I eventually retired to shore where my lovely partner wrapped me in a towel, gave me some warm clothes. He sat on the beach drawing love notes in the sand, while I dressed, rather unsuccessfully in the car (it is a two seated car- hardly any room to move, even with the hood down, let alone dress when you are soaking wet and shivering). Once thoroughly warmed through, I ran and jumped up behind him and we embraced in a wild tickling flush of laughter.... and suddenly, I was exhausted. The wild animal within me was beginning to tire and I could feel myself become weary... We both collapsed onto the silky frozen sand beneath us. We watched the sea crash into the shore as we listened to the distant sound of an owl twittering and the waves whirling metres from out feet. Fatigue took over so that all we could do was laugh, laugh at ourselves, laugh at the world, laugh at everything. We joked, giggled and chatted, until eventually, I became so tired that he put his arm round me and I closed my eyes, blissfully resting, safe and in peace. I had a wonderful time walking along the beach.... I always have so much energy that comes into effect and the beach helps quell my inner whirlwind somewhat.

Spoken Language and Behaviour

A mystery I have yet to unfold is that of the deep disconnection to the outside world which the Asperger's mind interprets all spoken language. I still find myself tumbling over everyday language used in almost every other sentence.

Such realisations do make me question how I understood anything as a child, and explains a lot of my behaviour.

I can't imagine how difficult it was for my family to safely control me and my behaviour. Of course, a child who misunderstands nearly everything you say will have difficulty understanding what it is you want them to do, and that is not their fault. So their behaviour could be considered to be 'bad'.

Here are a few examples of when I misunderstood common phrases used by my family to control my behaviour:

1. "Stop it, now." – I would always find this to be a very confusing statement as it is not very specific. What is the 'it' I am supposed to stop?
2. "Pack it in." – I would helpfully look around for packets to bring in; I'll explain this in the form of a story later.
3. "Joely, can't you see I'm not happy?" – My mother's face would clearly (to someone without Asperger's) be expressing anger and frustration, however, I was unable to recognise this emotion.
4. "Someone give me strength." – I would take this to be a very literal instruction and would stand by my mum's side and attempt to inject strength into her arm. Simply following a very literal, but very wrong, instruction.

Such behaviour, although unwittingly annoying and actually quite cute, was not amusing at first. Yet, as this quirk of mine continued my family could only laugh at my funny behaviour. It became cute that I would inject my mother with 'strength'. It proves that I really had no idea I was being naughty or rude, it was certainly not on purpose.

Children with A.S.D with the extra complications of additional difficulties do find it extremely bewildering to understand spoken and body language. For example, as a child, I was clinically deaf in my left ear and partially deaf in my right, on top of my Asperger's. I can only imagine how difficult my hardships made to positively control my behaviour for my family. My family could use specific and effective language for my Asperger's to understand, for instance they could say

"Joely, you need to stop running so fast, because you might fall and hurt yourself. Stop running, now."

However all words could often fall upon deaf ears – literally.

Autism's misconception of 'selfishness'

If someone on the spectrum appears to be acting selfishly, maybe having a meltdown in a supermarket, or another example, obliviously talking about their specialist topic at a funeral, it wont be a deliberate response, it will be a response that has been frantically created in a desperate attempt to cope with their manic surroundings – the confusion, frustration and the complexities, whilst also trying to do the right thing and behave in the 'correct' manner. Sometimes the disability can get in the way; overloads, meltdowns and brain fog and pain can make it hard or even impossible to make connections about the right or correct way to behave. consequently, so we operate on 'default'. Which so to speak, means communicating through specialist topic or other wise ignoring you, un less speech has been pre prepared. It may seem selfish – but it is not selfish at all, because being selfish mean you are thinking of yourself without a care for the right thing or other people – with people with Aspergers, this is not the case – as they always trying to behave and communicate 'correctly', -its not their fault that their disability can make it so hard sometimes, especially with the massive pressure to be correct, coupled with people negative perceptions – the most important thing is that they are trying!

Advice to Anyone Communicating with Someone with Asperger's

Use simple, clear and specific language whenever communicating with somebody who has Asperger's. I can't stress enough how important it is to be specific. If you do not tell them exactly what it is that needs to be done or changed, they are not going to understand you correctly. Effective communication is key to any successful relationship.

An example could be a child with Asperger's is meant to be painting a picture, but when you walk into the room they are doing something they shouldn't.

Instead of saying -

"Stop it"

It would be more helpful to say -

"Stop painting the wall and put the paint brush back into the paint pot"

Meltdowns – The Sound of 'War'

Do you hear that? It's the sound of clashing drums, it's the sound of leather strips slapping against armoured suits, it's the sound of thrashing metal, it's the squelch and stab of bone, it's the sound of death screaming out in desperation, it's the sound of your heart hammering out of your chest, it's the sound of agonized cries as panic sizzles your blood, and it's the sound of your rickety breathing as you count to calm yourself for battle, the stench of blood choking you with fear. Do you know that sound?

It's the sound of an Autism nightmare; It's the sound of war as it explodes from the mind.

It's the sound of an Autism Meltdown.

People who have Autism battle through their very own personal wars, every single day; going through turmoil after turmoil, battle after battle, as they fight meltdowns and information overloads for their rights to be at peace. These people that are amongst the most vulnerable in our society can also be the most honourable and brave; fighting daily battles that most of us would find it hard to understand.

It is possible to put yourself into the world of an Autism Meltdown; to see the battles as we do. To feel that overpowering panic as it bubbles like lava throughout your blood stream, the sense of never reaching peace again; fighting through your challenges, desperately trying to push aside those knights that represent your darkest difficulties, in battle after battle, to win your war and claim victory of peace of mind once again.

I am going to try and paint you that picture. Imagine you are in a super market...

Bright lights are flashing, blinking, ferociously bright, fragments of colour move around you as you blink and count to ten, desperate to try and see the world clearer again. Aisles of products seem to sway side by side, a mess of pixels, breathing; bright colourful. Numbers from prices jump out at you, creating illusions, and you find yourself desperately finding multiples of that number to try and calm the rising sense of alarm.

The drums of war I described earlier? Those are the sounds of footsteps as they crash to the floor, hundreds of them, ear splittingly loud, beating like a drum on steroids, vibrating throughout your veins as you try to solve any simple problem. Those leather strips and armoured suits are the rustling sounds of people clothes as they walk around the shops. Rustling clothes create this havoc wreaking white noise; overpowering, squeaking and ever enhancing the grimace on your face. That thrashing metal is the sound of the trolleys that squeak around the supermarket, clashing together, screeching to a halt; a cage of goods, patterned metal melting together to create one stripy grey blur. The sound of stabbing bone is the firing up overload as it controls your senses; little tiny needles stabbing your skin in all directions, prickling, painful, if anyone touches you now you will just scream out in agonised desperation.

And then there is the smell...

Every person emits this atrocious smell; that woman over there coughing into a hankie, smells like a wet dog with her chest infection, the smell rises thickly into the air like a menacing green fog; its gag worthy, but does anyone else notice it? Nope! The man's aftershave is so overpowering that all you can taste is his sweat, over powering, making you feel like you are choking above water, Where is this oxygen that all these people seem to breathing in with ease?

Through the mass of mayhem, someone asked a question; which colour would you like, green or purple?

Here it comes... the explosions of bombs going off all around you, the ground shakes beneath your feet, as your legs become week, trembling as you try to problem solve to create an answer; desperately standing your ground. You close your eyes to the debris and the mass of colours swirling around you, unable to see clearly though the thick explosion cloud of brain fog of confusion. Your hands fly to your ears, blocking out the shrieking white noise, of entire dimensions crashing around you. How can they possibly expect you to answer a question whilst you are fighting a battle like this? How can they be walking through this supermarket of horrors as if nothing terrible is happening?

Mash all these sensory overloads together, and what do you get? A battle to achieve inner peace. A battle known as a Meltdown.

The only way to cope is to count, to close your eyes and plaster your hands over your ears, to hit yourself, to flap your hands, to try and re gain some sense of clarity; desperately trying to control the offending sensory inputs with routinely and safe, sensory output. These reactions are entirely un avoidable and out of control. In fact these reactions are the only path left to take to try and win the battles that come with Meltdowns. These Meltdowns are made far worse by being expected to talk, walk, or problem solve. Imagine now, if this meltdown, is happening in a school, in a class room, when you are supposed to be learning? To me, it makes sense, that in massive desperation when meltdowns and overloads are wreaking havoc with your concentration, and usual abilities, that people on the spectrum 'lash out', or appear not to try, or participate. Behavior like this is for one simple reason, they have no choice; it's the only way they can communicate that something is really, terribly wrong for them. The last cause of action to take, while everything else appears to fail them. Finding the root of the problem, rather than passing off the behavior as the fault of the individual or the parents, is very important, because its only then that the support networks can begin to build to create the help, those with autism desperately need.

For instance, there could be any number of reasons in the classroom that can cause overloads, that could also be prevented.

These possibilities include:

- No room changes, or supported room changes
- sitting in the same space
- making sure the smells are neutral
- making sure that there is not too much to look at, perhaps stuck on the wall in front of them
- make sure their desk, and the teachers desk, is tidy and clean
- making sure the whiteboard is clean (No smudges) with not too much over powering writing
- controlling the class so they are not too noisy. Perhaps providing noise cancelling head phones.
- providing a soft stress ball, or stress reliever, which sits on every students desk (to not single out and be exposed to ridicule), if safe to do so.
- provide time out, to stand out in hallway with 121 staff, or friend of individual, for a 2 minute break.

- make sure the lights are not too bright / dim, make sure the blinds aren't casting strobe lights across the room, avoid any glares on the white board

The fact of the matter is that we are not naughty; no matter how are meltdowns are displaying themselves. We are not rude, we are not wrong and there is certainly nothing 'wrong' with us. We don't need a cure; we don't need people to tell us that we should try harder, that we should maybe stop hitting ourselves in times of overloads, that we should just stop listening to the mayhem around us... What we need is acceptance, care and sensitivity.

Autism Meltdowns and Shutdowns

Both are extreme reactions to everyday stimuli. Both tend to be the result of long-term unresolved issues (continuation of 'simple' overloads; for instance, school, work, changes in routine or general stress) both Shutdowns and Meltdowns are out of control for the Aspergers / Autistic person. With both, I get seizure like symptoms (which I called head 'surges' – a rush of energy through my head accompanied with severe white noise and an incontrollable shaking of my head or arms / legs). I pass out and my chronic pain enhances to such an intensity, that I can no longer walk or hold things. Autism Meltdowns is when Autism becomes a very physical and often un bearable disability; this is something many people don't understand. An Autism Shutdown is a type of overload and meltdown; it's basically a complete disassociation of all usual ability; an emotional and physical retreat.

Think how a snail retreats into their shell for safety, it's a bit like that. A shutdown is this feeling of complete numbness; watching life unfold, instead of living it. Shutdowns also come with an inability to talk with numb and slack mouths – you may have noticed people with Autism tend to dribble more, this is a reason why. Massive brain fog, blacking out, zoning out. Un-justifications from the past would circulate with my mind "What if" statements and these negative thoughts would be so out of control and extreme, that they sometimes cause repercussions with mental health problems.... When it comes to an Autism Shutdown, all our usual difficulties would be intensified to the point of impossibility. The only thing to rectify a Shutdown is to counter act any negative feedback they are getting from their environment (teacher, bullies, family) with calm soothing voice. Additionally, simply letting the Autistic person have the necessary Time Out, to rest is a must; and if that means having a day off school to sleep, then so be it. It would be entirely counterproductive to send an Autistic child to school while they were suffering with Meltdowns and especially Shutdowns – if anything, it could intensify the issue and make future learning or development seem impossible. For this reason, when I was 11 / 12, my Doctor wrote to my school to suggest I had every Friday off, so that I could rest and recuperate myself – with an additional session of weekly counselling therapy. This was entirely necessary, because if I didn't have this, I would have been in trouble constantly with teachers, for not attending (due to shutdown related illnesses / pain), or hiding in the toilets, unable to cope. Some people think Autism only affects basic things, it doesn't; Autism effects every second of my life, in a huge variety of different, complex, painful and frustrating ways. This is why I am grateful for volunteering for being so flexible and supportive; that even I, with my in ability to work, or sometimes, my in ability to walk or leave my house, even I have the rare opportunity to gain my life skills, and my happiness.

"Freeze, Drop and Roll" – Shutdowns and Frozen Defence Mode

Chances are, if you know someone who has a disability on the Autistic Spectrum, then you may have noticed their behaviours completely change; perhaps from being really hyperactive and energetic one minute, to staring into space as they stim, not wanting to say, or do anything the next. It can be quite alarming at first, if you are not sure why this change is happening, especially seeing that glazed 'out of body' expression that passes over their face. This is something I like to call 'Frozen Shutdown Defense Mode' – or "Freeze; Drop, and Roll!".

This becomes a very complicated reality, when sensory stimuli, general demands and Information is overwhelming, too much to cope with and too much for a person to process.

We with autism, tend to go into shutdown mode, operating at a basic shutdown level; we 'Freeze', 'drop' and 'roll'. We stop everything we are doing to try and recover, we freeze, we get frustrated, annoyed, feeling a lack of self worth, even though it really is not our fault, and we have to stop doing everything to cope with overloading stimuli. We then begin to shutdown. We drop; our physical abilities lowers, and drops, our minds abilities, lowers and drops. Then we start to stim to enable us to cope with the chaotic demand of life… and so, we roll. Yes, when it comes to stimming to recover from overloads, I tend to rock and roll!

My brain will initially try to shutdown (or in this case 'drop'), or block out the stimulation to avoid overload. To try and regain abilities, the person may start stimming (or in this case 'rolling'), shutting their eyes or cover their ears to block out further stimulation. This 'frozen deer in the head lights' expression, and their inability to do anything, is simply the person trying to recover their abilities, that have been lost through overloads, meltdowns or shutdowns, and keep calm, by not doing anything at all (freezing). This is because, people with autistic disorders, like all humans, have boundaries. The difference is that those on the spectrum will reach their limits far quicker, than those who are neurotypical, for example.

I believe that I operate on 'frozen defence mode' when I am forced to work, or do a job, while my body, and my mind, is having a shutdown. If I am forced to do things whilst having a shutdown, I can only function by operating at a lower setting, (Frozen defence mode – less able to do anything) in order to cope, and keep up with demands, for a very short period of time. This of course, is very un helpful, because it means all tasks that are completed during Frozen Shutdown Defence Mode are not completed to the best of our abilities; and that's not our fault. During a shutdown, we need to rest, and recover our abilities, and that is it.

With shutdowns, meltdowns and overloads, that change capability on an hourly basis, for those on the spectrum, this proves that our boundaries may change from day to day. What we could accomplish yesterday, we may not be able to do today, or even next week. Hence, why sometimes I can volunteer for a few days, maybe work on my website, write my book, maybe do a speech, (Not all of these activities but a few spread evenly over the week, with plenty of rest and support in between) but for the next week or two I will be unable to do anything at all, suffering with a shutdown of all my minds, and my physical abilities. Even little things like basic house hold chores (I'm being 100% honest and serious here) are too much, this is another reason why I have been declared by doctors, to never be able to work.

On the surface, we may appear able-bodied and as if there's not really any difficulty at all. I can be supported to do things, whilst in 'Frozen Shutdown Defence Mode', but of course, if I do that, which is rare thanks to my disabling shutdowns, it will mean the rest of the week (or two, depending how many hours I 'worked') will be spent in recovery (complete Shutdown mode), with no demands or jobs, not leaving the house, in too much pain to walk properly and functioning at a very basic level (even more basic than Frozen Shutdown Defence Mode).

"Half a job done, twice as much time"

Not all the time am I able to do what I want, or complete the mountains of work, that is required as an autism activist. In this way, school was increasingly difficult, as I was always in a state of shutdown, freezing, dropping and rolling. This is because of the countless stressful offences, daily life with school, demands of social life, bullying, and work, seemed to never end; without giving me any chance to recover, to enable me to be better again. Thanks to always being forced to operate at such a low level, my grades were affected. I couldn't concentrate, I was easily distracted, I couldn't understand or problem solve my way out of anything stressful. School was a nightmare because there was no understanding that the reason I wasn't doing well, was because I was operating in Frozen Shutdown Defence Mode, and therefore not able to do anything to my best ability, whilst also, having multiple days of sick every month. My family could see the issue, but the school didn't believe there was anything wrong, so we took the issue to my doctor. Thankfully, my doctor prescribed me every Friday off school to recuperate and do nothing, because it was the only way I could cope. I have never been more thankful than to be able to have time off to recover from shutdowns; I imagine it's the only way I could have coped with the chaos of School life. This is because people, including teachers, don't always understand the barriers to completing basic tasks, or why tasks take so long to complete. Such barriers include shutdowns and being 'frozen', and as a result I would get in trouble for no reasons beyond my control, and they would say some cruel or offensive things.

Behold! The (often unintentional) hurtful every day quotes…

"It is obvious Joely; just think about it" People would sneer, shaking their head in bemusement

"Haven't you done it yet? You have had so many days off this week…" People would chide

"Come on! Hurry up… what is taking her so long this time?" people would mutter in frustration.

"She could get higher grades if she concentrated and listened more, instead of spending all her time staring into space and biting her nails…" people would say

"If she actually completed her homework on time, it would help her, but she won't listen!" People would sigh, with misunderstanding.

"Oh for goodness sake, what is she up to now? Get back here!" They would cry

"I'm knocking on the front door, the lights flickering, but no one's home! Joely, I'm talking to you!" they would half joke

"Use your brain/your ears/your eyes/your sense of logic/your common sense" they would chortle.

These are circumstances that seem to come up all the time… and it's frustrating for me, that not everyone understands. I take a lot of time to do things, I get distracted, I become lost in thought, I become easily confused and unable to do things in any manner; and of course, pain controls my abilities. The truth is, in times of shutdowns, with frozen defence mode, I will be unresponsive, and there's nothing I can do about it. It is counter-productive that people say things like this to me, always pushing and challenging me to continue when I am really not able to do so.

The judgements of people with their negative perceptions, doesn't help in these moments of 'frozen shutdowns defence modes' especially when people seem to push us (on the spectrum) to carry on, when we have reached our limits, and need to just recover, in order to go back to our usual abilities. They don't understand the necessity for us to shutdown, instead of forcing us to freeze, drop and roll. But still, we are pushed, to our limitations – breaking point, with requirements, communication and rules. All this overloading hardships when our body's usual physical abilities has shut down, and our minds usual abilities has shutdown too, leaving very little other choice than to recover. Push! Push! Push! Pushing us to function in frozen defence mode, against our best interests. Then people wonder why we aren't performing to our usual capabilities at school or college, why we aren't behaving like normal, and they wonder why we have meltdowns?

"I wonder why?" I want to scream at them "You're pushing us to breaking point, and all we can do now, is recover, to regain our usual abilities – but still you push us! Stop telling us off for not participating, for not talking, for not making an effort, for having un controllable meltdowns?! Why do you THINK we are suffering with frozen defence modal shutdowns, having meltdowns and behaving 'bad'?! we have no other choice…Literally, just give us a break!"

A lot of people in life forget about the reasons behind the behaviours, or they simply don't understand. Instead they judge and assume it's a failure on our part, and that our explanations are actually excuses; perhaps based on the belief that we can't be bothered. Which is heart breaking, to say the least. Simply because they don't understand any better way. Yet, now it's my turn to wonder… If these people could see and understand the hardships those on spectrum go through, the sheer exhaustion, and pain that comes with simple thought processes, would they still make these judgements? If they could see, for instance, the invisible never ending shutdown, which is like being stuck in mud, unable to move, standing between me and what I want or need to accomplish, would they still say, "Just keep trying – don't give up just because you're a bit tired!". As if we have a choice; our only choice is to rest when we have shutdowns and meltdowns, so that we are able to try again later, and function to the best of our abilities later.

Don't Push us to Breaking Point – Advice for Parents

The thing is, if you keep pushing us when we are frozen, dropping or rolling, when we ultimately need to recover, and shutdown, then we will spend the rest of our days, not reaching our full potential, because we are always being pushed to complete every little task to the least of our abilities, and continuing to function worse as a result (here I mean that we are forced to function within an endless 'frozen shutdown defence mode'). If we have time to recover, then each thing we try and do will be done to the best of our abilities, because our abilities have been given the time to recover (whilst we are recovering in shutdown mode). It is a defence mode for a reason, these behaviours have a purpose, to defend us so we can get better again. We can achieve things with support, but we need to recover in between, to enable that to happen. It's not giving up; it is giving us the strength to carry on for the future.

If and when you do see this "frozen shutdown defence mode" response
A. Understand that the person is getting overwhelmed
B. Minimise further stress, perhaps by taking away all further demands, and be sure to keep your body language and voice neutral – lower your voice
C. Break down instructions into simpler manageable steps.
D. Quietly reassure them that they are safe and accepted
E. Be supportive, by being very patient with them.
F. Avoid asking too many questions and don't expect too much of them (even small things like house work), and offer gentle encouragement for even the tiniest of achievements they have made; leaving their bedroom, washing their hair; anything.
G. Allow them to safely freeze, drop and roll! Give them time to recover.

Try also to analyse the stressful circumstances to understand what may be overwhelming the person on the spectrum. It could be that there has been a change, even something small and preventable, like a table change and they can't cope, they could be overwhelmed by the noise levels, or the class activity. Or it could be as simple as freezing, dropping and rolling, due to anxiety of completing class task well enough or not understanding instructions.

Often, in cases with school or college for example, a person (well I certainly did) can recover simply be pulling away the demands of class, and lowering the stimulation. The best way to help someone who is having Shutdown, is to allow them to rest in sensory friendly surroundings as possible, I say rest, it could mean a few hours, or a whole day or two; whatever they need to recover and go back to their usual self again. Understand that 'frozen deer in the headlights' expression, allow them to freeze, drop and roll, because at moments of overload, those on the spectrum really need to, they need time out. They need to shutdown. 121 is essential to support the child. I have found that by following this advice, people tend to recover quickly and can continue the activity, later (although they will be tired and easily overloaded again).

Obsessive Behaviours

I am going to write about why I am obsessed with the replication of various disease cells.

Have you ever lay in the long grass of a large field, safely alone, with the sunshine beaming overhead and wondered how the earth came into existence? Have you been somewhere so peaceful, where branches from trees rustle with life, with leaves hanging down like luscious green water-falls? Have you ever been somewhere similar to this, and stared at the complicated mechanics of the tiny flowers growing in the tall blades of grass around you? Have you ever gazed at the light filtering through the gaps in the tree branches and thought of light and dark? Ever closed your eyes to listen to the sweet tune of birds singing their lullaby and imagined them breathing as they sing? Have you ever listened so intently that your own heartbeat, dedicatedly pumping life around your body, as it begins to sooth any stress? Have you ever watched as the light breeze makes everything in your surroundings sway and breathe a sigh of life...

Have you ever wondered what it really means, to be alive?

I have, on many occasions, taken time out from my hectic life style, and wondered just this; what is it to be alive? How does our body fix almost every problem without us so much as noticing there was a problem in the first place? I believe that life is wonderful, to be alive disabled or not, is an adventure of incredible strength. I think the process of life and the mechanics of how things stay alive is simply captivating. It is something that has always interested me. I just never had enough passion or time to research to become really knowledgeable upon any related subject before.

However, a desperately sad passion developed when my wonderfully amazing mother was diagnosed with cancer a few years ago. This was the moment in my life when I finally understood the term "my world came crashing down around me". You see, as my family and I sat around that table for dinner time, I experienced it for the first time. Upon hearing such heart breaking news, my world, our world, really did come smashing, crashing and hurtling down around us. I experienced tunnel vision for the first time on my life and struggled to cope. How did this happen to my amazing mum? The rubble of intense emotion tumbled upon my family, trapping us all under the heavy wreckage of despair that cancer had brought. After that, life seemed so fragile, so complicated so... lifeless. I became psychologically numb, the endless emotional pain cancer had caused was so consuming that it was corroding my happiness and lust for life. (Admittedly, those were the toughest years of my life, because there was a lot of badass rubbish going on in my life right then. I got diagnosed with Post Traumatic Stress Disorder and other physical illnesses that affected me daily). I always used to think, if mum's cancer is affecting me this badly- how was it for my mother and the rest of my beloved family? Even though statistics looked in our favour for a recovery, the sense of dread never really leaves you. It stays in the back of your mind, niggling away, reminding you of the terrible times that could start at any moment. We were walking on egg shells, around our own life. When happy times occurred, we never really knew how long they would last before cancer destroyed them. I soon learnt to live life with no regrets, because you really have no idea what is round the corner- and how quickly things could change to prevent you from doing what you want. So I say, while you have the chance – do what makes you happy before something changes. I live to this as much as I can every day. No regrets.

My enthrallment with life and how our bodies survive, grew and grew as I struggled to cope with the nasty news. I did extensive research on diseases like cancer, small pox and the influenza virus. I became desperate to find out the answers to my endless questions, the main question that burned through my mind was always –

Where did the cancer come from?

Here, began my new specialism of how cancer cells reproduce and how tumours form. I even did an art project upon the subject at my arts university, resulting in a Distinction grade. I became obsessed with researching cancer cells and understanding the process. Nearly every other interest, (aside from my family and friends) became less important. This was a project that fed my appetite wonderfully and really aided my recovery from the shocking news. Working on understanding the process of how cancer cells replicated to create a tumour, somewhat calmed my nerves. I guess even though in my heart of hearts, I knew I had no control over the cancer and how far it spreads, there was still a faint glimmer of hope that if I understood the replication process, I may be able to control it from spreading.

My research forced me to think about the matter rather than hide from the problem. It became a possibility that I may be able to seek comfort from the facts, and seek comfort, I did. My new obsession helped me cope with the horrid effect cancer had created in our lives.

There were negatives to my obsession, I saw cells everywhere and I became somewhat obsessive compulsive about germs. I would scrub my hands and body red raw to be clean of the bad cells and without even noticing I was harming myself. I would unwittingly scratch at my skin in an attempt to remove a fleck of dirt until my skin was streaked red. I spent hours every day researching and trying to understand the process, to the point where I stopped going out. It almost took over my life.

The day I found out my mother had cancer had been so tragic that I could not sleep for weeks (maybe months really) with anxiety and depression. My mum, being so ill was horrific to see and I am loathe to admit how many tears are trickling across my cheeks as I type right now. Although my mother is currently cancer free and strong as ever, I pray that we will all remain cancer free, healthy and happy.

Other obsessive behaviours

I like to think I haven't got an addictive personality because I have never done drugs or smoked and drink very little alcohol. I like to think because I don't get obsessed by one thing like a T.V show, I don't have an addictive and obsessive personality. However, strictly speaking, maybe this is not true. I have many obsessions that most of the time, I don't even realise are controlling my very existence (it's like I am being controlled by a giant robot, like a puppet). I shall list a few of them for you:

1. Cleanliness
2. Routines
3. Certain foods
4. Music

Cleanliness and routines can be categorised into the same section, because I have to have a cleaning routine that I follow daily. If my routine is interrupted, or I have less time to complete it, all hell lets loose. If I have less time or if my routine is slightly altered or interrupted, even if someone just stands in the doorway of my room, I go crazy. If anything happens to distract or prevent me from doing my full routines, I can't go out anywhere, I'm often late to meetings as a result as I often have to start the routine again, uninterrupted, no matter how close I was to finishing. I have written more about routines in 'My Big Bang Theory – Rigid Routines'.

Everybody (Autistic spectrum or not) has obsessive tendencies, while most are mild, some are very severe and greatly impact upon day to day life. People with Autistic Disorders are more prone to obsessive behaviours because they find comfort in facts. That means anything outside complete accuracy is incredibly unsettling because it is wrong and not the truth. When you live in a world that is confusing and difficult to understand, you develop ways to cope with this. People with A.S.D seek to understand daily realities by looking for the truth, because the truth can never be wrong. The search for the truth can become obsessive as daily life throws up so many questions, changes and deceit. In the confusion, seeking the truth (and becoming obsessed by it) is the only way to learn how to best cope with such situations. While obsessive behaviour can appear to be bad and disruptive, try to view them positively. Obsessive behaviour when nurtured in the right way, can lead to the person doing extremely well in that particular area.

Aggressive and Violent Behaviour –What Could it Mean?

A lot of people (generally children), on the Autistic spectrum tend to run around in frenzied circles, head-butt table legs (while sitting under the table, rocking backwards and forwards) and lash out at people around them. Some of the time, people lash out at others as a form of communication. I believe that if the person does not know how to express what it is they want; violent behaviour is the next step to take, to be understood. For example, if a child is in pain and they don't know how to explain or express that something is hurting them... they hurt themselves further (in front of a teacher or carer) because they know they will then be helped, and the initial pain, may be treated. Literal behaviour showing the person exactly what is wrong. In an odd way, it's quite clever really.

Another example is that, if you are in a classroom and someone starts hitting another pupil and screaming, the teacher will safely manage the behaviour and take the pupil out of the classroom (to avoid putting other pupils in danger) and isolate the pupil in a separate room or corridor for 'time out'. It only takes one spell of sensory overload for a pupil to realise that if they can't cope with the madness of the classroom, all they need to do, is behave aggressively and maybe hit someone, in order to be given some time out. When in reality, all they had to say was

"Please can I have some time out?"

But spoken language is not always an option, partly because it may be physically impossible or voicing such a necessity to teachers often results in ridicule from both teacher and students. Also, the teacher may not understand why you need time out in the first place.

When all other ways of communication are impaired, and frustration at being misunderstood takes over, bad behaviour can be the way to communicate. We just need to try and understand what it is they are trying to express, such as:

1. "Please help me"
2. "I want time out"
3. "Can't cope"
4. "I am in pain"

I believe that it is incredibly important to establish why the person is behaving in such a manner, rather than jumping to conclusions which are possibly incorrect. I have mentioned many times before communication is one of the key areas of difficulty for those with Autistic Disorders, this is why it is so important to understand the actions being taken, and try to determine the cause of the stress in the first place. Is there a possibility of a sensory overload? The reasons, I believe stem from both nature (genetics and personality traits) and nurture (what has been learnt through the environment they live in). Some behaviour can be so aggressive and well, strange looking, that those on the outside will wonder what an earth is going on.

Advice for Parents and Teachers – Managing Aggressive Behaviour

When a person with Autism is behaving in a manner that could harm both themselves and others... what do you do? In my childcare work, we have various guidelines (which are tailored to individuals). I shall share a few of the guidelines related to Autism with you.

Step one: **Work out the reason behind bad behaviour.**
You need to ask yourself:

1. Is the person in pain?
2. Are they trying to communicate something to me?
3. Are they experiencing a sensory overload?

You need to determine the cause of the stress in the first place. Once you have discovered the source of the stress you are more likely to be able to remove it.

I once looked after a child who would start acting in a terrified frenzied manner, seemingly out of nowhere, screaming running around arms outstretched and hands waving violently. Each time we safely controlled, comforted, and distracted the child's behaviour and wrote down the sensory happenings. It was only when we read through notes, that we realised the reason for the child's behaviour was because a plane had flown over head each time. It made perfect sense, the plane was noisy, distressing and reminded the child of a very stressful incident of noise, number of people and sensory mayhem they had experienced at the Air Festival my town holds each year. No wonder the plane upset them; they probably thought the sensory mayhem of the Air Festival was starting all over again.

Step two: **Distraction.**
If a child is behaving badly, perhaps self harming, as a means of communicating that they want something (perhaps a toy or food), it is often thought to be safer and easier to give in to the child and give them what they want – purely to stop them from hurting themselves. However, this will mean that the behaviour will never (or rarely) improve, and the child will always know that if they want something all they have to do is hurt themselves, and they will get whatever they want. The child won't try to learn new strategies because this strategy of

hurting themselves works so well and it is not necessary to learn something new, especially if the adult is not initiating any new strategy.

Clearly, no one wants the child to hurt themselves, so another technique may be necessary. You need to try to distract the child's attention by creating another, new un-related activity, which is related to a routine. A distraction could be spontaneous singing (child's favourite song) a favoured activity or hobby. If the distraction doesn't seem to make a difference, you need to attempt to calm them down. A calm manner is key here. Taking the child to a temporary sanctuary is a nice idea, maybe a sensory friendly place, the child's bedroom or a quiet secluded place like an empty classroom. This acts as a temporary distraction and displacement from the initial distressing scenario. Don't forget the child's specialist topic is usually a calming and interesting topic so try and introduce the topic into your relaxation techniques.

In most cases, this will stop the bad behaviour. In some cases of severe agitation or pain, additional steps need to be taken to help the child.

Step three: **Blow off some steam – Go running, dance, sing… Anything.** Sometimes, when relaxation doesn't appear to be working, it is best to let the behaviour run its course, where you could encourage them to burn off the bad behaviour by physical activities. Take them outside, safely, or to a large open safe space and tell them they can run around (providing the perimeter is completely safe and the child is familiar with the location for example a school sports hall if you are at school, or your garden if you are at home). This, in itself is a distraction, exercise is just another form of behaviour, but is a safer and more suitable behaviour to learn.

Step four: **Try to take control by talking.**
Once the child has calmed down, only then do you talk about the consequence of their actions. If you try to have this conversation when they are agitated or overloaded, you will upset and worry them further and they will be unable to communicate effectively.

Avoid mockery, long sentences, questions and confusing language. Make sure you are clear and specific with what you are telling them. You need to keep calm and avoid phrases such as "you're just being silly"

Or

"that's not how to ask for food"

Also avoid using exasperated, frustrated and angry tones. Any tone of language that is anything other than calm, will confuse and agitate the child further.

Step five: **Leave them alone.**
If all else fails and you feel at your wits end trying to cope with such behaviour, make sure the person is safe and leave them alone. Allow them to stay in a quiet room, with little things to break or throw and allow the behaviour to runs its course. Throughout, it needs to be ensured the child is safe. If a cushion is close by this could be used as padding for whatever body part they are hitting, they will then hit that instead.

If their behaviour is still really violent and their own safety is in jeopardy, a form of restraint could be necessary. By restraint, I mean a trusted adult holding the child, safely, so they can not physically hurt themselves or anyone. Obviously this is the absolutely last resort, and many may disagree with me, but I believe that this type of safe restraint does not harm the child. In fact I believe it of great benefit. Unfortunately I have witnessed situations where the child's behaviour had become so aggressively violent it was the only action left to take. I was present once in a child care setting, where a child was acting up. The behaviour became more and more challenging, to the point where the child was kicking, screaming, biting, hitting and flailing their arms wildly in frustration. The child in question, suffered with a disability that made their bones weaker and prone to breakages. This meant that even though other children had been removed from the situation, the child was in real danger of breaking bones. It was at this point that the teacher and the teaching assistant had no choice but to hold and sing to the child until it fell asleep from sheer exhaustion. I know this is an extreme example, and I hate the idea of having to control a child's bad behaviour physically, but I would like to think, no matter how horrid it may seem, safety and the wellbeing of the child, always comes first.

Advice for Parents – Don't Wrap me in Bubble Wrap

Often when a child behaves negatively, it may seem like the best option is to isolate them in a room where they are safe. While this is a necessary short term solution, I think it is important to look at the bigger picture. Children need to be able to learn from the world around them, and of course this is true of those on the Autistic spectrum. Not allowing the child to experience the outdoor wonders for fear of their safety or judgment from others, could have massive negative impacts upon development. While it is natural to want to protect someone, especially a vulnerable person, I think it is still vital that the child is allowed to explore, and learn from their surroundings. Children with Autistic disabilities still need to learn how to manage risks more so than other children without such a disability.

A child will normally learn how to manage risks through trial and error. They will be able to learn from their mistakes; whereas a child with Autistic Disorders will not. Children with Autistic Disorders will only be able to learn how to manage risks by being taught the correct routines, and repeating this routine over and over. They need to be able to take safe controlled risks, as part of a routine, (completely the same each time) with a responsible adult in order to learn, with time, what is safe and what is not. Children on the Autistic spectrum follow facts, truth and routines as if they were the law. When given a routine, they won't change anything, and would most likely follow it to the letter (exactly as instructed).

If you want a child with A.S.D to learn about the risks around them (e.g. crossing the road safely), letting them take safe controlled risks and allowing them to repeat the same process over and over, is a highly effective way. Controlled risks can include walking safely in car parks, playing in a play park with climbing frames and swings, road safety and walking to school. Such controlled risks are a necessary part of day to day life, and must be learnt in the interest of safety.

People on the Autistic spectrum have little sense of fear, mostly because they don't understand danger, or realise the importance of safety.

For example, if a child with Autistic Spectrum Disorders is out walking and they see something intriguing in the road, they won't think twice about going to have a look. They could easily run into the middle of the road without a thought to the consequences (moving cars). This is because they do not make connections. They would not make the connection between moving cars and them running into the road which could lead to being hit by car. So they would not realise they could be putting themselves in danger.

Considering this is an area where people with Autistic Disorders struggle, it is very important to take extra time to teach them what is safe, correct and dangerous. This is why letting children with Autistic Disorders take controlled risks is so important.

As a child I had been taught resilience and happiness through climbing trees, exploring forests, parks and rolling down grassy hills. All are fabulous controlled risks that facilitate and enhance holistic development with the certain beauty of giving joy. Now, it seems parents are afraid of the consequences of letting their children take any risks in an outdoor environment. I think that some parents get scared by the word 'risk', but the fact of the matter is that it is a 'controlled' risk. This means you are there observing and teaching the child how to manage the activity safely.

My experience of controlled risks

Mum and dad have always said that they will never wrap me in bubble wrap; which means they would never protect me so much that I stopped living life to the full. They didn't want to prevent me from taking safe controlled risks and stop me from exploring in an outdoor environment.

This does not mean my family never protected me, quite the opposite; as they supported and protected me constantly; they just knew where to safely and happily draw the line. This was in order to build up my independence, life skills and resilience and allow me to live my life, as I should – exploring and learning indoors and outdoors.

I love my family, for all that they have done for me; I never felt safer and more protected than with my understanding family; my loving and caring parents, my strong, kind, and brilliant brother who looked out for us all as if we were the most important beings in his world, and my wonderfully understanding sister who looked after me and made sure I got all the rights to which I was entitled. To be honest, my whole family did a mixture of all the above, because they are all dazzling like that. I could not wish for any better, this is why I respect their decisions with clarity of mind because I know it was the right thing to do, for me.

My family and I firmly believe that life is wonderful, and needs to be lived and explored, especially in an outdoor environment. My family have been adamant not to let my disability get in the way of me experiencing 'normal' life, and the wonders of the world. They have always helped me and protected me in every way they can, but have been careful not to help me so much that I can't do anything for myself. My family knew that doing too much for me would prevent me from recognising that I could actually do these things for myself. I firmly believe I would be a different person today, if I had not had the opportunities to learn and explore the outdoor environment. We explored the great outdoors, regularly as a family, taking long walks, sensory learning out in the fresh air, taking part in sports and normal family life. I was always encouraged to learn through play, and play from my own resources, both indoors and outdoors, enhancing and strengthening my imagination and social accuracy. It was wonderful and I could never thank my parents enough for recognising how vital such outdoor and indoor learning through play was for me to develop wholly.

Outdoor Sensory Learning

I think the best type of learning comes from the outside environment, not in a stuffy classroom with limited resources and paper work.

I would like you all to try something for me. Imagine you are in a nice forest. Imagine you are completely safe, content and comfortable. Now imagine you are surrounded by tall trees, a little shallow stream running on one side and miles of luscious green rolling hills. Imagine the day is bright, the sky is blue and the temperature is just right. You are relaxing underneath the shaded branches of the trees. The leaves shimmering in the breeze, birds singing to each other in the distance and you are happy, with no stresses from normal life burdening you at this moment. Close your eyes, breathe in, breathe out... relax. What a wondrous splendour you have created within your mind's eye... Isn't this place beautiful and calm? I must ask you a question, if you were a child visiting your imagined place for the first time, what would you explore first? Would you chase butterflies across the meadows, flap your arms and pretend to fly? Would you explore the trees in the forest, with their knobbly bark, cascading leaves, play animal games and endless possibilities of peek-a-boo? Or would you head straight for the flow of the twinkling stream, to splash about and try to catch a glimpse of a possible stream monster? I know what I would have done if I was a child. I would have happily spent hours skipping around the trees, climbing, splashing in the stream, pond dipping and rolling down the hills.

How lovely would it be to visit a place like this and learn from it in real life? You can! Whether you find these places at your local park, countryside, coastal areas or even in a back garden, there are endless places to be explored.

 I believe children and young people with disabilities especially benefit greatly from the outdoor world. This is because there are always opportunities of learning whether you realise it or not. Any child visiting new surroundings will automatically explore using their senses (looking, touching, smelling and hearing). The child would be looking at the trees and seeing all the branches and leaves, all the colours and animals. They are listening to the sounds of the water flowing and the sticks breaking beneath their feet. They are be feeling the rough texture of bark and the elasticised smooth texture of grass and petals, the cold wet feel of water lightly running through their fingertips. They are slowly but surely learning through exploring with their senses. They will be forming questions and connections about what they are experiencing. "Why do leaves have veins?" "What has created this shadow?" "Why does the water flow in that direction?" etc etc, the questions are endless.

The point I'm trying to make is that it is very easy to open a book and learn about a certain place or situation, but actually experiencing that situation for yourself is far more fun, therapeutic and beneficial.

Learning in this way – through interest and play is an effective way of all-round development for children and young people with and without disabilities. Sensory gardens are absolutely fabulous for this very reason. They are majestic places that are peaceful and unique and offer brilliant fun and sensory enjoyment for all.

It's all well and good imagining such wonderful possibilities and places, but obviously, it would be far more beneficial to go to the real thing. Go to a nearby forest or beach, or even your local park. Make the most of what you have around you, you would be surprised what amazing things you have on your own doorstep.

Play Behaviors – Learning Through Factual Play

Through my research into my disability, I stumbled across a rather interesting trait that is common for children with A.S.D. Apparently, children with A.S.D are more likely to play using facts and figures than be able to play imaginatively and play 'pretend' games. I find this odd, because growing up; all I ever did was play pretend games. I would go running around the park every day after school with my best friends and we would pretend to be jumping over molten lava or sailing in boats. We would be swinging from the monkey bars in my local play park and pretend we were hobbling on a rickety bridge with a huge gaping hole beneath us.

We used to pretend that we lived in the trees, like monkeys and we would literally climb up trees and swing from the branch of one tree to a branch of another tree- metres in the air. I don't recommend you do this, as these things are dangerous. Our pretend play was fun, exciting, subject to change (eek), unrealistic and co-operative... Not only that, but a lot of these ideas were mine, I was not following their lead completely, often I wanted to play 'let's pretend' games myself. Which is not particularly typical play trait's for a child with Asperger's.

Children with A.S are supposedly more comfortable with play that involves fact and figures and things that are true. Whereas, a lot of pretend play is not always real. It is also a trait that a child with A.S.D will be very rigid in their play routines, if they play with others, they have to play exactly how the child with A.S.D wants to.

Usually pretend games would be limited to specialized topics only and very specific to how the child with A.S.D wants to play. The friend is thought to be there more for the purpose of acting out the role to allow the specialized game to continue, more than to be there as an actual friend for the child with A.S.D to play with. It may seem odd, but in a way, the child with A.S.D almost takes control of play when friends are involved to ensure that the pretend play is 'accurate' and 'true'. I find this quite strange because, it is known for children with A.S.D to have difficulty with socializing, so to be able to control and organize friends to play the 'right' way, is quite impressive.

However, since this rather intriguing discovery, I have realized that I too, used to play pretend games using facts and figures. You see, during my imaginative play as a child, I used to pretend that I was in scenarios I had learnt about at school. More precisely eras and events I had learnt about in History lessons. Hence why my fascination with history grew and grew. I did not always have anyone to play with who shared the same ridiculous love for something deemed as boring as 'history'. Often, this was because I did not have very good socialization skills that allowed me to control topics of play... So I always had to make do with using my wild imagination and playing by myself. At the time, it may have appeared that I was being very imaginative with my pretend play, but actually I was carefully re enacting historic events.

My home became the place where my imagination ran wild... and wild, I ran. Every single room in my house was a different era in history with a special story to it. Usually, play stories would follow factual events or something I had learnt at school or read about in books. I had a deep fascination with all my play eras in history; I believe the historic topics had such a huge part in my play, which is probably why I had learnt so much from it. I believe this is certainly proof that you learn more as a child through play and through things that are already of interest to you. I loved history; I believe it was my specialist topic although I don't think I know quite as much about history as I would like you to believe. Although my family would probably beg to differ.

At such a young age, my bathroom upstairs was always Inca Peru, with giant stone temples surrounded by beautiful trees. Every time I walked in my bathroom, in private, I would be literally ducking past tree branches, brushing leaves out of my face, blinking in the streaked sunlight. I would be hopping across stones in my imaginary river, looking up at the fast flow of an almighty waterfall just metres from my feet (the shower). It was incredible and made it feel like I was escaping the stresses just walking in there. My goodness it was only a bathroom but what it meant to me was so much more than that. Of course my bathroom looks nothing like an Inca Peruian Rain forest (what bathroom does? I sound ridiculous, I do know) – My bathroom is simply just clean white tiled like any other bathroom... but in my imagination, that is what it was to me. Beautiful. I have no idea if my family know this crazy quirk about me or not.

My landing was often a market place for whatever era in history I fancied. My favourite play theme for this area, was to pretend to be a Vestal Virgin of Ancient Rome, priestesses of Vesta, (Vesta – goddess of the hearth-protection of the city of Rome). I would sit on the landing, protecting the sacred flame of Vesta from ever diminishing. A few times, I pretended that by cruel circumstances of misfortune, the flame went out, a punishable offence by death. I pretended that I got caught by the guards, and summoned to be scourged and then death by court order (because I had allowed the protection of the city to go awry). I pretended that I was forced to dig my own grave (as was protocol – to ensure I died 'willingly' to abide by Roman law),in the Campus Sceleratus, aka "Evil Fields" (an underground chamber). I travelled down my staircase, and pretended to dig (one step at a time, digging 'deeper'). Once the task of 'digging' my own grave had been complete, I would pretend to bid my tearful farewells to those too sickened by me to face me, and take my first steps into the chamber. As with Roman law, I would take 3 jugs of water and some bread to sustain me until I, too, perished from the devastating effects of lack of oxygen, hunger and fear. In Roman law, it is unlawful to bury the dead within the city, but to bury them alive within the city, is not technically breaking the law, hence why burying them alive – willingly, with bread and water was necessary. (Don't quote me on any of this, my memory is not fantastic and I was very young when I learnt all of this, so my memory may not be accurate). Although in reality, I only had a chocolate Kinder egg, a fruit shoot and a treasure chest lid to lie in, not quite 3 jugs of water and a piece of bread, but hey – ho- it still seemed real to me. These are all things I had read about in books and learnt at school. It all very much fascinates me today.

My hallway was anywhere I wanted it to be, on occasions I would stand at the top of my stair case, and pretend I was up a large mountain in Africa. I would pretend that I was overlooking a bay, hiding from slavers, (people on ships looking to captor people for slavery) watching from afar as my community got torn apart. This would be my favourite, and I have written many stories upon this subject. I would sit / perch on my staircase pretending to be crouching in the branches of a tall gnarled tree. I would peer over the top of my staircase and stare down, my eyes portraying my intense emotions at the horrifyingly distressing scene below me. My imagination, running wild, was allowing me to see miles of sea and sand, hundreds of lines of slaves chained together, making their slow and painful process to the boats to take them out to the slave ships. Sweat glistening off of their bare backs, marks on their precious skin from where they had already been unfairly disciplined. Men, woman and children, all chained separately, by shackles around their neck, ankles and wrists. The sounds of despairing cries rang shrill and clear in the merciless air. The true horror of the families ordeal, sounded out by the tragic cries of separated children and fearful parents. The eerie silence, of those grown accustom to the disciplinary beatings. Eyes downcast as the hundreds of slowly diminishing hopeful hearts, gave up on justice, one by one. After looking down at the lines of imagined slaves, I would look out to their feared destination – an uncertain and unjust future. Several ships anchored out to shore, swaying in the oceans wavy furnace. The people capturing slaves, were roaming around on horse-back, barking out demands to dirty sailors in a strange, foreign tongue. The suits on their backs were clean and carrying foreign flags. Their canes looking immaculately clean, cruel and distinct in the early morning chill of despair. Near the shore, in the crystal clear shallow waters, I imagined sailors wading through the water, carrying wooden crates of food and water out to boats, to be rowed back to the main ship. Shoals of colourful fish could be seen swimming around the men's feet as they splashed through the masses. I would imagine a cool and wicked breeze on my face, as I sat, watching such a distressing scene unfold below me. (I would pretend) My body trembling in the hot, humid heat of the morning, a single tear rolling down my cheek as my heart thumped in my frail chest. One question burning through my mind… what has become of our lives?

Sorry, I get carried away with descriptions. Anyway, I went into such great details, because I feel it is important for you to all understand the sheer intensities of my play, emotions and passion… This is why I learn so much. If, I am interested in the subject, I can become a walking encyclopedia.

In reality, I also used facts and figures to play, which I conducted by myself and was based around true stories and factual events. My play may have been very imaginative and bizarre to onlookers, but it was merely practising facts that I had learnt about and envisioned during class. So I guess, we all learn through play differently. Eventually what was once pretend play soon became ideas and opportunities for the endless stories I would write. In a way, I still play pretend, when I write my stories.

Story of "Pack it in"

On October 13th 1999, when I was seven years old, something very amusing happened; a story that will be told in my close family for many years to come.

It had been a long, tiring day and my mother was looking after me, while dad was at work. My mum was exhausted looking after three children all by herself, on only a few hours sleep. It was a trying day for me also, as we were tired and communication mishaps were sky high. I had been on the go (running around with endless energy), from the early hours of the morning. Constantly restless, energetic and causing utter chaos everywhere I went. Mum recalls that it was one major incident followed swiftly by another. I had been sprinting from one room to another, tipping toys out all over the floor, breaking things, knocking furniture over, being noisy, trying to talk and sing, being my usual whirlwindy self. I was being a rascal, but not on purpose. My mum, naturally, was getting frustrated (this didn't happen often) This example might make my lovely mum sound bad, don't let it cloud your judgement; for my mother has the patience and understanding of a saint, she is truly wonderful and I couldn't wish for better. This was the only time she ever lost her temper with me. So, as I sprinted into the kitchen, she followed me in frustrated exhaustion to check I hadn't pressed any button on any cooking devices (which I had), and I started sprinting around her in tight circles. As I ran around her, I started opening and banging shut the cupboard doors, creating a therapeutic rhythm of banging cupboard doors, in perfect harmony and order of each other. I did this because I was tired, and unable to express that I needed a rest and was close to having a sensory meltdown. My mum, bless her, was also close to having a meltdown and needed a rest from me.

Amidst the noisy chaos of me running around her in circles, she shouted at me

> "Get out. Go into the garden, now. GO."

Her face was apparently twisted into very clear signs of anger – I, obviously, couldn't tell. I stopped running and looked at her, in confusion I believe, because I didn't understand why. My confusion and lack of understanding must have frustrated her further because she then asked, angrily

"Can't you see I'm angry, Joely?"

I looked at her face to check, oblivious to the raging signs of clear anger, and shook my head.

"No"

I said, grinning at answering the question 'correctly'. My mother shook her head and pointed at her face,

"Does this look like a happy face to you?"

She practically screamed in my face.

"I don't know"

I said quietly and cutely, with a shrug, struggling to understand what was happening, completely oblivious. My mother sighed loudly,

"Just GO. Just go into the garden and will you *pack it in.*"

My mother had said dismally in frustration, now calmer, and pointed vigorously at the door to the garden. She had meant for me to stop my whirlwind behaviour, but I hadn't understood the language she had used. I ran outside into the garden, to do exactly as she had told me (from my understanding). I, however being the kid that takes everything literally had gone into the garden and started searching. My mother started making a cup of tea, relieved to have a moment of peace, and glanced into the garden to check on me and watched in confusion as I walked slowly up and down the perimeter of the garden, bent over, and picking things up. So, despite herself, she had to see what I was doing, she came out and said

"Joely what are you doing?"

I had looked up, and apparently said

"I'm looking for packets"

And I continued searching like it was the most normal thing in the world. My mother's mouth dropped open, in quite obvious surprise. She was utterly bewildered at this point and stared at me as she tried asking me from a different approach.

"Why are you searching for packets, Joely?"

I looked up again and said in a confused manner

"I am looking for packets in the garden, to bring in... I'm packet-ing it in;
Like you told me to".

I thought she was asking in a weird way if I could bring packets in the house. I just assumed she had missed the 'bring' out of the sentence, and that she was meant to say "will you *bring* pack – it (packet) in" It was logical to me anyway. For someone who doesn't make connections easily, or understand language; I had to interpret it someway... and this is just one of those times where the results of me understanding language wrongly were just hilarious.

Like I said, my mother really is the best. I really couldn't wish for better, she's amazing; in fact my whole family are all incredibly understanding and supportive. In this one example she was angry at me, don't let that create a judgement, because the fact of the matter is that my mother and my whole family are all saints, sent from above (metaphor, not literally). All my family are understanding, helpful, wonderful, supportive and we all love each other dearly, nothing is more important than family. This incident happened over 15 years ago, but it is a story we all still laugh about now.

> *My Mothers Advice for Other Parents of Autistic Children*
> You need to take time out for yourself. Losing your rag and shouting at your child does not work, it just makes the situation worse. Take time out, breath, and return to the situation with a calmer outlook.

Secrets Of My Mind

I think hidden disabilities are similar to mental health issues because they are both similarly misunderstood. Asperger's, is a fairly hidden disability, it is not obvious for anyone to see that the disability is there. As disabilities go, Asperger's is hidden, and therefore judged and misunderstood. Sadly, mental health issues are also a hidden disability for some. In fact, I have some mental health issues of my own, some of which terrify me to my very core, others that make me feel so alone, that I wonder if I merely exist in a post apocalyptic world. Let me tell you something; to feel so isolated in a world surrounded by people, is a terrible, dreadful thing.

Regardless of the difficult trials having mental health issues can bring, it is something that someone can learn to deal with and accept as an interesting part of their personality. Providing that the sufferer has support from family, friends and organisations such as councillors and health professionals, the person may, with time, get back on the road to recovery. A rollercoaster ride to recovery, it may be, with many ups, and downs and terrifying dips into darkness… Never forget, every roller coaster comes to a safe end.

I have had mental health issues, sadly like many others, but that doesn't mean that with support they can't be positively controlled. My main mental health issue is my diagnosis of PTSD, aka Post Traumatic Stress Disorder. I have PTSD due to lots of things that happened many years ago now. My PTSD is so much better now, but I feel I should reveal an insight into how difficult it really was, not only to build an understanding but to reveal how someone could try and overcome issues themselves. I am writing this section because many other books I have read from authors who personally have Autistic spectrum disabilities have shied away from mental health issues. I feel it is important to address such a scary topic to better help those in desperate need. Also, I am writing this because I believe mental health difficulties are something that will affect nearly all of us, in some stage in our lives. We must address the issue so we can learn how to help others, and ourselves.

I say all of this because, according to my 'safe places' research (please see 'Schools Out – Volunteering) it is statistically common for people with disabilities to be victims of theft, robbery or violence. If anyone falls victim to such things, it can be very distressing and very unjustified. It can be horrid to deal with, especially alone. Victims of such cruelty could start suffering with depression disorders and depending on the degree of the trauma, they could get PTSD, like me.

When bad things happen, it is incredibly important to realise that support is out there for people who are suffering (perhaps with depression) in the dark. I wish to help by writing this section. I have PTSD, this often means that I hear voices, I see things and I get flashbacks of various things that have happened I also used to suffer from depression. Fear not, I am much better now. Depression no longer affects me and as it happens I am very happy, in fact I have come out stronger and I am currently the happiest I have ever been. You see, despite the horrid difficulties that comes with PTSD, at this stage in my life I am achieving more happiness and opportunities than ever before. It is possible to go through the darkness and eventually see the light on the other side. None of this would have been possible without the tremendous support I received from my family, friends and voluntary sector.

Hearing Voices and Seeing Things

For years I was convinced that I could hear a female voice calling my name and asking if I was ok. It was really strange because even in my teenage years I was hearing these voices. It went beyond a phase of fear. Although I had thought about the possibility of being haunted (when I was young I didn't really have much understanding of mental health so it was not a possibility to me at the time, funnily enough being haunted seemed more plausible!) it had never really seemed possible, I just honestly thought I was going a little bit crazy.

Sometimes it was just a female voice and it always sounded really far away like she was calling from down stairs and other times she would sound like a person talking to me or standing right next to me. Although it freaked me out on more than a few occasions I am thankful for the fact that the voices never told me to do anything. It was just always mindless talking and sometimes questions.

"Stop that, now."

"No"

"Joely…"

"Help!"

As I got older, the sounds I heard developed from a female voice to multiple voices. I wouldn't hear the voices all the time. But often at times of stress and sometimes many times a day, but then very little for a few months.

I was about thirteen or fourteen when I started to hear voices quite often and really strange things would happen. I had a tendency to also hear door handles turn, knocking on doors, creaking floorboards and also a door opening-brushing across the carpet or wooden floor. Sometimes I even saw things. I would like to tell you about two minor occasions when I experienced these strange happenings.

Example 1

Once my brother was washing his car and I had the shock of my life when I saw, for a split second a big pool of blood dripping down his car. Before I could even stutter out an explanation of my jump of fright, I looked again, and BAM The blood was gone. It really scared me. For a split second seeing that blood made me honestly think my brother had seriously hurt himself. Even though it was all in my head and there was nothing actually wrong, the fear I felt was very real.

Example 2

I was lying on my bed reading a magazine. I was on my front facing away from the door. I was really calm and I don't recall being stressed, I mean it was the summer holidays – I was having a great time!
Suddenly, I heard my mum's voice calling from downstairs, saying

"Joely – Come here."

At first it sounded really far away but then a few seconds later she called again and it sounded closer so I started to move off my bed to face the door but was still reading my magazine I hadn't looked up yet – I was still captivated by an interesting article.
Then, I heard it again crying out the words

"Help."

I was very used to random cries of a sarcastic nature, so I did not move from my lying position. Then I heard louder, creaking floor boards outside my room. I paid no attention to it- I mean you don't pay attention to floorboards you just expect there to be someone outside, you don't instantly think there is a ghost or something outside your room. Then, I heard the distinctive creek and squeak of my door handle turning and then the sweeping noise of the door pushing against the carpet as it opened. I said

"Hi, what's up, Mum?"

I was still reading a particularly interesting story in the magazine – I still had not looked up. Then the creaking footsteps stopped at the side of my bed by the radiator (which is particularly creaky bit and very distinctive). It was only then that I look up from my magazine with a smile, I was fully expecting my mum to be there, so I was half way through saying

"What's up?"

when I looked up, I saw that there was no one there. My shock and fear came instantly; my heart was suddenly in my mouth. I shuffled back on my bed and looked at my closed door, suddenly I felt like I could not breathe, scared, really freaked out and confused. Why an earth did I just hear all of that stuff and there is no evidence of any of those noises being real? What's wrong with me? Am I going a little bit crazy? It sure felt it. I looked around in utter confusion and suddenly started feeling a chilling expression giving me goose bumps. That was all the creepiness I could handle. I jumped out of bed (on the other side of the bed because I did not want to run into a potential ghost- Honestly, how silly I was) and my goodness, did I run.

I really freaked out. I ran down stairs, to see my mum by the front door, I hastily asked my mum if she had called me and she shook her head

"No Joely I have only just got in"

The moment that she registered the look of sheer panic on my face and started to look concerned was when I realised I was alone in the house when it happened. She looked at me with a funny worried expression on her face, she calmly asked me,

"What's wrong Joely? What's happened?"

My mum could tell something was wrong and so I told her everything I had experienced. The words just tumbled out and months of weird experiences and hearing voices came flowing out of my mouth in a fifteen minute word frenzy.

This was the first time I had ever mentioned hearing voices, or sounds to my mum, so as you can imagine she was rather shocked. The next day she phoned for me to be seen by a psychiatric nurse. I'm really glad my mum made the appointment because I got the support I needed, thankfully. I had kept a few of these incidents to myself but I told her everything then.

I started seeing various specialists. Eventually therapy started to work- and for years I heard very little and was absolutely fine. I finally had peace of mind and it was a wonderful relief. I got told it was my past memories catching up with me, the things I was hearing were all real, but they happened a very long time ago. I was just reliving certain things I heard (or someone had said) in a very peculiar way. Apparently hearing these voices and reliving experiences like this is a completely normal reaction to an abnormal situation, as part of PTSD. My psychiatric nurse told me that the best thing I can do to help myself was to ignore them completely, distract myself and not think about them when they happen.

PTSD – Post Traumatic Stress Disorder

I used to live in the depths of despair with mental illnesses such as Post Traumatic Stress Disorder, anxiety and depression. Due to my PTSD I used to have flashbacks multiple times a day for years. I say 'used to live in the depths of despair' as although I still technically have PTSD, I have learnt to cope with it much better. Now I only get anxiety attacks and a few flashbacks here and there which is a vast improvement on before as I am no longer living in the 'depths of despair' with PTSD.

When my PTSD was bad many years ago, I struggled to cope effectively. The terror of flashbacks use to grip at my very soul as the memories intoxicated my dreams, depression would errode at my happiness and fear would crush my lust for life. That was how I used to be, now I still get flashbacks and 'bad days', and I suspect I always will because the trauma will never really go away, but I am learning to cope better and do things to make me feel happier every day, so it does not affect me the way it used to.

Trauma is not all about soldiers from war. The sad reality is that it can happen to anyone. It is in fact a very normal reaction to an abnormal situation.

Every day I used to get flashbacks, but it was hidden, because I was scared to let it show because there was always so much going on. I just didn't want to worry my family by revealing the extensive truth. One preventative was that my beautiful, strong, lovely and amazing in every way mother had cancer when my PTSD got really bad. I couldn't possibly stress her out with my problems; especially because I felt they were my fault and I was guilty (bad people are good at manipulating your thoughts and twisting your sense of reality so you feel guilty even though you have done nothing wrong). My worry was that it could have made her cancer worse. For that reason, I had been hiding behind a smile for far too long. Some people might think that because I act ok, I must be ok. Quite simply, that is all it is – an act. In reality I was far from ok, in a sense I felt like I needed to be brought back to life. At some point, after flashbacks, hearing things and hallucinations it felt like PTSD was controlling my life. Literally clawing at me from the inside of my heart and wrenching away my life, making the gloom of depression reign everyday on my very being.

It got so bad that I was seeing and experiencing things that weren't true (but I was, and still am, convinced that certain things did happen), my sense of reality was warped, and confusing me and after a while nothing seemed real. Whenever I was left alone in my house, even for a minute while my parents popped to the corner shop, I completely freaked out. I would hear things, see things, shadows would chase me (I believed shadows caused by people, out to get me), the darkness of fear engulfed me... and I would be convinced I was not alone. I was so scared... panic stricken does not cover it. It really was a case of 'fight' or 'flight' hormone, and my choice was 'flight' – run away and hide, and if necessary, fight for survival. I would tear through my house, bang into my bedroom, grab the nearest object to be used to defend myself against the intruder and hope for the best. When the fear of being found got too intense, I would sit and hide in my bedroom wardrobe or somewhere, sometimes on my rooftop, hunched over, rocking myself. If I was in a wardrobe, I would make my hanging clothes conceal my shaking body, head down, eyes closed, hoping there was no need for a battle this time. When I was hiding elsewhere, I would carry pillows with me, covering my head and my vital organs because I was convinced someone was in my house. Many times, in the middle of the night I had nightmares and woke believing they were real, a few times, I climbed out my bedroom window to hide somewhere safe while I dialled 999. Things were bad, I was often confusing realities with flashbacks, nightmares and hallucinations. I was in a dark, hell like place where no matter how hard I squinted down the long, never ending darkness of the tunnel; I could not see a glimpse of light to guide me through.

Thank goodness, I found the strength to tell my mum, because that led to receiving the support I desperately needed. Needles to say, I am not like this now, I am happy to inform you that I can be left alone now and (at worst) only have very minor panic attacks.

When you're in a terrible place, like this, it's easy to do nothing and hide away from the world, but, you have to do positive things, to help yourself because psychiatric help, (although brilliant) is not always enough. I found that if I couldn't make myself better, the least I could do was try and make life easier for other people, to ensure they don't suffer in hell like I did. I motivated myself to spend time volunteering. One way to help with feelings of depression is to bring back your lust for life, you can do this by building a friendship circle, confidence and doing something that is not for you, instead do something that helps others, it's very rewarding. Volunteering your time with local organisations is a great place to start- there are plenty of opportunities out there and once you start, with time, you'll notice a difference because suddenly there's more to your life than the pain and bad memories. You have got to make your life one you want to live. You have got to make yourself happy.

Flashbacks

What is a flashback – my interpretation
Flashbacks are when you relive (or remember) something really terrible and traumatic that has happened. Usually a flashback is combined with seeing things you saw when the traumatic event(s) happened. The experience is so real; you literally relive the event as if it was occurring again. You relive everything exactly as it happens the first time; you see, hear and smell the same things that were apparent during the original trauma.

Being 'stuck' in a flashback
Complex traumas that lead to severe flashbacks can cause the sufferer to become unable to distinguish between a flashback and reality. This is simply because the flashbacks make the victim genuinely believe they are re living that trauma all over again, no matter how much time has passed. So much so, that they could look around them and not see anything at all, only what they would have seen in the flashback (the original memory). From that point on, they are unreachable, except through hearing. If I was in a flashback this severe, someone with me, would gently call my name, and quietly remind me of where I am, making sure not to touch me, unless to protect me from myself. Sometimes it would work, and I could find myself back in reality again, other times I would be too consumed by a flashback to hear them at all, in which case I could relive the traumatic memory until the end. I could stay like that for hours. My flashbacks are not all like this, although they used to be, especially when I was at University. Nowadays, I get them when I'm stressed, talking or thinking about the past or trying to do too much at the same time. I just get flashes a few times a day, with voices, but they don't last long and then I'm back to normal again. It's ok now, it's bearable, and I won't let myself be afraid of life again, life's for living, even if it's a struggle, not for hiding and making things worse.

Some of you may read this and have the 'stiff upper lip' approach to life – There's no point crying over spilt milk, stop dwelling on the past or 'keep calm and carry on'. Maybe some people will read this and might think that all these problems are in the mind, which means I can control my problems and get over it... which is a theory that has been proven by researchers and scientist not always to be possible. This is because the 'mind over matter' approach only works once you are past the initial battle scar, once you can remember the traumatic event. However often, if the trauma is still too fresh (not a memory), 'moving on' is too dangerous and could create greater damage later on in life because you wouldn't have given your brain the time or effort to remember the painful chunks of memory.

If you Could See, What I Can See; You Would not Judge me

My research has shown that traumatic events don't immediately process as memories; instead they appear as flashes of detail here and there. This is why a lot of victims of trauma won't remember strings of events or the flow of what happened to them. The trauma is still too early to be processed by the brain. Until the person is emotionally capable of coping with such trauma, the trauma will remain a flashback (their brain is still in shock, if you like, and shock can last for a very long time if unsupported or nurtured). It is only when the person can cope with their ordeal that they will begin to remember the trauma, instead of experiencing flashbacks.

I would now like to tell you about one of my flashback experiences.

Manipulate

I had been at a party, and it got too much, too quickly. One second I was smiling with friends, relaxed, happy and laughing along to their joking, the next second my heart started to palpitate and my skin grew clammy. I was having the beginnings of a panic attack and I started to feel faint. I looked down at my hand, holding a cup of water, and noticed that I was visually shuddering, my hand shaking so badly that water was spilling violently over the edge of the cup. I looked up in a fresh wave of dizziness and the light strained my eyes. Thoughts started to come into my mind, memories I had no control over and I could feel my mind sliding and being drawn into the darkness and gloom that is a flashback... Suddenly dizziness swept through my very being, and pain, almighty pain seared through my head. The people surrounding me were fading into the light; their voices quiet, ethereal, like they were not real, not even there. Someone's hand had been on my shoulder, trying to see if I was ok, but it did not take long before I couldn't feel it. My chest became tight as if someone was pressing down on my lungs and I gasped out loud suddenly struggling for breath. Blinking wildly, the tiny whisper in my head spoke to me, and I became desperate to remain in control of my body and mind, thinking to myself 'please don't let this happen to me now... not here...' and then there was nothing but shrieks for help, screaming from my mind alone. Another surge of dizziness and pain and my eyes clamped shut as the voices (in my head – not real voices) started taking over my sense of hearing; screaming in my ear for help, drawing me in. In an instant, someone's hands were on my hips, my legs, holding me still, touching me, tickling me.... no, no, no, no. I shuddered away violently thrashing about... What's happening to me? I shrieked in my mind, desperate to try and get the sound to issue from my lips, but to no avail. I force my eyes open, desperate to try and seek out the reality, but all I could see is darkness, and shadows leaning over me, hurting me. It's not real; it in the past... says a tiny voice in my head that is partly overshadowed by the bellowing screech of my flashback... Confusion explodes within me... it's happening now... I can feel it, it must be happening now...no. I feel a sharp pang, stabbing at me, a stinging sensation and I wheeze out in pain, blaring out in terror, hammering out my fists and knees, franticly searching for a way out of this hellish nightmare. My heart beats on, as my voice struggles to be heard, my mouth is glued shut; and now I cannot move at all, I'm now paralyzed with terror. It is in the past Joely. None of this is real. My eyes flew open in terror, as I gulped down huge portions of air. This time, colours blink through my tears, and I realise where I am; I'm at a party, surrounded by friends, who are all staring at me. I start to wake, and I realise no one was touching me at all, as everyone had formed a very large circle around me, metres from me in all directions. I looked up at their jeering, confused faces, to find I had fallen on the floor, looking up at the faces, blinking laughing and swerving beside me. Why, were they laughing at me? They probably thought I was just drunk like everyone else. Silly fools; why would I put myself in such a position of danger like that? I barely drink alcohol so there must have been something wrong with me, but did they try and help? No. After struggling to stand upon my two quaking feet, and failing, finally I received a little aid from strangers who perhaps took pity upon my state of unease, graciously I accepted, even though I was frightened I could be overwhelmed by a flashback so easily at the touch of someones' hand. I stood up, wobbly and uncertain, anxious to get out of that situation to distract me from the trigger of a flashback, while I still knew what reality was. You see, once I become engulfed in flashbacks, I won't be able to recognise anything in reality, or my surroundings at all... I completely relive the flashbacks as if it were still happing. The flashback, becomes reality, it's hard to distinguish between the two sometimes.

In reality, I was at a party having a panic attack, followed by a flashback. Why? Well, it happened because the joke the people had been talking about had merely mentioned a word that triggers nasty memories for me (manipulate... It sends a cold shiver down my spine, it really does), and that was it... I had to get out before I got worse. There were people milling about everywhere, and everyone (apart from me) was drunk and I couldn't cope with the chaos that issued from every corner of that sensory mayhem place. I ran out the house, apologetically pushing people out the way as I did so, distracted from polite pleasantries to rid myself of that sense of alarm. Outside, the air was cold and it was pouring with rain, and I looked up at the night sky, with tears mixing in with the fat rain drops that were beating down onto my upturned face. Someone was still screaming in my ears from the flashback, trying to draw me back in, and pain still roared through my system. I cried loudly into the chill of night air. My breath came out in clouds of swishing beauty and I outstretched my arms and twirled round; watching the raindrops beat upon my face and swirl round in encircling patterns of speckled delight, closing my eyes to the twirling lights in the clouded night sky. I stopped spinning, and opened my eyes and found my gaze had fallen upon a tree. I looked into the tree and saw two birds sitting on a branch, high up above, looking at each other, and tweeting. I took a deep breath, and counted to ten, and looked down at my wristbands, trying to remind myself of my happy realities. I looked back at the birds again, and noticed how sleek and shiny their feathers were, they were soaking from the rain and still tweeting their beautiful songs, with such passion that I felt a swell of beauty surge within me. I smiled despite myself; this is my reality right here, in the pouring rain, looking at these beautiful creatures sing to one another. A wish to sing along stirred from deep within my heart, and I smiled and sang random notes, out loud. It was a momentary relief of happiness, and it cheered me up a treat, to release my angst in a positive way. No matter what you have to do, to enjoy the little things – do it, to keep you smiling, to keep you happy, to keep you sane.

I'm NOT a victim

After a while, I realised that I don't want to play the victim anymore, I wanted to be the winner, the survivor. I wanted to be the person people look at and feel inspired by what I have been through, and how I have come through stronger and happier than ever before. I want them to smile at my achievements rather than feel horrified at how my experiences have negatively shaped me to become very unhappy. I decided to not let PTSD control me.

I got past the stage of needing the reassurance that the things that have happened were wrong. Once I learnt to accept the bad and focus on the good, I realised that I was not guilty and the relief of knowing this, made me stronger than ever. Once you get past that stage you are closer to recovery than it would ever seem possible. That is how I got better – by choosing to get better.

The trauma is not all gone, but I am happy... the happiest I have ever been. I chose to fight my mental illness and not to let it take over my life. I chose to give my life purpose and give myself a reason to wake up every morning. Sure, the traumas are still there, the memories still upsets me, but I'm no longer scared by my memories; they no longer effects me the way it once did.

How to Cope with Flashbacks

Below is a list of the things that helped me cope with my flashbacks. If you are experiencing flashbacks they may help you as well.

1. Carry something you like with you at all time, to serve as a reminder of the good things in your life. These are called 'grounders' as they keep you grounded in the real world – away from the flashback.
    I have Glastonbury wristbands. When I look at my wrist bands, I am instantly reminded of happier and brilliant memories.

2. Talk to yourself if you have to, tell yourself a funny story, make it up on the spot. I made one story up the other day about an Inca palace and its rich temples and flowing waterfalls. Make sure the story is different to the situation you are in.

3. Sing (or whisper) a catchy tune, out loud, despite the looks you get from onlookers.

4. Think about a project you are doing, whether it is a school project, a fundraising event or your specialist subject. This should distract you with thoughts of how you can help others.

5. If you need to cry, cry. Don't let anyone tell you it makes you weak. Crying DOES NOT make you weak, crying is a sign of being strong for too long.

6. Slowly count to one hundred, try and only think of the numbers, picture the numbers as you count, it may help as time goes on

7. Talk to your family, friends and Doctors, get help, if necessary the Police.

8. Escape – and enjoy the little things.

Gaslighting – Autism

One evening, it all got too much. The darkness was menacing me, my zombie brain felt fried, nothing made sense, and the self doubt and self loathing was making me chew my nails with self destructive anxiety. What happened? I realised that my memories didn't add up, that what I thought was true, was actually wrong, incorrect... I realised that I felt insane, which made me feel ridiculous; Of course I'm not insane (which is what all insane people say). Besides, isn't insanity for people in the movies? No, there must be something wrong with me. I panicked, and so I finally reached out for help.

I messaged a family member; gasping for air, worried I was spiralling out of control, fingers trembling on the keyboard, desperately asking "Am I a bad person? What is wrong with me?" Finally, after a long pause that made me re consider my entire existence, I finally received a very unexpected response...

> "Joely, no. Someone's gaslighting you. It's not you, it's totally them. They are controlling you. They are making you feel this way. You are brilliant; don't you ever give up on yourself."

I read it, again and again, tears confusing my eyes, and the more we chatted the more reality slowly sunk in... and I begun to listen, I slowly started to believe my them. Then came the terrifying first step; understanding and admittance.

"... What an earth is gaslighting? Am I on fire?"

I had thought to myself, as I sat there trembling within the furry confines of my soft blanket. Figuratively, yes I was on fire. I felt like I was burning, and my home of familiar memories and fondness of myself, had crashed down around me in a blazing, painful fire. Nothing felt safe or real, nothing made sense, until all that was left was the fiery remains of my muddled mind, crashed down in smoky debris around me. Realising what Gaslighting was, and admitting it happened, and that it wasn't my fault, begun a long and difficult journey of self discovery. Learning to establish who I am as a person, and an activist, and work out how I had been transformed from a happy fairy, to a numb depressed 'selfish' zombie; by this gaslighting zombie virus (not literally). Gaslighting, mate crime and bullying are serious offences, often punishable by law; so why did it take so long for me to realise that I wasn't in the wrong... How did I not understand that this zombie shell I had grown so accustomed to, was simply a (non literal) virus plaguing me, due to gaslighting and abuse? Well, let me try to share some insight, you see, now that I have survived the zombie plague and my zombie shell of self-doubt has fallen away, I have suddenly been enabled to see clearer than ever before.

According to google, the definition of 'Gaslighting' is 'to manipulate (someone) by psychological means into doubting their own sanity.'

When I was being Gaslighted, my judgement was clouded; making me believe negative and horrible things that were not true, about me, and my family. Gaslighting infected my brain with twisted theories to alter my memories of what had actually happened, making me see the abuse, bullying or gaslighting to be ok, to be a correct result of me being stupid, incapable or selfish. Which of course, I can see now, that it wasn't ok at all. I had done nothing wrong, nor my family and friends; but the gaslighting makes you believe negativity, until all of your own self worth and confidence in yourself has dropped so low that you don't even question someone when they tell you that they had to be cruel to you, because you are 'too difficult for a normal person to deal with'. Also that what you thought you understood was wrong, and they were right. They change your perceptions on right and wrong, they purposely highlight your difficulties and then do things which they know would confuse or have a phycological impact. I shall write some examples now, but please note, that none of the below examples are 'true', these examples are not my experiences and have not happened to me (similar, but un related things have happened though), I just like to create a clear picture, when I write.

For example, someone who is gaslighting you may lie to you; perhaps stealing your money, and then while you are frightfully searching through your belongings, they would say something like

A. "I can't believe you lost your money? Again?! You are useless. You shouldn't be trusted with anything. Good job I'm here to help you, eh?"

Or another example, they could convince you that something you thought to be true (and is true) was wrong, it can start off small, with things like

B. "Don't be daft, of course the homework is due in for Thursday. Weren't you listening? Good job I'm here, eh? But Seriously Joely, you need to get your head checked out!"

When for example, in actual fact, the homework was due in on Monday, and even though you could have written the homework into your diary, self-doubt would eventually, make you feel like you somehow did something wrong, to end up with the wrong information. Not only that, but you believe that the people gaslighting or abusing you, are doing you a favour, or even helping you, when this is rarely the truth.

Another example of someone gaslighting you is their denial in the face on confrontation.

C. "I didn't say that to you, Joely. Why would I say or do any of these things? I'm trying to help you. You are going nuts, again. You just need to start listening more. You are pathetic making silly accusations that you obviously don't have the potential to understand. I know your Aspergers makes you a bit daft sometimes, but stop taking it out on me. Honestly, it's really annoying and upsetting when you do this to me, after all I have done to help you…"
When confronted, they would make excuses that confuse, trick you, or make you feel guilty, turning the accusation onto you. With all that psychological

manipulation, they would appear so calm and reasonable, for instance, not shouting. This would make you believe that the problem is you even more, and that you are over reacting or insane for believing things that aren't true.

So yes, it starts off small, but it can grow, to making you believe that different things have or haven't happened. For example

D. "Babe, did you not realise you called me? You totally did. It was really late, you sounded asleep. I'm so embarrassed for you, you were babbling on about your little secret... Gosh do you really not remember? That's crazy!" and you would be thinking, what secret? When? How? Because, low and behold, there was no phone call, and definitely no secret. They manage to convince you that you must have been half asleep, and you both agree that it was just a mental lapse on your behalf, and you end up laughing about it. Yet that niggling doubt still frustrates you; after all, why would your friend lie about this? Answer: to gain control of you.

E. "No, you are wrong. That didn't happen, you are so daft. No, what actually happened is that you were going crazy, screaming, shouting, waving your arms around like a phyco which was like totally embarrassing, and then I asked you to stop nicely, and then you pushed me away, and then I slapped you really lightly on your hand. I had to help you! I had to shock you out of your manic behaviour somehow!"

In this example (do remember these are all examples, and not my actual experiences) At first, you could recall having an meltdown and trying to calm yourself, you could not remember pushing (because you didn't) and you could feel the stinging sensation on your cheek, but if they say they slapped your hand, then you begin to believe them. It becomes you who is crazy for remembering events wrongly. It changes your perceptions, so that you doubt yourself as a person. You end up believing that you were in the wrong for acting out and starting a fight, not them, and especially that they reacted in a reasonable manner; you deserved that light slap on the hand.

It was such a slow process, that I can't even recall when I started to feel bad, when my memories started to change and when I started to become a Zombie. Gas lighting is a terrible, traumatic thing, and yet I hadn't even realised I was being gaslighted, or even what gaslighting was, until years later.

My Mental Health was affected, My PTSD, my depression, everything. I didn't feel human. I was a Zombie, plagued with a brain that was wired wrong, and human memories that were not my own, incapable of anything humane or human related skills. I was a zombie, and therefore, I was wrong.

Who can gaslight?

Here it gets a little more complicated to understand. As I learnt more and more about this fascinating subject, I found that it is actually very common for those on the spectrum to be victims of gaslighting; although they are not always gaslighted by bad people, or even intentionally. This is because like me, people with disabilities on the Autistic Spectrum face many hidden challenges that the majority of people don't understand and can't compare, and often because they don't understand Autism experiences, and the Autism experiences is not the 'norm' (to them) they tell us that our experiences, are either not real, are exaggerated or can't even be possible. This changes our own perceptions of our life, in similar ways to the examples I was describing earlier. Simply because they have no understanding of a reality different to theirs (and people say we with Autism disabilities have no theory of mind!).

Having Asperger's Syndrome, has actually felt like a lot of people, anyone from Doctors, Teachers, Friends, and other professionals are unintentionally gaslighting me. The truth is, it's not just bad people that gaslight; because many who are trying to help us, and don't have any understanding, un intentionally gaslight us, and make us believe things that are not true, for us.

I'm sure some of you can understand when I say that experiencing life when you have Autism is different to those without the disability. This is because of many of our hidden hardships. Our sensory perceptions for example are different, we notice details that others do not, we are over sensitive to textures, lights, taste etc. We get told that it's not possible to be so sensitive, to stop complaining about labels in clothes, because the average person does not have this difficulty. It makes us the problem, making us believe there is something wrong with us, for feeling this way. In this way, gaslighting can be anything from being told not to be so literal, to listen, to focus, to try more, to be more empathetic, to stop behaving so bad, or that your experiences or feelings are not real or necessary, when your reality means you are not doing anything wrong, nor are you able to change in the manner that they expect you too. Some quotes that spring to mind are along the lines of:

"Joely, the light is not even flickering that much, how can your eyes possibly hurt?! Stop complaining about something that is not even an issue"

"Oh don't be daft; the walls are not moving. It's just your mind playing tricks on you."

"Stop being so naughty! Just calm down, there is no reason for you to behaving in this ridiculous manner" (when in the midst of overloads, meltdowns or shutdowns – which of course, is not my fault).

As a result, we on the spectrum, spend our entire lives believing that there is something wrong with us and that we need to be corrected. The psychological effects do have an alarming impact on sense of self and mental health. If anyone is told, or taught, negativity in this way, especially that what they experience every day, is either wrong, or isn't real, they will likely start to suffer from the psychological affects, too. So actually I believe this is a form of gaslighting, no matter how unintentional it may be.

As a result, of gaslighting, I have doubted myself, constantly believing that there was something wrong and that I needed to be normal, when of course I didn't. I began to believe that I was insane, for feeling things and seeing life in a way that were not 'real' to the average person. I recall writing to my friends on a separate occasion, explaining how I needed to be put in a straight jacket in a padded room and left alone, forever. I believed that nothing I understood would be right, I believed that my memories were twisted and wrong, and that I was wrong, because I was selfish for not trying, for not behaving, for not being able to concentrate. I was wrong, simply for being me.

My perception of gaslighting, may be different to other peoples, but I believe that people on the Spectrum are particularly vulnerable to this type of abuse, simply because of the way our disability affects us. This is because I am on the Autistic Spectrum, I do take things literally, I do believe that everyone tells the truth and my theory of mind does mean that I don't always realize that other people have different knowledge to me, therefore they don't understand my hidden hardships and my disability like I do. I don't always make connections that as a result, people could mislead, manipulate, or express their wrong or incorrect thoughts; my understanding of my surroundings does not allow me to realize that other people, also, can misunderstand and spread incorrect information as a result. Therefore impacting how I understand the world and myself from listening to, and believing them. In a world where everything is black and white, there is no in-between, so we believe everything in which we are told, as part of how we develop and process information. Unfortunately, as much as a disability can be full of quirks and positives, it can make us vulnerable too.

I've believed all the people in my life, who tell me what my reality should be. For example, people who say things like

"You should be able to work; you are not even that disabled, really. You have all this time off, why don't you do something constructive and earn some money? Stop relying on everyone else. It's not good for you"

Professionals who have told me that that it's not possible for my body and mental abilities to stop physically working when I am under too much stress. To them, it's all in my head (and therefore easily overcome- how wrong a perception!), and they have started making me believe it, no matter how these shutdowns affect me. People who scold me for not liking new showers, with different water flow gages because the water feels like needles. That's not normal; I must be mad, right? Wrong. Just because other people don't understand my daily experiences, or the realities of life on the spectrum, doesn't mean I am doing anything wrong, or that I am 'faking' or 'exaggerating' it. It certainly does not make me insane. It's hard to survive with positivity in a world where everyone tells you what is right and what is wrong, and that usually, you are wrong, or need to be corrected to fit in with 'normal' people. As a result, I became controlled, desperately seeking 'correction' and for me to finally be in the right, or the norm. I would try and stop myself from appearing Autistic; I know, how sad is that? I was obsessively controlling my behaviors, like stimming, or rocking, and making myself stim by doing something less obvious, so I would be more likely to be perceived as 'correct' and not Autistic. I would force myself to look someone in the eye during conversations, even though it made the rest of my usual abilities completely useless, as I could not concentrate on my surroundings or what the person was saying, because I was too busy desperately trying to maintain eye contact. All so that I could possibly be perceived as normal, so I can finally be 'correct' like I was always being told I should be. I had meltdowns in private, giving me shutdowns of my usual abilities, making me more disabled than I could be if I was simply allowed, and enabled, to live the way I needed to (having meltdowns in public rather than stretching myself so thinly and becoming worse off much later). I would stare at my pitiful, tearful reflection in the mirror, with tense stimming hands, and whisper "Stop it! Stop reacting like some sort of freak. No one else is... You are wrong. Be more normal." I scolded myself for seeing and experiencing the world in the wrong and incorrect manner.

I know it sounds odd, but the more you are gaslighted, whether it be intentional or not, the more you turn on yourself, and start gaslighting yourself. I would shame myself, for being wrong all the time, for behaving badly, for never understanding the truth in my realities. I would shun myself for behaving ridiculously, and reacting extremely to situations that shouldn't matter, literally crying over spilt milk. I tried so hard to be correct, be like other people, to understand the ways of the world and people, the right way. But I wouldn't succeed, I wasn't trying hard enough... Or as I understand now, I couldn't measure up to these impossible odds, no matter how hard I tried. In the end, gaslighting changed me, and my perceptions of myself, depression caught up with me, and I hated myself, simply for being me.

Advice

To try and avoid unintentionally gaslighting someone, you first have to it least try to understand the hidden hardships of Autism / diversity, and try not to judge or compare. Every two individuals with Autism, or Aspergers, will display very differently. Just because one seems to 'function' better than the other, does not mean they have less of a disability, so try to avoid making them feel like they are 'faking' or have something to prove. It may seem like a compliment, but it is not, because life with a disability is hard no matter how you display. For me, it seems like I am always fighting to remind people that just because I present quite normally, does not mean my disability does not affect every second of my life, just like for others on the spectrum. It does not mean I do not need much support, because the truth is I need 121 care in pretty much every aspect of my life. My disability is my reality, not yours, and other peoples disabilities are their reality, and not mine, so we all need to try not to judge or compare disabilities or diversity, because that is how unintentional gaslighting begins.

Try to avoid

- Presuming anything about capeability or hidden hardships
- Do not express your thoughts on how incapeable they are; if someone believes they can not do something, they will become unable to do

something, this is part of something called the 'self fulfilling prophecy'

- Doing everything for them and thus, teaching learnt helplessness, learn to strike the balance so the person you are helping does not feel useless or worthless, or that they have no say in their surroundings
- Telling them off for misunderstanding, when it may not have been their fault
- Pushing your experiences of normality onto other people, because we all experience life in a different way. What reality is to me, is completely different to how your reality is.
- Telling people how they must be mad, or wrong for showing diversity to you, for working out problems differently, or having thought processes that differ to you

Managing my Stress

As a child I found it difficult to cope with any type of change (a common trait of Asperger's). So much so, that my parents had to plan each new event very carefully, so that my stress levels were minimised. Below is a story about how my parents tried to manage my stress levels.

As a young child I was pretty good at swimming and would always win all the awards at school with ease. Consequently, I was picked to swim for Dorset Youth Games. My parents were worried about how I would cope with a changed routine and the stress of competing. For these reasons, they did not tell me I had been selected, they instead told me that I was going for a normal swim.

We got to this swimming venue which was hours away. I thought nothing of it as we were always travelling up and down the country for my sister's swimming events. I just assumed we were there for my sister to swim because she was constantly in really important swimming competitions swimming for South West England. She's amazing like that; my sister has always been my biggest inspiration.
We got pool side and then I got told to go and get changed into my swimming gear so I could have a swim if I wanted. Literally, this is what happened, my mum asked me

"If you want Joely, you can swim two lengths now?"

I said yes because I adored swimming (still do). I did not think twice as to why I had to wait for everyone else to get in the pool, or why I then had to wait for a loud beep until I could start swimming. Please remember I was only seven years old and always did as I was told.

No one told me I was in a race for Dorset, I just got told to wait for the loud beep and then to swim to the other side of the pool and back. My mum even checked if it would be a horn, a gun, someone saying "ready steady GO." or a whistle" to make sure I started swimming at the right time.

I started the race late because the beep signalling the beginning of the race made me jump, I started swimming a few seconds later when everyone was frantically ushering me to start swimming. So I swam to the end of the pool and back at my usual leisurely pace – as fast as I could! Even though I did not know it was a race I was not half competitive and I wanted to beat the boy next to me. I did beat him too!

I won a silver medal; the other taller and older guy who had trained for this (I didn't), beat me by a split second (literally), so I like to think if I had started when everyone else had I would have won. Cheeky, I know.

I am not a bad loser, honest.

Why did no one tell me about the race?
No one told me because in all honesty I would have completely freaked out and would not have been able to race at all. I did not handle unexpected stresses well back then.

All in all though my family made the right decision that time because the experience was brilliant and I did really well – had I known about it I would have been stressed and unable to compete at my best standard (if any standard at all). It worked well all round. You might think it's strange that I did not know about something so important, but on this occasion it really was for the best.

Stress Diary, Things That Make me Smile

When my eyes swell red, and stress seems to be the only path for me to take; in my moment of madness, I stumble and fall, desperate to get back up, but uncertain of how to. Sometimes things are so desperate, so hectic just so bad, that I feel I really can't think of any good at all. In times like this, I take comfort from the little things in life that can offer me even the slightest of smiles. Search for the beauty in your surroundings. I shall search until I find a reason to replace my tear stained face with a memorable fond smile. As my family has advised me, I keep a diary of all nice things that put even a momentary smile on my face. Sadness and stress is a long trodden path; delicate with unease, the route of sadness and stress winds on, restless, complex, until it falters and stops, thankfully picked apart by gaping holes of light, pouring in to enlighten my smile with happy memories. I linger not for a hasty retreat. I know memories make me stronger; I am no longer left weak, shuddering in the pale speckled light of night. I have to make myself see well in every situation. If you and I think about the negatives all the time, we are going to be sad, but if we force ourselves to think of some positives, no matter how small, it can really help in the short and long run. Sometimes, it's a case of 'mind over matter', as my nana would say.

Diary entry 1:
In times of displeasure, I take a stroll along the beach, because that is where I feel most at ease;

where seagulls shriek high up above the sea and sandy dunes. Where surf rolls in, crashing with white waters frantic waves. Almost instantly, my mind become at ease. I look at the foot and paw prints of animals in the stippled sandy mounds and notice with a sweet acknowledgement that the golden sands rest with not just the expected golden sandy colour but within each dip lies a shadow; dark and inviting. Yet on one side of the tiny footprint there is a blue shadow, beautiful and bright and bright like electricity while on the other side the sand is golden and yellow, beautiful and soft, as you would expect it to be. To see the golden yellow sand, with dapples of cool calming electric blue colours created by shadows from the early morning glow. It put a smile on my face because such a sight is a rarity, an unexpected beauty. I smile despite myself, I feel better already due to that simple pleasure.

Diary entry 2:
As I walk, I glimpse a thing of splendour, delicate, sad, but ultimately beautiful. It was for me a wondrous, yet insignificant sight. In the distance, I see a quaint chocolate wrapper. Sighing with life and fluttering, swirling its edges in the gentle breeze. I watch the wrapper dance. Despite how sad it is to see that someone has thrown a wrapper on the road to pollute the environment and do the world no good, I remind myself that I can always pick it up, and put it in the bin (unless its recyclable). I gaze as the wrapper pirouettes down towards me, sometimes fast, energetic, other times slow and gradual as the last wisps of wind picks up its tail end. It arrives at my side, and I walk and I run, along with the wrapper, I glide. I find myself dancing, alongside the wrapper, joyously with the winds striking tide. Admittedly whenever I see rubbish fluttering in the winds, it upsets me, but then cheers me up once I watch its dance sequence. I am reminded that I should always put the wrapper in the bin, do my bit for the planet earth. Above all, the sheer concept of something that ultimately has no life, to show a swaying breath of life like that, to be able to dance, and swish with kinetic energy is simply fascinating to me. This is something that cheers me up, despite being really quite worthless. The concept of what makes one's life, alive, is something that truly captivates me with intrigued curiosity. The thought that anything, no matter how lifeless, can have a joyous moment of beauty, a stir and sigh of life, movement, is heart

warming to me; it reminds me that even in dull or nasty times in life, there is a moment or two awaiting us all, of pure happy bliss. As even something with no life at all, such as a chocolate wrapper, has a chance of flying excitement when the wind comes along and sweeps it out of the rubbish bin. Contented times await us all, that remind us what life is really about, happiness, acceptance, understanding, love and support. This is something that lightens my mood on a dreary stressful day. Simply seeing a chocolate wrapper, fluttering within the breeze, or a plastic bag flying the streets, reminds me of that concept.

Diary entry 3:

I am in my room crying out in pure desperation, from the early morning stress taking over. Tears dart across my cheeks, stinging and draining my cheek of colour. I wipe away a tear and decide to try and cheer myself up, I was fed up with feeling sorry for myself, I won't make myself feel better if I just sit around crying, will I? If I let myself cry like that or think negatively like that for ages, I would never be happy. I stand up, put some music on my C.D player, and become frustrated with the machine that would not work. Sighing in frustrated annoyance, I reach over to my curtains to open them, hoping for some light so I could see the buttons on the C.D player properly. For a split second, I was dazzled by streaks of light filtered through the gap in the curtain. Distracted now, I watched mesmerised, as thousands of tiny specks floated in the air around me, only visible in the blinding light sifting through the curtains. Dust particles that were so tiny, danced and flew about, whirling in glory, creating patterns, free, delicate, streaking in swirling fashions of white. As I watched, I fixed on one tiny dust particle, and watched as it bounced and splayed about, spinning, rotating, gracefully flying and bumping into other specks, and suddenly it neared the edge of the light streak and it disappeared entirely. I smiled and opened the curtain all the way so my entire room was filled with light and dancing particles. Maybe, I thought to myself as I became captivated with the whole room's dancing sequence, just maybe, I should open the windows and do some dusting. This cheered me up a great deal, I like dusting; if I wear a mask I can dust and watch dust clouds develop in the atmosphere, it's one of life fascinatingly boring jobs.

Diary entry 4:

I was swimming in the sea with my dad, and he says to me as he is doing breast stroke;

> "I'm not saying I'm overweight, but I can't move... my belly is beached
> on the sand!"

We were laughing for ages; it really tickled me and cheered me up. In his defence it was shallow water, and my knee kept hitting the sand, but still, the thought of someone swimming and getting beached upon the sand, was quite hilarious to me.

Diary entry 5:

Driving home from a distressing incident one day, we took a long route through the countryside with ACDC blaring on the radio. All around me there were miles of rolling hills and luscious grass, and yet I still could not bring myself to appreciate the beauty of my surroundings. I was too shocked by my last ordeal. It was a baking hot day, stress levels were high, and tears were sliding down my face in unwelcome quiet shock. I tried my best to hide the tears from the driver but I think even he knew something had happened but could not bring himself to ask. I felt the need to cover up and slowly wiping tears away with my sleeve, too scared to make any sudden movements as if the driver found out and saw me hiding the tears, oh the trouble I would be in later. I looked up momentarily to catch my reflection in the window, just to check if I had red eyes or any swellings, and then through the window, from a distance I caught a glimpse of the most marvellous of things. Distracted now, I gaze beyond the car up ahead, and saw a huge herd of magnificent horses, galloping across the road, clouds of dust swirling from their hooves, fast, powerful and majestic. I watched, intrigued from their majesty, as they galloped away, under a tree offering brief shadowed shelter before they sprinted off into the harsh heat of the light. As I watched, I saw how their coats gleamed in shabby extravagance, how their tails whooshed and swept behind them. Momentarily forgetting about my tears, and even the experience of why I had been crying, I leaned out to get a better look. I soon saw what the horses were rushing towards; a glistening lake which was just off to my right, with shimmering waters sparkling and gleaming with magical inviting intrigue, providing the sweet promise of refreshing relief from thirst. I learnt further forward in my seat as we drove closer, my mind at ease, distracted, and feeling much better. I was now excited to witness the horses grand, splashing entrance to the cold waters. The road I was travelling upon had turned and we drove towards the lake they were heading for, and now we were just metres away. Now closer, I could see much more detail. They gallop onwards, faster, bashing, bumbling and rocking their necks from side to side in their haste, their beautifully unkept hair swinging from side to side. One horse distinctly leading the pack, runs tall, unafraid, with a coat of gleaming brown, dappled with white, strength shining through the bent legs. As the leading horse's hooves met the shallows of water, even from a distance I could see tiny spots of water fly up into the air. Droplets in their thousands, were throwing themselves high, around the horses legs, rainbow colours catching the light in the miniscule seconds of their flight. The force of the gallop onwards caused the glistening water to stream back, against their legs, now in larger, more defined water splashes. As the waves and splashes swept back, the other horses ran in behind and the water at their hooves, swept in swirling beauty. Before long, the entire herd had splashed in chaotic magnificence into the shocked tumbling waters. As they slowed, the water rippled to a slow gradual pace and the reflections dancing and combining with the blue skies mottled together with exquisite colours. The horses were now trotting lazily around in the brilliance of the cold waters, and I smiled; it cheered me up a treat. I felt so privileged to see this act of nature, one of its most natural, the need to cool down and have a cool sip of water, on a stressful hot day.

So there you have it, my little diary of all things that cheer me up for a while. Whenever you feel sad or stressed, maybe you should also consider creating your very own stress reliever diary.

Anxiety

I am going to write about anxiety because people with Asperger's are more prone to anxiety related disorders than those without. I'm no expert on this topic but I do believe I know a fair bit about it because of my own experiences. I just hope that my personal insight into this topic can help somehow.

Someone once said to me many years ago

"I know it's tough, but try not to get too bogged down by everything"

Oh what a funny one, I definitely took that one literally. After hearing 'don't get bogged down', in my mind's eye, I was suddenly wading through a boggy marsh land, tumbling deeper into sinking mud, surrounded by trees and boggy marsh land. It sounded to me like 'don't sink in the boggy marshland'. Not, what the person meant, of course.

Luckily for me, I swiftly realised it had absolutely nothing to do with wading through a bog. The person actually meant 'try not to let bad thoughts make you sad'.

If only they had said that the first time, eh?

My friend was trying to help, but the language easily confused me and it proved unhelpful. Even if they had used appropriate language by saying "Try not to let the bad things make you sad" it still would have proved difficult as you can't easily control your emotions. It is a common opinion that people with anxiety can 'get over' their anxiety and stop worrying so much. Unfortunately, anxiety is a complex disorder and can affect different people in very different ways. For this reason simply 'not worrying' is not possible or going to fix the problem.

What is Anxiety?

A small reminder, I am not an expert on such a topic, I write from personal experience, and experience only. My understanding is that a person with anxiety may worry so much over things that are deemed as improbable, that it affects their daily lives. I believe anxiety can prevent people from carrying out normal day to day activities, such as working, attending a school or going out to meet friends. There is so much stress and worry involved with every tiny thought process, that anxiety swiftly turns to panic attacks, where the cold start of horror can claim you at any moment, and leave you a quaking, crying, shivering mess in the wake of your worries.

So what can cause Anxiety?

I believe anxiety starts from many different things. Sometimes the stem of anxiety (the stem meaning the point in which it/anxiety began) can come out of nowhere, people with a loving family, lots of support etc. Most commonly, anxiety has its roots in various traumatic events (This could include abuse, emotional negligence, bereavement, loss of job / income, car crash or other people doing bad things to that person or someone they know). They could simply have watched something terrible that has happened on the news on television and then got anxious that it may happen to them.

What is my Anxiety like?

I am very aware of how little life skills I have, and how much support I need hourly from my family. This makes me stressed at the best of times because I feel as if I can't achieve my dreams without someone there constantly to help me. I wonder, how am I supposed to travel the world and volunteer abroad ... how am I supposed to achieve my dreams, if I can't even answer the front door to a stranger or walk to the corner shop to buy lunch? This makes me feel unable to do things for myself so I try to over compensate by worrying and thinking about things that can happen and what I need to do to help. I do this as a preventative and learning strategy to make things better, but it does not always work, of course, hence the reason why panic attacks often occur.

When I get stressed about things, I'm constantly going over the 'what if' statements in my head. Such as – What if I got robbed? What if I got lost? What if someone beats me up in the street? What if something really terrible happens to me or someone else? What do I do then?

I think of these 'what if' statements to try and work out a plan of action and risk assessment of what to do in the event of any of these 'what if' statements happening, even though they seldom do. In an attempt to keep myself and others safer, it is designed to make me feel better but it does not always do the trick. However the stress of what could happen to me really freaks me out even if I don't always feel it, and thinking about all of these things affects me in horrid ways.

Symptoms of my Anxiety
1. I get so shaky that I can hardly stand
2. I suddenly experience a lot of pain, back, legs, tummy, head, toes... everything begins to hurt a lot
3. I become even less capable of problem solving, usually resulting in meltdowns
4. I get heart palpitations
5. I suddenly feel hot or too cold usually resulting in severe itchiness and discomfort
6. Everything seems louder, brighter and more disturbing to process than usual

'Getting over' Anxiety

To outsiders it may appear like the person with the anxiety disorder is worrying over nothing and that they need to just 'get over it'. This is important because quite simply, they can't just 'get over it', they certainly won't 'get over it' with rubbish support from their peers like that. People with anxiety need help because coping with it is very difficult and really affects one's ability to carry out day to day tasks.

The only way the person with anxiety can learn to deal with the symptoms is if they have the correct support and help that they need. This would include visiting a G.P. to discuss feelings and symptoms. Sometimes therapy, medication or counselling or a combination could be prescribed. It all depends on the individual and their personal anxiety, there is no cure that suits all.
Of course strength from within is vital too, which I believe everyone has, even if it does not feel like it all the time.

Anxiety and Connecting the Dots

From experience of working with Autistic individuals, I have noticed that it is very common for children and teenagers with Autism to ask endless questions, (if they can, I mean) in times of Anxiety, and that sometimes, this can increase levels of Anxiety. "Why is that?" you ponder to yourself, well let me answer this rather fascinating question. But first here are some examples.

"But why ..."
"How do I..."
"When do I..."
"What does that mean..."

To clarify, these children are trying to cope in a world of constant chaos and change – they are not being naughty. These questions are very important to us as Autistic people, and they do serve purpose. When we are trying to find reason within a world that just does not make sense with illogical demands and tiresome rules, Autistic people search for understanding through endless questions. For instance, why do we need to put our hand up in class, to ask a question? Why do we need to eat with our mouths closed? Why can't I put my elbows on the table? Why am I expected to shake a stranger's hand, when there's no reason to touch any other part of their body? Or, Why do I have to put my shoes on to go outside, it's not even raining? These little rules, that we are all expected to do, are all a part of acceptable social normality's, even though there is no logical purpose to a lot of these rules (that make immediate sense to someone with Autism). When those with Autism are asked to do anything, no matter how little or well practiced, it represents a big pressure that something out of their control will go wrong, and they may be become exposed to ridicule. In this way, children and teenagers on the spectrum are confused, and equally frustrated, in their attempts to overcome their challenges by trying to learn from more information, in a desperate attempt to control what they don't yet understand.

Children with Autism need information, and lots of it, in order to process and understand the reasons behind the confusing or illogical demands of their daily lives; to answer the questions and make sense of the things, that others, wouldn't even have to think about. Such information would preferably be broken down into easy chunks. Those with Autism also require justice and understanding to try and connect the dots, and make the connections that most people don't even think about. Doubt is a major factor in those with Autism developing anxiety and depression. With all of these questions, and the desperate necessity to learn from more data, comes the adrenalin, the sheer bubbling panic at not understanding or worrying that you might do something wrong; especially when you don't receive sufficient explanation or support from those around you. People not answering questions is beyond frustrating and can be a cause of anxiety and panic attacks, because when you are fighting to understand your surroundings, and your place and what you need to do, nothing is scarier than not understanding, change or not being included.

There is also the slight complication, that thanks to Autism, and it's many hidden hardships, despite the necessity of needing more information to learn and cope with life, those with Autism can also become over loaded, and suffer from anxiety anyway. It's a vicious circle. If the person with Autism is already suffering with overloads or changes, then they are not going to be able to understand the information given to them in a way that can help them find the connections they desperately seek; this also turns against them, making them feel like they are failing, for reasons beyond their control, in turn anxiety and self doubt increases, damaging mental health and their sense of self. This does make it very difficult to help someone with Autism who is always seeking answers, but can't always cope with the information given to them. Its unhelpful to say things like

"Just stop talking"
"You won't feel better if you do that, calm down"
"Why are you so stressed? There is no need"

This is because, true to un intentional gaslighting, saying things like this is actually really counter-productive. I understand how sometimes constant questions, can be frustrating to those caring for them, I have seen many people who have just responded with a roll of their eyes "Just do it; because I told you so". Do you see the problem with this reply? It belittles, and gives no information; it certainly does not answer the questions, it makes us feel that our worries are being trivialized and that we are foolish to have questions that are not 'important'.

People say that we with Autism lack empathy, but in times like this, I wonder if it's really just us, who lack empathy? In order to help, we need to remind ourselves that those with Autism will find their world so much harder to cope with, and that is not something we can judge, or say that "It's not so bad". Accept the hardships, and try to understand the very root of the issues, and try to help the child there. Answer their questions, no matter what, go into more detail if you feel they can handle it.

How to help answer questions
- Talk in precise, specific language
- Avoid rambling or distractions (turn the TV off, or on mute, for example)
- Use easily understandable language and examples
- Avoid judgement and offer support or 121 guidance to help them understand, or cope with overload
- Visual prompts

Depression

My personal experience of depression is somewhat strange. This is because it never occurred to me that I was depressed at the time. I can't actually pin point when my depression began because it must have begun so slowly that feelings of numbness became normal. I just assumed my negative feelings and dropping self esteem was normal as everyone at school was depressed, self harming and emotional all the time (not that I was self harming). Of course it is really sad that so many young people suffer like this and it does make your own feelings appear normal in comparison. When exposed to that much depression in day to day life at schools / colleges, when you experience the first symptoms you just shrug them off and assume that your feelings of depression are normal and of no worry, especially as in society where statistics of teenaged depression have rocketed due to bullying, family issues, trying to be 'impossibly beautiful' and comparing themselves to airbrushed, photoshopped and covered in make-up models. It is odd, as you don't always realise that the depression is there, grinding away at your self esteem and emotions until you feel so horrendous that you feel like you are the only person on the planet suffering. This of course is not true, although I always would have preferred to have been the only person suffering, because the sheer thought of the horrific amount of other people dealing with the unimaginable daily pains and stress of depression terrified me and made me very sad. I hate the thought of others suffering like I did, I would rather be the only one suffering so that others could be happy.

I experienced a lot of malaise. I do remember, however, waking up every day and going to school/college and just not feeling alive. I mean, nothing felt real, I felt like an outsider looking in on my own life, it just felt fake – to me and certainly not real. I felt like I was watching a film and some puppeteer was in control of my actions – I was just being stringed along. I, for once am finding it hard to describe that feeling of emptiness, the sheer chaos of loneliness where nothing seemed to have a real effect on me. Looking back, I suppose it's easier to pin point the depression now because I was acting so quiet and so withdrawn. My work was affected badly, I was always tired, had no motivation, my lust for life was disappearing rapidly, I stopped doing things I enjoyed and I was always in the most ridiculous amount of pain (physical side effects became very real and I often suffered with expanded intestines).

Despite feeling emotionally numb, I faked a smile all the time. I was walking around smiling like the Cheshire cat. When I thought someone was looking, I made sure to appear normal and happy, as not to arouse suspicion or have to explain myself (due to my communication problems and emotional barriers I was very bad at explaining how I felt, but having to explain something I did not understand was near impossible). I became very good at appearing to be normal and happy. When alone, I had no one to hide from, I could just be myself. Quite frankly, I very much preferred it that way, I often just sat on the floor in my bedroom and stared into space for hours without realising that any drastic amount of time had passed at all.

A few times, I would lie on the floor, and listen to the sounds of the house, the electricity and water gurgling and so on. The quiet sounds soothed me, and I would lie there, with my ear pressed against the cold hard wooden floor. It seemed to be one of the few things that could sooth me. Obviously my family knew there was something wrong, and they sorted me out, without me realising it. We went out lots, had lots of family trips, started hobbies (yoga) and things to do (I threw myself into my art work) with lots of encouragement, I started seeing counsellors (I would have every Friday off school for my therapy sessions). So my family definitely knew, despite my attempts at feigning happiness and they definitely helped. In many ways I have been told I overcompensate for these things and in many ways people can now tell when something is majorly wrong with me because of how overly happy.

I feel a real need to reassure you at this point, despite what has happened. I have never had any thoughts of suicide. Although I have wanted an end to my suffering, I did not want that, I wanted to be happy, not sad. Contemplating such a tragic thought has never been a possibility for me because it doesn't answer any questions nor does it solve any problems. One thing I have always known is that whoever you are, however lonely you feel, there is always

someone out there who would be badly affected if you were to kill yourself.....
family, friends, teachers, co-workers, boy/girl friends – many people. The
impact would be larger for your family. It could tear them apart, their jobs,
their lives and they could end up feeling as terrible as you, and the cycle would
start again. The nastiness of depression is that you genuinely believe that the
world would be a better place without you, but this is not true, please find it
in your hearts to believe this, even if you have to look at yourself in front of
the mirror each day and tell yourself that you are a good person and that you
are trying your best in life. Each and every person is valuable, and worthwhile,
especially if you don't believe you are. No one stays in that scary dark place for
ever. There is a lot of support out there for people with depression. Visiting a
G.P. is a good place to start as they can refer you on to many different places
that can help.

I overcame my depression initially by counselling and therapy with specialists.
They helped me understand and deal with my feelings better. Due to the
success of the counselling and therapy I was able to start volunteering which
helped me in a variety of ways. Volunteering was originally a distraction from
how I was feeling and gave me something positive to focus my time on. It
was not long before I discovered how much I adored volunteering. I found
it so rewarding that it changed me, and my whole outlook on life. It took a
while for me to recover from depression, but the combination of therapy,
counselling, support from family, and volunteering really worked for me.

Why are people with Autism more prone to Mental Health Issues?

I am a very positive person and I truly do see my disability as a gift, but the
hidden hardships I face daily are extremely challenging and hold me back
from achieving my full potential. I get a lot of Information Overloads due to
my ability to notice everything in fine detail. These Information Overloads
give me extreme Meltdowns and chronic pain; sometimes I find it hard to
walk, with migraines, seizures and extreme exhaustion every day. I believe that
Meltdowns turn Autism into a physical disability. Due to my Meltdowns I have
an uncontrollable habit called 'Stimming', which is where I focus all of my
negative energy on one repetitive movement in the hope of drowning out my
offending overloading senses; controlling negative sensory input with sensory

output. 'Stimming' is a very common necessity of Autism. My 'Stimming' includes flapping hands and fingers and hitting myself on the head.

Which leads me on to my next point – Meltdowns strike those with Autism apart, and can be used as a disgusting excuse to abuse. As a result of bullying and abuse I have Post Traumatic Stress Disorder (PTSD). A few years ago my PTSD used to plague me with hourly flashbacks, turning me into a shadow of the woman I have thankfully become now. Flashbacks used to corrode at my happiness. Depression ceased my desire to seek change; eating away at my ability to see positively. Anxiety created a warrior; desperate to break free from my chains of panic attacks and despair, to fight for my right to be happy. It was as if I was simply watching a movie of my own life; feeling numb as if I weren't really living at all. I felt isolated, pained and desperately alone. Those flashbacks I described are actually traumatic memories; it is hard for traumatized people to remember the actual traumatic memories because their brains can't handle it. The brain literally goes into shock. Instead, you get flashbacks of these memories until your brain deems you emotionally stable enough to handle the full memory. Every day I was transported back to my darkest moments by flashbacks; forcing me to relive the un just pain, as if it was happening all over again – and there was little I could do to stop it.

Some reasons why those with Autism could be more prone to Mental Health Issues:
- **Autism general difficulties**, like communication, self expression, and behaviours, and knowledge that we are indeed, different to others.
- **Un/intentional Gaslighting**
- **Autisms difficulty with perceiving problems** to be bigger or more scary than reality.
- **Social Imagination and Problem Solving** is very challenging, having problems with finding safe and flexible recovery systems.
- **Lack of self belief** perhaps induced by so called 'failings' or mistakes
- **Lack of understanding** in surroundings, or themselves
- **Inability to cope** with in-justice or change in routine
- **Information overloads** shutdowns and meltdowns

All of this can come together as one sticky mess, to create mental health issues. It seems completely reasonable to me that a person with Asperger Syndrome could become depressed or anxious. In these ways I think that people with

Autism are generally more likely to develop certain Mental Health Issues such as Depression, Anxiety and OCD. This is due to Autisms diversity, the way people with Autism Spectrums Disorders brains are wired up differently, we are affected in different ways to those who are neuro-typical and as a result our brain functions and coping abilities are different too. Every area of life is difficult and overloading, there is always possibility of 'failing', whether in the eyes of other people, or in the eyes of yourself. Becoming so aware of your flaws, or failures, and the massive frustrations in not being able to avoid failure, or making mistakes, results in a scary possibility of bullying or abuse, and so, I think it is also natural that someone would become introvert and wish to avoid situations like this entirely, increasing risk of sadness and lack of belief in themselves. The resulting belief that you are wrong, and others are right, and not recognising yourself in a healthy way, creates this dreadful sense of isolation or lack of identity.

Autism and coping with injustice

One of the most well known aspects of Autism is the necessity for truth and honesty in all areas of life. Following exact rules and routines may seem simple enough, but it allows for zero error or impromptu change. This means that anything out of routine, or that is 'wrong' (incorrect experiences, injustice or behaviours), are wildly upsetting – causing meltdowns.

Those on the spectrum are more sensitive to life experiences and the 'insignificant' everyday experiences can massively impact them, causing anxiety and meltdowns. These tiny things that most people can 'get over' within seconds, like a change in toothpaste, a lost set of car keys or a late bus, have huge implications for someone on the spectrum and can potentially ruin their whole day. This is because such tiny hardships have the potential to negatively affect their abilities more than usual; often resulting in overloads and meltdowns. If meltdowns and anxiety are a symptom of daily life for those on the spectrum, just imagine what happens when a real big change happens; something really unjust and wrong? Something like experiencing bullying, hate crime, changing school or university, or moving home?

What happens then?

I think that it is rather logical that if daily normal life is so upsetting to cause multiple meltdowns – then abnormal and unjustified life with Bullying or

Disability related Hate Crime is actually traumatizing; creating a much bigger emotional reaction of Anxiety, Depression, OCD and sometimes PTSD.

Advice for People with Mental Health Issues – The Roller Coaster Road to Recovery

Recovering from any illness, mental or physical can be a long process, especially if the symptoms are not correctly identified. Mental health issues are so complex that diagnosis and treatment can be difficult, but with the right support they can be resolved. I have already talked about my personal experiences and what has helped me, but I would also like to give some general advice on how to cope with mental health issues.

1. **Write a list of the good points in your life.** Family, friends, school/college good grades (or improving grades) that you are a nice, caring person etc
2. **Keep a general daily dairy of it least one thing that has made you smile** that day, no matter how small, insignificant or momentary. Read through it every night
3. **Keep a diary of the things that worry and upset you.** You can use this to see if patterns are occurring and to determine what your emotional triggers are. An action plan can then be formed to help avoid or overcome triggers
4. **Do things that you enjoy**, for example, your hobbies
5. **Contact your G.P**, who can refer you for appropriate counselling and therapy.
6. **Start exercising.** Regular exercise does wonderful things for the mind and body. Not only can exercise help you stay fit, but it can help you feel motivated and positive. This will enhance your mental health and wellbeing and you will start to feel happier. Exercise does not have to be about losing weight or building muscle strength- it can be as easy as taking regular walks in the fresh air, cycling to and from work or school/college, or playing a game of football down the park. Do whatever you feel comfortable with and enjoy. It also helps to exercise with friends or family as you can motivate each other.
7. **Eat a balanced and healthy diet**, it may seem terribly cliché but it absolutely works. If you are not fuelling your body with the right nutrients

you will not be able to function properly or operate to the best of you ability. If your body can not function effectively, then neither can your mind.

8. **Take some time out of general routines.** Personal relaxation time is very important. Whether this is listening to music, reading a book, art, or doing yoga or meditation, you have to do something to take your mind off of the daily stresses.

9. **Speak to friends and family, do not suffer in silence.** I am sure if somebody you knew was feeling alone or depressed, you would want to help them.

10. **Try to have something with you at all times that reminds you of happier times.** This can be an easy way to distract yourself, and bring you back to reality. For example when I get sad, I look at my Glastonbury festival bands on my wrist. I am then reminded of how overwhelmingly happy I am at that festival and all those brilliant memories come flooding into my mind and I feel a bit more at ease again.

Advice for People with a Disability – Staying Safe in Public

This is a section of upmost importance; because safety is paramount at all times, nothing is more important than safety. Staying safe in public can decrease the chance of various unpleasant things happening.

"So how can you remain safe in public?" I hear you cry (I told you I was psychic). This is my little list of advice:

1. **Tell your parents/carers where you are going before you go out.** One must do this to remain safe and content, if anything happens they need to know where you are to best help you.

2. **Make sure you take money,** I usually take a bit of money in my purse which I keep in a zipped compartment within my zipped up bag and some in my securest pockets in case someone unfortunately steals my bag. Only take as much money as you need. If your lunch will cost £4 and you need to catch a bus (if you live in England then hopefully you should have a free bus pass if you have a statement stating your disability) then you need roughly £7-£8

3. **Take a suitable bag with ZIP compartments** (over the shoulder bags are good because they minimise the risk of someone stealing your bag).

4. **Take a mobile phone.** Make sure it is fully charged and has credit on it so you can ring someone in an emergency.
5. **Try and walk with groups** (friends that you know well and trust) especially at night.
6. **If it is dark, use routes with lit up streets.** Walk there instead and try to avoid dark places that have little light, houses or people.
7. **Know where you are going.** Know how you are getting there and what you are doing when you get there.
8. **Look and listen before you cross the road.** Even if you are in a rush, there is no harm in waiting, safety comes first.
9. **Don't take risks.** If someone is pressuring you to drink alcohol, you don't have to, and if you do, don't drink a lot. Drinking impairs your ability to function properly, so even easy tasks become more difficult. You can very quickly find yourself in a vulnerable situation.
10. **Communicate and keep people updated of your whereabouts.**

If people approach you, or start harassing you
1. Ignore them, it is best not to respond to them
2. Try and walk away
3. Call a parent or carer or someone who can help you
4. Try not to react in a bad way, if you call them names, start acting violently you will be as bad as them. If the police need to be called you can get in trouble too – even if they started it. Just don't get violent or shout. Instead warn them to stop or you will call the police

When is it suitable to ring the police?
Only warn the people harassing you with the police if they have done something wrong, or if you feel like you are in danger. Every situation is different, and the police may not be required every time, for example if you are at school or college you could tell a teacher who could help you instead.

Examples of when it could be appropriate to call the police:

1. If you have been touched inappropriately. This can be touching you in your private parts or shoving or pushing you around.
2. If people are acting anti socially, crowding round you and trying to intimidate you.

3. If they start to follow you
4. If they hurt you in anyway
5. If you feel you are in danger

If you are out alone and you feel vulnerable and/or worried for your safety, you could walk into a shop/anywhere with people (not a house) and ask for assistance there (this is what my Safe Places scheme is all about). Shop assistants and managers should be willing to help you if you ask for help.

If you are not sure if it is necessary to call the police telling your parents/carer/someone you trust is a good option as they can advise you. If they think you are in danger they may be able to come and meet you.

Don't:
1. Get into a vehicle with any strangers, unless it is a registered taxi
2. Give strangers money
3. Talk to strangers (there's a new one, like you have not been told that before. Sarcasm people, sarcasm)
4. Meet up with people you don't know or have not met face to face. (For instance if you have met someone on the internet and they suggest to meet, say no. They may say they are your age and safe but there is no way to tell if they are lying or not, they could be dangerous)
5. Lose stuff. Try to keep your belongings as safe as possible.

Overcoming Stress

This is a story you must not try at home (or anywhere).

The instant I realised my mental health will improve came to me at a very peculiar moment. The moment of clarity in which I realised that I won't let my memories corrupt me anymore was a very striking and memorable experience. This is a story I have not told, even to my family, purely because it is embarrassing; and dangerous and I feel a fool to let them worry.

To start with, I must explain a little background. As a child, I often practised the strangest things. I used to hold my breath, underwater, for long periods of time, trying to beat my record each time. I did this under the strange belief that, if I can hold my breath under water, I can do anything. After things that happened, when memories started to corrupt my mind's eye, it became a stress reliever. I would go under water, sinking into the cold, quiet eerie world that is the underwater buzz, and held my breath to calm my stress. It became a strange, delightful new world which I had not explored nearly as much as I had wished... I delighted in the fact that I could escape the world of noisy mayhem as easily as one, two, three and I found mercy at the hands of water, many times. Holding your breath underwater, is something that could kill you, and if you come so close to an uncertain death, to come straight back to the land of the living again, in one swift, almighty, breath of air, is something quite incredible. Also, out of fear, I used to practise holding my breath under water, in case I ever found myself in the situation where I need to lie in water, and pretend to be dead, as a preventative for being killed. Yes, I know, I have an overactive imagination and I am really crazy. Yet, because of this weird belief that if I could hold my breath under water for a certain amount of time, I can come so close to something unimaginable, death, darkness, loneliness (or heaven, whatever you may believe) to then bop back to life again, I could overcome anything. It may sound like I had a death wish, I have never had one, I was just very, incredibly... stupid... In fact, words can't describe how stupid I was.

So, to contain this stupid belief of overpowering challenges in this way and relieving my stressful memories by proving to myself that I was stronger, I practised holding my breath for as long as I could, all the time, whenever I got the chance; in the bath, the swimming pool, the sea, and dangerous as it was, it calmed me down; it allowed me to make sense of the things that troubled me. I don't recommend it, because it is so very dangerous and could put your life in danger. Don't do it. One time, I was in a desperate situation, my young childlike self had experienced something that was unpleasant, traumatic really, and I found it hard to cope.

The very reason my mother got PTSD, and one of the reasons for mine, is what affected me, and probably everyone else in my family, also. A long time ago, when I was seven or eight, someone had broken into my house, in the middle of the night. I witnessed some nasty things, which I don't wish to speak about, and found it hard to cope at the time. I managed to cope by escaping the worlds loud madness by swimming to the bottom of pools or sea banks, and holding my breath.

For years, I couldn't remember anything that had happened. Suddenly, the memories came back to me, when I was roughly thirteen. The memories came at me in forms of flashes, and maybe I have had PTSD, for a lot longer than I ever had known. The memories, confused, angered, scared and frustrated me. One time, it all got too much and I felt like I was going crazy. Along with finding out about my disability, at a similar time, I had many memories like this that would come to the surface of my tired brain that I couldn't make sense of it. The memories shot through my system, memories of the struggle, the confusion, and the frightful night terrors of awaking in a cold sweat. This is a story describing, in detail, what happened one time when I held my breath under water; and the joyous relief to breathe at the end. I have told it in a story format because I wanted to show how detailed I write because of my disability, and to capture the true essence of why the water is both soothing and terrifying to any that dare compete with it.

One time, I went swimming with my best friend, when I was young perhaps aged nine or ten. This is a time where my parents had just started to let me go to the park and our local swimming pool; by myself (providing I was always with my best friend and all the usual safety check precautions had been met). We were in a local swimming pool, just the two of us, and I started practising holding my breath under water. The stress was so unbearable, the sensory overload, the memories, everything was unimaginably painful, emotionally and physically... and I needed some peace. I knew that the peace of mind I much craved could come from something so simple... a different world of eerie, soothing silence. So I took a breath, and practised what I had been practising for weeks, months even. I swam slowly to the bottom of the pool, as my best friend counted aloud from the sidelines.

"1, 2, 3, 4, 5...."

I stopped swimming now, as I had reached the bottom, and I just hung there, letting the water calm my nerves. The noise that frustrated me, had disappeared almost instantly and now was replaced by a series of whooshes and white noise, a ticking noise from generators and the calm beauty had soothed me instantly. The sound of my friend counting slowly grew quieter as I slipped deeper into the bliss of water. At first, fear quaked through my body and I felt unable to compete against my usual average which was a time of 58 seconds (my best time was 73 seconds). However, then a relief swept through my very being and I felt calmer than I had done in months.

"I can do this" I thought to myself, "I am at home, water is my home… I can do this."

Something wholly strange happened, as the seconds ticked by and the icy slickness of the water lapped around my body, the memories felt less magnified, less terrible…. I stopped being scared. The fear from the memories melted away into darkness and the fear of not breathing; died away in an instant. Distantly I heard my friend counting aloud,

"17, 18, 19, 20, 21…. "

I could feel myself drifting, my mind at ease, snapping apart from my ropes (metaphor, here I mean memories) that had tied me down. I relaxed, and let my body flop, no longer rigid, arms and legs floating away from me in the water. Drifting up… up, like a fairy; delicate, flimsy, spindly arms and wings outstretched. The water was making me float, dancing to my very own tune. Obscurity engulfing my very being as the calm serenity of the liquid, held me weightless in it's almost unbearable arms. I exhaled some breath, slowly, meaningfully and watched, fascinated as the eruption of tiny bubbles flew out my mouth and disappeared into the water in streaks of white. The water lapped at my body, soothingly, coming at me in simple ripples of effect, calm, comforting. My hair, that had come loose from its pony tail, started weaving gently around my head and shoulders, fanning out like a majestic lions mane. Now I focussed on my sense of hearing, I could hear muffled cries and laughter of the children having fun above water level. An even vaguer noise, was my friend counting, patiently waiting, confident for my return

"36,37,38,39…"

I watched people's legs kick, underwater, and thousands of bubbles erupting from the force, streaming in swishes of unimaginable beauty. I displayed my hands in front of my face, and saw that my skin had tinged a light blue, reflected from the water and the tiles surrounding me. Light reflected on my skin, in patterns, making me see myself as a blue and white cheetah, mottled spots, outlined thickly, light streaking and patterns beautifully rarely seen, appeared briefly on my skin. My fingertips were becoming shrivelled, lined and numb, goose pimples sailing up and down my body in uncomfortable streaks of cold shivers. Suddenly, metres from me, an almighty force burst from the surface of the water, disrupting the easy calm.

Thousands of bubbles dived down, surrounded by white water, swishing in vibrant bubble cloud formations. Diving down through the bubbles, emerged a little boy, pale arms outstretched above his head, a brown plaster on his elbow, long finger nailed hands together, diving down through the water. He looked at me from the distance. His cheeks puffed out, filled with air, skin red from the water, eyes dark but strange and distorted behind his goggles. As he wiggled and swam towards me, I noticed a little graze on his left knee, with a water proof cartoon plaster hanging off on one side. I swiped away a stray hair that was annoying my face, and proceeded in more comfort to watch the plaster flap along with his kicking. Satisfied with the rhythmic flapping, I looked back up at him. He had swum closer now, and floated for a moment or two in front of me, before extending his hand and waved rapidly at me, grinning widely. I merely watched, uncertain if I should risk my breath and concentration to wave back, instead I smiled. He pointed up towards the surface of the swimming pool, I gently shook my head "No, not yet," I had thought to myself, although the urge to breath was growing stronger. As a distraction, from the urge to break free from my spell of airlessness, I preoccupied myself with the little boy's momentary presence. I noticed his belly button, his rib cage protruding beneath his milky white skin, a little pop of belly, six freckles (that I could count), long toes on tiny feet. He swayed for a moment, waving his arms. His short blond hair swashed back with the waves, his lips pursed together and a look of almighty concentration on his childlike face. He waved again, and swam away, his legs propelling him up to air. Air, air... enchanting air; I imagined that little boy, now breathing, at ease, above the water, my head started to spin. I could feel myself start to struggle now. 'No, I must prove to myself that I will not let these memories beat me. I can do this, I am strong'. I thought to myself, willing myself to forget the need for oxygen running through my veins.

I watched the kicks and bubbles from his escape for a moment or two, and then I closed my eyes. Eyes stinging worse now, the chlorine harsh, I sank back into the easy darkness, darker than I could have imagined. The battle almost, but not quite won, I felt a new lease of life... just when I could almost lose my life at any moment, either to memories corrupting my mind or the desperate need to breathe. It felt that although I could not breathe, the water was breathing for me... a sigh of life, stumbling and uncertain. The water swishing around me in forms of bubbles and waves, breathing, alive; whirling to waters own breath. Breathe the very sign of life, an almost forgotten song that had always been such a constant figure of certainty... I shall always breathe... until my last dwindling second. Oh, the beauty of breathing.

"Not long now. Keep going, you can do it Joely."

This thought barely crossed my mind, "56, 57, 58, 59... " I could hear white noise and the faint glimmer of screams, but they seemed so far away, so distant, in a different world, a different universe, screaming at a different me. Everything was so dark, so beautiful... so calm. Trickling air droplets formed across my back, popping, moving, tickling and tailing my goose pimpled skin, upon my neck now. Uncomfortably I shifted, desperate to rid myself of the tickling sensation and was greeted with something much worse. My eyes flew open as the buzz in my ears fired up, popping loud, and unimaginably screaming at me, "Breathe, Joely... breathe." A spasm shot through my body, fast, unafraid, shuddering now. My lungs! As the burning pain in my chest excelled, I fixed my eye line on the tiny tiles littering the base of the swimming pool; in all shades of blues, whites and greens, tiles missing here and there, the pattern, zig-zagged and spirals. My eyesight swaying now, I blinked my eyes shut again, back to darkness. My lungs heaved, desperation taking over, I can't do this much more. I have to get out. I slashed about, the water beating out in violent waves of bubbles. My lungs bucked and bailed, uncontrollably heaving for air. Air, air, air. Water, water, water... I opened my mouth to the gush of water sweeping in, and I was almost shocked that it was not the necessary air I so desired. Choking and spluttering now, I splashed about with uncertainty. What did Corinna always say? Her face came to me now, her beautiful smiling eyes, but completely serious in the nature of her tone;

"When you're swimming, and water goes in your mouth, you don't have to swallow it – spit it back out."

Did I ever listen? No. Had I remembered in the jolt of despair? No. I wish I had. My vision disappeared as fluently as it had appeared and I realised with a cold start that, if I don't break into the surface of air soon, I could die.... The water was cold and greasy in my mouth, forcing itself down my throat, lurking dangerously in my lungs, the chlorine stinging my nose and eyes. I chugged, uncontrollably for air. Searing pains in my lungs grew hotter, stronger. I started to feel dizzier than ever before. Suddenly, the reality of my situation literally sank in and I felt a new sweep of terror grip my heavily beating heart.

"68, 69, 70, 71…"

The distant chime of my best friend's voice grew faded and vanished entirely. I panicked, I know I shouldn't have, because it didn't help the situation but the panic was unavoidable. My arms flailing now, I must reach the surface, but where is the delightful air I so desperately seek? I escalated the remains of my long held breath, far longer than usual, rickety and fast. The force of my eruption of air, created bubbles in the water, which caused me to sink back further into the depths of despair. I looked from side to side, vigorously. My knowledge of up and down, distorted now, as the panic overwhelmed my being. I squinted in the tumbling water around me, my eyes burning, tears streaking, bubbles shattering out my mouth in wordless shrieks of terror. The calm serenity, disturbed by my wake, as I chugged for breath. I flailed my arms, and started what I sincerely hoped was swimming, my legs kicking hard as an attempt to boost me upwards. My arms, once desperate to start swimming, were unable to move because the strain on my lungs made me choke in water. The pressure burned my lungs and they felt fit to burst. I realised with fear that swimming would not work.... but what will? A little further, Joely.... you can do it. When you get to air, you can overcome anything... You can do it.

The fretful seconds ticked by, caressing my nerves to pieces... I closed my eyes, seemingly at a loss of what to do; I can't swim, I can't breathe, I might actually die... no! I'm too young, I'm too vulnerable, and I have too much to give, to die like this. I mustn't die. My mind raced with terrible thoughts, and the pain blazed through my being, in another terrible wave of sickness... then suddenly, with my eyes flickering shut, darkness taking over, there was nothing. No thoughts occupied my mind and I drifted into a calm darkness, down, down, down... where there was little escape. Floating, as if I were an astronaut on the moon, calm but surreal, slowly spinning in the cold water, I floated down, eerily. I could feel my hair loll lazily at my head, at first tickling my face, but slowly any sensation melted away into nothing and I drifted into the dark, tiled bottom of the swimming pool, lonely, and emotionally numb. This darkness, this desperation, this loneliness, this pain...

Is this how it feels to die?

Darkness stretched in front of me, a never ending tunnel of anguish. I was so far away from my physical being, that I could hardly control my limbs anymore, floating, dying... My head bopped down, every time I lost consciousness and I fell deeper down from the force, completely oblivious now, of what was

happening. In the midst of darkness and sub consciousness, I found myself
bump to the bottom of the pool; A slow bump, that rocked through my body,
like dominos, a jolt ran through me, pain, almighty pain... and for a second,
I was back. My eyes flickered open, and in the hazy shades, I found myself
startle with fright once more, I sluggishly looked at my legs bent beneath me,
swaying lazily in the waters tune. A thought miraculously, filtered through to
my tired brain; 'No, Joely, you can do this'

This is when I realised I was right where I needed to be, to escape.

I laid my hands out on the floor, feeling the bumpy texture of tiles for a
moment before I miraculously managed to see through the intense dizziness
and pain, and managed to right myself to a crouched standing position. I
stumbled and clumsily planted my feet firmly on the tiled swimming pool
floor. Closing my eyes, praying to anyone that cared to listen, for survival, I
bent my knees and pushed hard as I could against the tiled flooring, and shot
up, up, up. My lungs blazing, I exploded up, fast, majestically powerful.

I broke the surface of the water, where water meets air, where death, meets life. My head blasted out from the waves of the jeopardising water, the cold of the air hit me instantly, swarming into my head, cold air tingling my skin. I found the delighted air I was so desperately seeking and through splutters, I inhaled, deep, deep, deeper. My eyes flew open, light affected my vision and I shut them instantly, gratitude seeped through me, glazing my eyes with pleasure. Oh, to breathe again. I gasped, air pushing through my lungs, brimming through me, electrified, beautifully like an answered prayer. I gasped, over and over. Waves of nausea and dizziness gripped me tight, and my head swam in the water around me, lolling heavily from the pressure of air. Suddenly my ears popped, and a wall of sound hit me, like a gunshot; lots of people were shrieking, screaming... at me? In my confusion, I smiled, laughing through splutters of breath, the hilarity gripped me tight, and I could not stop. I had done it. I had probably beaten my record. If I can do that, if I can be so strong as to get through something like that and still live to tell the (stupid) tale, I can get through anything. I laughed aloud, splashing about, my head and whole body bobbing up and down with the weight of my laughter, my relief at succeeding. Suddenly, during my splutters, a strong arm hooked around my waist and hoisted me up, with ease. I opened my eyes to a flash of yellow, red and the blinding lightness. I blinked in the white room, hot fiery tears reverberating through my eye lids. And as I was laid on the swimming pool side, I smiled. My mind at ease, a stupid battle as it was, I had won. It was at that moment that I realised that even in the darkest of despairs, when death or insanity is so close, there is still hope, still room for improvement. I lay there gasping with wonderful oxygen, the cold wet floor, stinging the skin of my back, my head feeling woozy, and the sights spinning from side to side. My eyes squinted open, in a daze of light headedness, the white blinding my eyes, and several blurry shapes appeared to sway at my side. I focussed and saw hazy faces, peering at me, with unreadable expressions on their faces, although I now imagine they were concerned or scared for my safety. As the feeling of dizziness left me, the life guards did their job, although they mostly just lectured me to not do it again "It's a stupid thing to do, baby doll. You could've died down there in that water." the life guard had said with a heavy Australian accent.

I lay there smiling, breathing heavily, and I felt like the most powerful creature in the world. I had won, nothing can beat me now, whenever I struggle from now on, I will remember this time and I will gather strength to move on.

Escaping the dizziness more now, I smiled, widely, and stumbled up to stand, and was greeted by several hands pushing me down in haste. As I looked at the faces, everything still blurry, the flash of yellow from the lifeguard and my best friend miming at me from the side lines, the thumbs up signal... was signifying to me that I had done it... I had beaten my record; I closed my eyes in happiness and rested my head back down on the smooth ground.

As crazy as it may sound, it was at that moment, when I came up for air, I realised with certainty that everything would be ok, the memories, as painful as they were, could not control me. I realised that I could stare any challenges in the face, with this new found knowledge, and know that I will try my best to overcome any struggles. I have since found a far better way of coping with the madness the of hectic world in my wake, for instance writing stories, art work, hobbies, enabling positive change in my community through volunteer work, soft things, my favourite comfortable clothes. So I am a lot safer now I have learnt how to cope better. Despite the clarity of mind I was given, I certainly don't recommend it, and I won't be putting myself in danger and doing any more 'diving' that's for sure.

Infinity and Beyond

First up, I would like to ask you a question. What is the reason you wake up every morning? What is it that gracefully wakes you from the slumber of dreamland? Is it motivation to achieve something more or is it the sensation of necessity?

For me, it is the knowledge that I am happy; it is motivation that wakes me up. Every day I am fortunate to have the opportunity to make a difference; I can campaign about my passions as they explode with reels of inspiration from within my mind. I can resist the temptation to fall back asleep, and I claim the day's victories in kindness – no matter how small they may be.

Everyday I wake up, ungracefully, I should add. I sleepily open one eye, bleared with dizziness, half the duvet on the floor, (Tracy Emins messy bed springs to mind) my hair a mess, body mangled with pain, and with desired sleep calling me back to the realms of rest; and I jump out of bed. Awake, ready, motivated to do what I do best – Autism Activist work and Random Acts of Kindness.

Random Acts of Kindness – Autism Activism

I am a firm believer that random acts of kindness are the difference between feeling accepted – friendship, and loneliness; and in extreme cases, life and death. Random acts of kindness are opportunities that appear in daily, often hourly life. If you have dreams of making a difference in lives of others, but opportunities seem to be tainted with mist; it is hard to realise when these opportunities arise, and what the best cause of action is to take. The best cause of action to take is something incredibly, mind blowing simple. It is something that we take for granted, something that a lot of you already do. Something I live by everyday to become a positive person. Something that is really quite easy...

Be a person who is interested in others, be the person who would safely help an old lady cross the road, be the person who gives to charity, be the person who would comfort others, be the person who would help someone pay for a meal, be the person who smiles and says hello to the homeless on the street, be the person who makes small talk to the elderly on buses; be the person who would go out of their way to help a stranger in need. You just have to believe in yourself and your abilities of kindness; because kindness is within us all. It is our human nature to want to help one another in our survival. We are all humans, despite our differences and we can all help make a difference; momentarily changing stranger's lives and changing our own lives, and our outlook, for the better. The relief of knowing you are not alone can be the sole push towards a future with an positive outlook.

I am going to write a short story now to try and capture your imaginations, as to just how a random act of kindness can make a difference; one of the main reasons I became an Autism Activist – to help others through hardship. Just imagine this:

"Rain drizzles down onto the dirty window pane, clouding the view. Harry leant against the window, one hand outstretched, his palm flat on the cool of glass, the other hand drumming restlessly on the seat to the side of him. A sense of dread rises within him as the train sits at the station. He shudders, his thoughts a violent mess of bubbling frustration and fear, the train judders into life and powers on again, picking up speed now; taking him away from any hope he had left. He sighs and shifts, feeling shaky, blankly gazing out the window with glazed and tearful eyes. Wild abandoned hope, that sensation of pain and fragile being, seemed to hold him tight in a grasp of panic; one question burning through his mind... what an earth could he do to salvage this situation? Eyes closing, he leans his head against the train wall, noting with dismay that his heart was palpitating and the shuddering train was making him feel sick. Anxiety rose along with his desperation. He couldn't have a panic attack here. Please not here. Not in front of all these judgemental strangers... He shakes his head, his breath coming thick and fast now, fingers restless, drumming fast, hopeless, agitated and sore. Through the cloud of pain and confusion, cutting through his battle to remain calm, comes an sudden unexpected warmth that rushes through his finger tips, the feeling resists on his hand. A gentle squeeze, it was comforting, but what was it?

"I'm real sorry you're feeling unwell... can I help you at all?" says a soft quiet voice, ethereal, sounding like it was speaking from miles away. He looks around to see his unlikely saviour, the source of the glowing warmth that has since rushed from his hand to his heart, warming him through, demisting the panic of judgemental strangers. His eyes take in someone gazing at him, as they sat beside him, smiling sadly. He looked down to find their hands carefully placed on his own battered and scratched hand. He looks again at this stranger, this incredible person who has decided to try and help whilst all these others sat, wrapped up in their own lives, ignoring and careless. His eyes prickle, his fingers that were once tense and hopeless suddenly relaxed, hope swelling. He looked at this person, his eyes widening, his breath slowing. That warmth tingled within him, as he calmed. Removing his hand from the window he accepted a tissue and blew his nose unable to believe his luck that this stranger was trying to help him. This person wasn't judging him to be weak or inhumane for his anxiety attacks. He wasn't being made to feel like an alien who was pretending to be normal; he was human again. This person was treating him like a friend would; if he had any. Suddenly an emotion rushes through him, something unrecognisable, something warm, glowing ... it was nice; it was hope.

The relief courses through his veins and calms the raging sense of alarm that sizzled there just moments before. He had been scared of having an anxiety attack in front of judgemental strangers... but look at this, this stranger was helping him. Shaking, he squeezed their hand and removed it, suddenly feeling like he didn't want to push his luck. The comfort of warmth from their embraced hands now gone, but the feeling of hope lingers. The stranger smiled at him, suddenly embarrassed at holding his hand, and there was that warmth again, firing up within his heart as he realised with a new found certainty that people do care – this stranger has just proved it by putting themselves in an potentially awkward and embarrassing situation, just to help him. Going out of their way to help him, when he had been feeling so desperate, so alone, and burdened with his problems. They sat side by side until it was time to go, he stood up ready to depart and suddenly felt a massive necessity to thank this stranger. He stood up tall, no longer slumped and shaking, exhaling, feeling much more relaxed, he looked the stranger in the eye and said "Thank you... so much. I was in a bad place and you took time out of your own life to try and help me. A stranger... That meant a lot. Thank you" A little smiles slips onto his lips and he nods in farewell at this stranger, who was smiling from ear to ear, eyes brightened. "Goodbye" The stranger said a little choked up, voice catching with the sudden pleasure. Their eyes interlocked, both of them remembering the sensation of being appreciated and being helped. They waved a cheery farewell and he stepped off the train; exhaling as he shook his head with a little laugh, a smile spreading along his lips; he may have his problems but people care... if a stranger cares, then he is not alone. That is all that matters.

The stranger sat on the train, bristling with pride, chuckling to themselves. "No matter what people say... I am NOT a bad person" with a smile, hope rushing through them, appreciating their own glow of warmth that glazed through their heart, they shut their eyes awaiting the long tiresome journey a head of them; the stress of peoples harsh comments washing away now. They knew they were kind and that they cared and made a difference today... that was all that mattered. The train rattled on, taking these two strangers away from each other, never to see one another again, but never away from their experience today. The impact of such a random act of kindness was too great for that. They would be forever etched into each other's memories and hearts, when times grew too hard; they would become that glowing hope that enlightens the path with hope and clarity of the good in the human race. That, is all that matters"

Thank you for reading my little short story; I hope it wasn't too long winded! My message is this – be that person who cares, who wishes to understand and help diversity. I suspect, that you already are! Becoming a person who is interested in others, and indeed the beautiful and fascinating diversity of the human race, is ultimately the best way to begin your journey into your dreams. From experience, the reward of being the sole reason for someone's smile is beyond measure, truly priceless. If you help a stranger, (or even someone you know) with a random act of kindness, then that feeling of clarity will remain with you, enabling you in your own darkest moments, and provides hope, for them. It is an emotion and warmth that you simply don't forget; something that can push your forward, clearing any mist of confusion and allowing you to see what is really important in life. Once you realize that, you are that much closer to reaching your dreams, you will realize what path to take, and how to pave your own way to a brighter future. Trust me, I have seen many people blossom like flowers in the sun, from simple acts of kindness – it works. This is the basis for my love of Autism Activism, and why I adore what I do, no matter the shutdowns it gives me. So a little suggestions, next time you are struggling to wake up, give yourself a goal to help someone during your day, to understand a little about different people and their plights. Slowly but surely, you will wake up to Motivation and understanding of diversity; Wake up to Random Acts of Kindness.

Thanks to support, I have been enabled to see the positive quirks within my disability, and use my disability to achieve my dreams of helping others within our Autistic Community. As a result of my families, and voluntary sectors dedication and sacrifice, I have been empowered to become a multi-national, and world award winning Autism Activist. My Autism Activism is something I adore, one of my specific narrow interests and passions.

My current list of Awards (2016)

1. **World Winner of 'Community Achievement' Award**, with ANCA, Global Naturally Autistic Network Consulting Agency 2016

2. **World Finalist of 'Community Achievement' Award,** ANCA, Naturally Autistic Global Autistic Network Consulting Agency 2015

3. **Team Winner of the National "Accessible Britain Challenge" Award 2015.** I worked alongside a fantastic team, to help design and implement the 'Safe Places Scheme' in my community. The Safe Places Scheme gives disabled people public places of safety they can easily access (shops etc) should they need help; for instance if they have been a victim of bullying, hate crime, or theft. Staff at these locations are trained to deal with any disability or situation that may arise, to best help any disabled people who need help.

4. **Winner of the Prime Ministers "Point of Light" Award 2014.** The "Point of Light" is a National Award which recognizes outstanding volunteers and inspiring individuals who are making a real difference in their community.... and I am one of them! At the time, Prime Minister David Cameron said:

"Joely Colmer has not just overcome huge personal challenges in her own life; she is helping other young people in a similar position. Through the Safe Places Scheme Joely is helping young disabled people to feel safer and more independent in public. I believe it is my duty as Prime Minister to hold up examples of great volunteering and service as an inspiration to others. Through her hard work and dedication she is making our communities stronger, and our country a better place. Joely's courage and determination is inspiring and I am delighted to be recognizing Joely Colmer as a Point of Light"

5. **Winner of the National YMCA and 01 Telecom of the Year 2013.** A National Award which celebrates the transformational work YMCAs and YMCA volunteers do; to honour the young people who have made exceptional progress within their personal lives and their community through volunteering. Blair Crawford, chief executive at Bournemouth YMCA, said:

   "We are incredibly proud that Joely has been given this award. She has shown immense talent and an extraordinary amount of courage and determination in transforming the lives of disabled young people..... "Joely is a true inspiration and we are honoured to have been able to celebrate her journey so far."

6. **Regional Winner of vInspired's National "All Round Commitment to Volunteering" Award, 2014.** The vInspired National Awards recognise and celebrate young people (under 25) and youth workers who have made an extraordinary contribution to their communities through volunteering. vInspired believes in giving young people the recognition they deserve and we want everyone to know about the great things young people are doing. Upon my recognition as a Regional Winner Terry Ryall, vInspired CEO said:

   "Joely Colmer is a complete inspiration...(Joely) demonstrates a complete dedication to volunteering and shows how she has built positive relationships, brought people from diverse backgrounds together and strengthened communities. Joely has done all this and more and should be immensely proud of her achievements."

Higher Education

When I left school, I went straight to college to study key skills; maths, literacy, cooking, care and physical education. I was not expected to do well at my GCSE's, so I got enrolled onto this particular course which was created to bump up my grades. However, when my results came through, I had wowed everyone, and my results were too high for the level the course could cater for. As I had already enrolled in the course I decided to stay, in the hope it could enhance some of my basic life skills. Unfortunately I gained very little from the course and so I left after a year.

I then started at the Arts University in Bournemouth, studying Art and Design. After two years (and three A levels) I left Art University to be a full time volunteer, and that is a decision that remains the best of my life. I love volunteering for what it has allowed me to achieve within my community, and myself. Now, I am still a full time volunteer and still loving life. I currently have a few voluntary awards under my belt, plus runners up for other awards. I was over the moon when I found out that I had won these awards because it's great to be recognised for something I feel so passionate about. If winning these awards helps others become more aware of the beauty within disabilities, and encourages others to volunteer, and enhance themselves and their communities holistically, then it's a double bonus.

I would now like to go into more detail about what I did when I left school, from higher education to my voluntary work

When I was 19 years old, I took a higher education course to help improve my maths skills. I didn't get the best GCSE grades when I was at school, so I decided that now was the right time for me to learn and understand maths. I took the course with an aim to get a grade C or above and I achieved my aim.

Below are some extracts from my diary that I kept while studying on this course.

I had forgotten how busy a class room at school is, although there are fortunately only two other students here today, it is still very distracting.

There is loads of evidence of work covering every inch of wall space. My class room is multi coloured mayhem. Goodness, they even have 3D work hanging from the ceilings. It is

a jungle in here. So consequently I find that I am always distracted although I try not to be. I don't count everything like I used to but I do look at everything in detail purely because everything is constantly jumping out at me and grabbing my attention as it wanders.

My tutor is fantastic and although it's Maths – I'm enjoying it.

SHOCK HORROR.
My Maths course is really good for me, I'm so happy because the stress has gone from Maths now. Now I can take Maths at my own pace and in my own way and not feel ashamed about it. Maths is finally making sense because I can really focus on it. Whereas, at school, I had loads of other subjects zooming through my head so I could sadly never be truly focused, even if I wanted to be. Because of my parents not pressuring me to do well and instead giving me endless praise, help, support and encouragement, I managed to shock everyone with really good GCSE grades and good enough to get into University. Go me! That would not have happened if I was pressured, that is for certain.

Knowing how much I disliked maths at school, I was nervous about having to retake it. I was worried I would still find maths so difficult to understand and that I would not pass the second time round either. As it turns outs, the learning environment was so brilliant that even I, with my appalling maths skills, was still able to learn everything I needed to pass the exam.

I think I was able to pass because:

1. I was older
2. I could give maths my full attention (I wasn't distracted with more projects)
3. There was less distractions and fewer pupils
4. The teacher was extremely patient, kind and understanding, and taught me very well

I know a lot of people would frown upon having to re take an exam, but for me it was the best scenario for me to get through my GCSE's. When I was at school I was able to focus on the subjects I felt I could do best in. I left Maths, which was my worse subject, for another time.

Voluntary Work

I do lots of volunteering because I enjoy it and I love helping other people and my community. When I was 19-20 years old I was doing roughly 20 hours a week in different voluntary projects. This is a list of voluntary work I did during a five year period.

1. **Chatterboxes**

   Chatterboxes is a youth group for disabled young people. The group gets together once a week. The aim of the project is for them to produce a quarterly magazine. The magazine is designed for young disabled people in our local community, it showcases what the 'chatterboxes' have achieved, what voluntary work they do and what events are coming up in the community. The magazine is distributed to local youth groups, schools and day centres. The Chatterboxes has currently been running for four years and has won a multitude of national awards.

   I have been volunteering with the Chatterboxes for 5 and a half years. My role was a Peer Mentor and Assistant Magazine Designer. As a Peer Mentor I was responsible for supporting the young people to help them express their views and opinions so that they could be included in the running, design and development of the magazine. As an Assistant Magazine Designer I was responsible for assembling the work the volunteers had produced, I would bring together all of their wonderful articles and ideas to produce the finished magazine using Indesign software on the computer. Sometimes I travel the country to give speeches at award ceremonies regarding life with disabilities. At these events there are often workshops which I help plan and run.

2. Safe Places

I'm privileged to say that our 'Safe Places Scheme' has won a prestigious national award called "the National Accessible Britain Award'. After viewing a similar project on the news, my youth worker and I decided that our local community of Bournemouth, Poole and Boscombe would be perfect for a similar scheme. The aim of Safe Places was to make Bournemouth, Poole and Boscombe town centres safer and more accessible for young people with disabilities by turning shops and local public areas (Libraries, cafes etc) into 'safe places'. We wanted to make sure that when young people with a disability visited the town centre they had somewhere safe to go if they felt vulnerable, scared, lost or if they need help with matters ranging from missing their bus or train, losing their phone or witnessing a distressing event.

Each Safe Place location will have the Safe Places logo displayed in the shop window, this is so a disabled young person is aware that if they need help they can find it in that location. Each disabled person in the area will have their own Safe Places identity card to carry with them when they visit the town. If they become distressed or need any assistance they can enter the Safe Place and present their identity card to a member of staff who will be able to assist them.

My role in the Safe Places scheme was to choose the safe locations and approach those locations for their support. I designed the Safe Places training manuals for the staff members n the chosen Safe Place locations. I went into them (Beales a large department store, Bournemouth Library, Specsavers, Boots, Bournemouth Odeon to name a few) to train staff members about the running of the scheme. I helped illustrate all the paper work and visual aids to be placed within the locations.

3. ANCA, Naturally Autistic – World Ambassador – UK Representative

The ANCA World Autism Festival is 'one of its kind' and famous for excellence; a world platform to showcase all the wonderful innovations and contributions to the positive growth of Autistic people, from around the world. Attendees are invited to learn first-hand from the autistic culture -global community, in an environment that strengthens the very fabric of our societies, to change lives. Attendees range from world leading Autism experts, Business organizations, community leaders, cultural organizations and diplomats as well as other Autistic people like myself, who are finding inner success with their disabilities.

I am honoured to say that during the ANCA World Autism Festival, in Vancouver, I won the prestigious World 'Community Achievement' Award, and become a World Ambassador, with ANCA, Naturally Autistic, people awards. Words can't describe the shaking beauty that surged through me, as the understanding dawned that I had actually WON the World 'Community Achievement' Award. Yes, words can't describe the emotional whirlwind, as I was awarded with the honour of becoming a World Ambassador; the hyperventilation as I struggled for breath, the laughing hysteria, as tears of utter joy poured down my face. It was amazing, and I am very grateful for my past experiences for teaching me and for my supporters who have empowered me so that my autism activism does create an positive impact; because that all that has mattered to me.

4. **My positive Asperger's website – www.aspergerworld.co.uk**
    My website provides a world of information, guidance and inspiration for the autistic community. My websites is where I show case Autistic Role models, and show the world what the quirks in Autism, really are – from a wide variety of people affected by this wonder filled disability.

5. **Motivational speaking and teaching presentations, and role modelling**
    I adore public speaking and creating speeches. I have given speeches about my disability to over five hundred people at a time. The events I have spoken at include Diverse Dorset, Schools, Colleges, Universities, Charities and local councils. A few years ago I would never have considered public speaking, let alone in front of hundreds of people. Since I left school, I have gained so much experience and knowledge from all my voluntary work, that my confidence has gone from strength to strength. I have put myself in uncomfortable situations, (speaking in front of about four hundred people, when the microphone stops working, when I have only just started a ten page speech, that is rather uncomfortable) but it has always worked out for the best. If I didn't constantly challenge myself, I would never achieve anything. I now adore public speaking and feel

very confident in that role. I have just realised that as my public speaking is vastly about Asperger's / Autism, I am effectively talking about my specialist topics, how very ideal for a classic 'Aspie' like myself?!

I also design and give out teaching presentations about Asperger's, tailored to each event that I help with. Often my audience members are professionals (perhaps from my local council) or young people, who wish to learn about Asperger's syndrome and different disabilities. When I am more experienced, I hope to start charging for my appearances and turn this area of volunteer work into a part time flexible paid career.

My Role Modelling sessions are usually 121, or close knit workshops with young people who have, or know someone, who has just been diagnosed with Asperger's or Autism. The forum is about building an understanding and changing negative perceptions of Asperger's, so young people can equip themselves with a better understanding of this disability in the future. I do this with positive role modelling, through doing a speech about what the disability is and what I have achieved with support, easy to understand interactive activities about Asperger's difficulties and talking through the difficulties I had at school, and how I overcame those difficulties.

Why I Love Volunteering

I am a multi award winning Public Speaker and Disability Awareness Workshop Presenter and Designer . These passions have enabled me to achieve my dream of creating positive change for people in the Autistic Community. My aim is to change lives; by raising understanding and awareness of the hidden aspects of the disability. I do this by going into schools and conferences and speaking to professionals, parents and young people alike about what the disability means and challenging misconceptions. With every one of my voluntary projects, and my passion to make a change, have come national and world awards, which is incredible to say the least, but most importantly, making a positive impact into the Autistic Community. The realisation dawned on me, stunning me to beaming silence; all the pain, the bullying, the isolation and frustrations of Autism... it was all worth it. Because it had taught me so many valuable lessons on how to help others through similar difficulties, and now, with these awards, I know with a certainty that I am making a difference.

That's all that has ever mattered to me; that is why I adore volunteering.

Through the power of my words I can mesmerize hundreds of people, and coax them to delve into the depths of a world so different to theirs. My lived experiences, coupled with years of volunteering has made my disability my biggest motivation and my specialist topic. As a result I have become quite the walking encyclopedia about my disability; this means I am very honest, and I can articulately bring clinical information to life, with stories that inspire hopeful hearts and usher tearful eyes. I can give my audience a gift; the gift of understanding and inspiration.

You see, volunteering as an Autism Activist is more than a job; it is my biggest passion. I love what I do, and I adore watching the change in the people I work with; blossoming like flowers to the sun with a new understanding and acceptance. I love being able to bring an understanding of the disability, but more importantly a positive outlook. I love talking to about the difficulties and pointing out their positives, and leaving with relieved smiles, a can do attitude and a mind full of the possibilities. I adore making a difference within the Autistic community; and the standing ovations, wonderful reviews, and of course my awards, are testament to the fact that I achieve these hopes, and much more.

People don't always understand why I volunteer, but you know what? I do it to help make changes in our community, I do it to make a difference and I do it because helping others is my dream job. I am living my personal dream right from the start… and I love it.

At my busiest I was working 25 hours of voluntary work a week. People say

"Wow; that must look really good on your C.V."

Why must they say that? It has nothing to do with my C.V – I don't care about that. It never occurred to me that doing all this work would make my C.V look good. Surely, the important thing is helping to make a difference – that's why I do it. Why does money, or making yourself look 'good', have to get in the way of all good intentions? It's ridiculous. Why do people only want to help others to make themselves look good? How could something so selfish influence one's desire to help, where in reality, they only wish to help themselves? No, the impact my joyous volunteering has on my C.V has hardly flickered across my mind's eye.

I am somewhat careless of society dictating that I should have a job, just for the sake of earning. I might not have a 'proper job' but I volunteer. Choosing to volunteer means I am dependant on myself for motivation, volunteering does not mean I lounge about all day, not working and relying on benefits. I work hard, every day, whenever my disability allows me to, just like everyone else. People with little understanding of the true extent of my volunteer work, say things like

"Why don't you want a proper job?"

Well guess what? I do have a proper job, in fact I have several 'proper jobs', just because most of them are unpaid does not mean it is any less a job.

I am very lucky that my mother is able to employ me on a part time basis; this gives me the freedom to live out my dreams through my charity work. It also enables me to manage my disabilities hidden hardships (such as shutdowns, which stop me from working 'properly'), illnesses and mental health. I could probably get a part time job in a supermarket, but I do not feel this would suit my personality and my aspirations. At least by volunteering in my dream areas I am living my dream from the beginning. Eventually when I am healthy enough to want a full time paid job, I will be able to get one in my dream area (working with young people and children with disabilities and public speaking) because I already have loads of experience and knowledge. Perfect.

Quite frankly, I think that life shouldn't be about earning money while hating your job, it should be about enjoying your life because you never know what might happen in the future. I don't want to sound scarily cold, but there is little we can do to see what the future holds... Who knows, when our final days are drawing closer, do you want to look back with regret? Where there is regret or a struggle, there are opportunities for both change and motivation. I feel you should stand up for what you want to do, and always try to look back happily with the knowledge that you enjoyed yourself and lived your life the way you wanted to. Volunteering is the way I want to live my life because it makes me happy and I know I won't regret it. I love volunteering, seriously I feel like I'm on a high when I get back from work. It's tiring but I don't mind. I'm living my dream, I don't have to try and fit in to society rules. Why should I get a paid job I don't enjoy when I can help make a difference to our community, for free? I love volunteering, that is why I volunteer.

A few years ago, I was lying in hospital bed undergoing countless examinations and it suddenly dawned on me the reasons I am inspired to help young people and give something back to my community. With my hand attached to a drip, verging in and out of consciousness and on a heavy dose of pain killers, I realised that due to my disabilities, mental health and illnesses, it is unlikely my dreams would become a reality. Especially not without the intense support I received day to day from my family, partner and the voluntary sector.

Even then I would have to rely heavily on other people's patience and good natured wish to care and make a difference. My blood ran cold (Not literally, this means that I had a sudden feeling of dread) when I realised that there are hundreds of young people out there who don't have opportunities like I do. They don't have the support from family, school or the voluntary sector. This means they are not being wholly motivated, challenged and supported to achieve or aspire to their dreams. The realisation hit me like a cold shower.

How difficult life is to achieve your dreams or be able to dream at all, if you are forced to survive without such support.

I believe that we all deserve a dream that we can achieve in to become happier in life. Happiness comes through a variety of things, which can be tailored to individuals: support, friendship, self-esteem that is close to ones 'ideal self' and a sense of accomplishment in their aspirations. I lay there in that bed for the whole night and the rest of the next day thinking long and hard about the complex scenarios young people face day to day. I imagined to myself what it would be like if I had all of my disabilities and difficulties but did not have a loving and caring family to go back home to. I realised how dramatically different my life would be. What if I did not have a home to go back to? How would my dreams and my lust for life be affected? How would I treat other people if I was without such valued support? The answer is too much for me to truly comprehend. I lay there crying with silent tears, overcome by my emotions and traumatic turmoil of how disastrous life can become... and how much more so if I had no support.

I lay there then trying to capture in my mind what I had to do to help encourage young people to imagine a dream for them to follow, and then what I had to do to help them along the path of happiness. I decided that I have to at least, try. One tiny little step at a time. If you are dedicated enough, change can happen. Just like I came through the deepest darkest despairs and saw the light on the other side.

I still remain confident that you can help change communities for the better, one step at a time, by dedication and caring enough to try. I think you need to sort out various problems from the root, in order to make a solid change. Many problems stem from individuals environments, how they grew up, lack of support, low self-esteem, bullying, cultural differences and lack of education regarding other people's differences. If you help someone (anyone) feel confident and give them the support they need to develop and become the best that they can be; they can be easily transformed to have dreams that renovate their self-image, self-worth, self-esteem and therefore impacts on every other thing too. I truly believe that I can help to make a difference by volunteering, so this is why I shall continue to give and support my local community. I also believe that you can help too, anyone can; it is within our human nature to help each other, in order to survive.

Why I Don't Have a Paid Job

One of the main reasons I have never been able to have a paid job is because of my disabilities hidden hardships (shutdowns and chronic pain) and illnesses. My Asperger's and all the anxiety that comes with it can prove difficult because employers don't tend to use understandable spoken language. Also, my anxiety can prove disruptive to my daily routine. If I had a job I would be forced to work to my contract unable to take time out if I needed it. When I get panic attacks, flashbacks and anxiety attacks it can take me weeks to recover, because I am already constantly ill with various diseases (hypercalceamia and hyperparathyroidism) it becomes impossible to juggle tasks such as leaving the house. So working a few hours a week, from home with my mum became my only option.

The beauty of volunteering is that because it is unpaid I can do as many hours as I wish when I wish and at my own pace and can still gain a lot back in return. I am still learning everyday and I am still achieving more than if I was in a paid job. Quite frankly, I know I am much happier than I would ever be if I was forced by society to get a paid job and suffer hell in consequences. Volunteering is very rewarding and life skill enhancing after all.

I have tried one full day of work experience, once a week for nine months, this was a fabulous experience and I did really enjoy my job. I worked for a natural beauty company and I like to think I learnt quite a lot about the products and was good at my job (I remember making a lot of money for my fabulous bosses, so surely I was not that bad) However even after one day of working and my usual routine with college and voluntary work, I was so exhausted I had no choice but to sleep through the whole of the following day, sometimes through the whole weekend. I was unable to function or concentrate on anything meaningful. I couldn't even make a cup of tea and a sandwich- which is a life skill my family had been teaching me to do for years. My body simply would not allow me to continue. This is why holding down a paid job with a contract and rules would be damn close to impossible for me to cope with physically and mentally. Much to my distress obviously, if I could, I would quite like to have my voluntary job as an actual job so I can save money for my future, but my body has never really listened to what I ask it to do.

I am constantly trying to make myself better. I am not giving in to my illnesses and feeling sorry for myself. I am not letting myself become unmotivated and unhappy. I know my limits of what I can cope with and I am slowly teaching myself to get better and safely expand my limits. There is no way I am going to let these bad things rule my life, because I wish to remain happy.

Shutdowns and Working

I get overloaded very quickly from normal un-stressful life, chores, activism, leaving the house, 'socialising'; due to the frequencies of these stressful daily occurrences, this makes me operate in my special 'Frozen Shutdown Defence Mode'. My Shutdowns get worse, the more I am forced to participate in any jobs or work when I am suffering in 'Frozen Shutdown Defence Mode', and needing to recover my bodies and minds abilities. Then I get shutdowns. I become completely disassociated of all usual physical, emotional or mental ability. I suddenly can't talk, without over whelming dizziness, or being literally unable to talk without dribbling and slurring. I get seizure like symptoms (which I called head 'surges' – a rush of energy through my head accompanied with severe white noise and an incontrollable shaking of my head or arms / legs). I pass out and my chronic pain and muscle cramping enhances to such an intensity, that I can no longer walk or hold things. In this way, when it comes to an Autism Shutdown, all my usual difficulties would be intensified to the point of impossibility.

The truth is, my wonderful disability, which makes everything in life difficult at the best of times (got to love it though) has its ups and downs when it comes to committing to a job. I have been severely ill with shutdowns for a long time, on top of other painful diseases, mental health issues (which 'cripple' me with flashbacks and disgusting memories every day, every hour). Combined, these all make daily life a terrible struggle because I was always in so much pain, over tired and so ill. I always felt like I had the flu due to my illnesses and I always felt quite mentally unstable because of my mental health issues.

With shutdowns, meltdowns and overloads, that change capability on an hourly basis, changing what I can achieve day to day (every week will be different). What I could accomplish yesterday, I may not be able to do today, or even next week. Hence, why finding a job that can be so flexible that I am allowed to stop working at a moment's notice due to shutdowns and pain (usually after only working a few hours), and also not have to go into work so many times a week, and cancelling work days due to sudden onset of chronic pain and shutdowns, is very unlikely. Let alone the fact that if a job like this were available, it wouldn't come to enough money to survive on. So what's the point, in making my disability harder, if I can help others, and myself, as a volunteer Autism Activist? I'm still working, and changing lives, my passion for Autism Activism is still the same, but I'm working in a way that's flexible and helpful for me; I give myself plenty of rest when necessary, and I don't push myself too hard to do too much work, so that in the end I can help more people – which is all that matters to me.

Autism and the Workplace

Asperger's can bring many positives traits to the workplace; honesty, hardworking, passion, motivation and working well within structure and routine. People on the Autistic Spectrum can be considered assets to any employer and it is these positive traits that should be focused on when looking for a suitable job. For example, I am mathematically challenged, so I would never work with money or behind a till. Finding an appropriate job, with understanding and patient bosses, is key to having a successful job that can aid development and well being.

Advice
People on the Autistic Spectrum need work experience and/or extra time to learn new tasks. It may take people on the spectrum longer to learn new roles, but if the employer is willing to put in the additional time with training, it is likely that they will become a highly valued member of staff. It is also very important that the workforce has an understanding of the disability as this is key to Autistic workers feeling welcome and accepted and means they are able to deal with any tricky situations if they arise. It is likely that those on the spectrum, will need a lot of time to adjust to their working roles and will need more breaks during work hours, this is vital for their overall health and well being. This is also where volunteering can be very helpful indeed, because if someone on the spectrum starts off on trial runs, within a volunteer role before paid employment, they will be able to learn new skills and get a taster for the 'real world' without any pressure. Then, once someone on the spectrum is ready for employment and they enjoy and are safely capable of completing the job, I imagine it will become a main focus of their life, just like a special narrow interest. They can easily become dedicated, punctual and hard working and certainly less likely to intentionally break rules, and best of all, they will do everything to the best of their abilities .

Advice for Parents

If you have a teenager with Asperger's, what do you think about them getting a job? As you probably know, forcing your child to do something they are not ready to do can be counterproductive and incredibly distressing. I am sure you have experienced many situations like this when your child was growing up... maybe starting a new school or doing anything out of their normal routine.

My advice is simply to wait until they are ready and until they want a job. They can't be pressured into it. If you pressurise a child with Asperger's, the outcome is likely to be bad. The reason being that if you insist on your child into doing anything (even if it is meant to be for their own good like getting good grades at school or getting a job for money to survive on) they will get stressed and anxious (not good), they will begin to think you don't think they are good enough and they will, with time, begin to resent both themselves and you (definitely not good). This is really bad news if your ultimate aim is to help them, which no doubt it is, your child may not always see it that way.

Look at it from their point of view, they think that you are nagging, are annoyed with them, don't value them because you want them to do more and are always on at them because you don't approve, understand or like them. It's difficult striking the fine line between nagging and pressurising to being gentle and supportive, but it is possible. Good luck.

Applying helpful pressure
You need to make sure your child knows you appreciate them, yes your child is likely to be hard work some times (goodness knows I was, sorry parents for my whirl wind antics) but if you are proud of your child (even if it is something really small like travelling on the bus by themself or doing something they could not do before) then let your child know. If your child feels appreciated and knows that you are there to help and support them, then they are less likely to reject you when you try and apply pressure to help them. Your child should always remain more important than your wish for them to do well.

My parents were constantly proud of me, even if I came home with failed tests results and a lost jumper (that happened a lot). They were supportive and never told me off because they knew that would make my performance worse (they only told me off when I had done something deliberately wrong). They have always been proud. I absolutely love them for it, they are wonderful. It is because of them I am doing so brilliantly today (Bigheaded much?).

I believe that a lot of children with Asperger's are the same and would react similarly to me so I can only suggest that you don't push or pressurise them too much. You could unknowingly be making their lives a lot harder. If you feel your child should learn about life skills and improve many other skills I can only advise that you let your child try. These are the things that my parents encouraged me to do, to try and increase my life skills:

1. Volunteering (there's a surprise!)
2. After school/college clubs
3. Activities I enjoy
4. Exercise
5. Work experience
6. Holidays or weekend away, a slight change in routine. Maybe try camping, it can be really cheap and that experience of trying to make a tent / food could be very helpful for you as parents. Just be careful with sensory overloads.

If you have help, you can smile through anything

Summary

You need to encourage your child and apply appropriate praise and pressure. You also have to support them to try new things without being forceful and putting them in a situation too stressful for them to cope with. I know there is a fine line between forceful pressure and helpful appropriate pressure, and it may be difficult to find the balance, but it will be worth it in the end.

Learning My Basic Life Skills

I would like to tell you about my journey as I attempt to learn life skills. Since leaving School and College I have learnt a lot from my family from the environment and friends about how to conduct myself on a day to day basis. These are the sort of things that I have never have been able to learn at school, in a classroom. However, such life skills are extremely important. Before I begin I would like to clarify the reason I find learning these life skills so difficult. I learnt to speak, and hear late (about six years old) and therefore all the things I should have learnt and developed in my early years were not developed until years later. This created a ripple effect of problems, as the things I should have learnt as an older child did not develop until I was a teenager and so on. Also, to add to this, as a child I suffered dreadfully with sensory meltdowns which meant there was no room in my thinking process for learning new things and making connections. Due to my slow processing speeds and inability to multi task my thinking strategies, all the skills I had to learn late, still took an awful lot more time, than a child without my difficulties would have taken.

Needless to say, the reason I don't have much practise in life skills is because I have simply been learning all the things I should have learnt earlier. I have simply been surviving in a world where sensory meltdowns are an hourly occurrence, leaving no room for anything else. All these reasons combined, and having to wait for support from others to help me learn these things is why I am still learning such basic life skills now and the reason why it has been a long winded and trying journey. As much as its going to be, and has been, very tricky, I am determined to learn such life skills, and more in order to achieve my independence and my dreams of helping people. After all, imagine all the people I could try and help if

I were more self-sufficient and more confident in different life skills. My motivation to learn is key here and I won't stop trying no matter how hard it gets!

I would like to discuss four key areas that I find difficult:

1. Using a telephone
2. Cooking
3. Cleaning
4. Money and finances

Using a telephone

Simple things such as talking on the phone and small talk are very hard work for me. If you take my usual problems with communicating, understanding and processing information, and then add a phone, the initial problems multiply and become magnified. I have to have my phone conversation planned out and scripted right in front of me, even now at 22 years old. I have to have what I am going to say, what they might say, what I can say in response to an unexpected question and also be prepared with an idea of what to say in case the call goes to answer phone or someone unexpected picks up r indeed anything unexpected or sudden happens.

For most people, having a phone conversation would be a simple procedure carried out without thought. You are simply just talking, listening and talking again. Yet, I literally freeze with fear when I am on the phone to someone. It is becoming a problem that is more serious than simply being shy. It requires a lot of thought to make a phone call because I am terrified of making a mistake and sounding silly. The thing is, the person at the other end of the telephone could be unaware of my disability and my troubles with phone conversations. Consequently, they may not make any allowances for me. It takes me a lot longer to process information and respond, so often the person on the other end of the line will become angry or frustrated. This only makes its worse because I don't know to cope with their frustrations. It really scares me when that happens, because I can hear the person getting frustrated but there is nothing I can do about it and the more I try the worse things get.

I don't cope well under pressure at all. It makes me even less able to do what is necessary to talk on the phone – Ahhh, the embarrassment and guilt causes complete and utter mayhem of crushed confidence.

I tackled this problem by practising with scripts, when my confidence had grown a tad, I had to answer the phone every time it went off (I disliked this a lot, it made me mighty uncomfortable, but it helped a bit). My mum would still have to stand beside me telling me what to say, supporting me. I would also be encouraged to ring other people when necessary (for instance my school). I still have similar difficulties but not to such a degree as I did back then.

This is a very difficult skill to learn, but it is a very important one as we use phones in our day to day lives. I won't give up and I do keep trying, because practise makes perfect, right?

Cooking

At school I used to really enjoy cooking, once I was in the zone. I would just get on with it and get the job done to the best of my ability (I don't have much cooking ability, but I always tried). It was a shame school only taught us how to make biscuits and cakes rather than foods I would actually consider cooking for daily use (you know, food to eat for lunch and dinner; practical foods. Biscuits and cake for lunch and dinner may sound yummy but that could become really unhealthy). As fun as cooking lessons were, they were never of any practical use; and so I still don't know much about cooking foods that could actually help me in daily life.

I am not so good with hand eye co-ordination and fine motor skills. This makes things like buttering bread and stirring a cup of tea, a messy business. When I cook, it does not always come out right, I am not one to forget about something in the oven and burn it, I don't usually forget given instructions either (if they are specific), I usually just don't know how I need to carry out such tasks as I should. Reading instructions on packaging is fine, that's not the problem; its understanding what the words mean, and then carrying out the physical task. I simply don't know how to conduct myself. Even very specific instructions are not specific enough, and even a tiny task you have to do in one simple operation can be difficult and complicated for me to complete.

How do you describe making a sandwich to someone? How specific must you be in order for someone to actually get it right? I have heard of a fabulous training exercise where two people sit back to back, one facing a table with sandwich making equipment and ingredients; one with her back to the table. The person not facing the table has to tell the other person how to make a sandwich. The other person has to follow the instructions precisely as they are given, forgetting all of their previous knowledge about making sandwiches. The results could be quite disastrous. The inside filling could have been scraped on the outside of the bread, butter in the wrong place, bread on the wrong side, filling not spread properly because the person failed to specify in which way you must hold the knife to butter with... The possibilities of how such an exercise could go wrong are endless.

I believe that such teaching exercises show why it is so important to give specific instructions when teaching someone with Asperger's how to cook. If the instructions are not specific enough, the results could be mayhem as we follow instructions and language precisely as you say it and don't make the connections to use any former knowledge.

Every time I had a food assignment, my father was brilliant; he always took his time to go through different recipes with me and we would always spend the evening cooking together. Being a chef, dad loved us cooking together and to be honest, so did I. He would be very specific and tell me what to do, how to do it, when to do it, what to do in the mean time and best techniques to use. Honestly, it is not as easy as it looks, to get it right, which is why having such a fabulous cooking mentor is invaluable.

Advice to Someone with Asperger's
Do you want to start learning the life skill of cooking? Ask someone to help you learn, maybe you could ask a parent/ carer, sibling, friend or teacher to help go through different ways of cooking. You could try and create a time once a week where you can cook something together, going through techniques and recipes (simple things like making a sandwich to start with).

Once you feel that you have mastered the basics, turning on a cooker and safely preparing basic food, you could enrol yourself on a beginners cooking course.

Currently, I sadly don't cook a lot. Learning how to cook is on my list of life skills to learn, I just have many other things that are considered of greater importance in my daily life twhich I need to learn first. I am terrified of cooking purely because of the prospects of knifes, cookers, fires and food poisoning. I am fortunate to still have parents who can provide food for me. When necessary I buy food and cook it, but usually it is salad, wraps, food that is stir fried or microwavable like soup etc. Terrible for my health and diet, I am trying to learn how to improve, though.

Cleaning

"Oh no, where did the maid go?"

As my lovely father would say. I try to keep on top of chores and tidy my room, but often I get distracted or feel too ill to move (not an excuse; honestly, disabilities and illnesses are exhausting beyond reason). My organisational skills are terrible which means that organising my time so that I can tidy more, is rather difficult. I would love to be the perfect role model and be able to say that yes, I tidy up after myself and have no problems with doing so but in all honesty, I am far from that. I have techniques, it is called cleaning as you go (I am being serious, mother). I figured that if you tidy as you go, the tidying will get done where as if you say you'll do it later because you are busy then the job will not get done, or at least it won't get done as effectively, and by then there would be a lot more tidying to do anyway.

Advice for Someone with Asperger's – Organising your Space

I am not talking colour co-ordinating and alphabetical order – although obviously you can if you wish. No, what I mean is simpler than that. You work out where you want various objects to go and you always keep them in that space dedicated to that object.

For instance, I always keep my books on my book shelf and on my bed side cabinet (Oh, how my sister had laughed when she read that bit; books – kept on a book shelf? Who would have known?!). I always keep various garments of clothing in my drawers and my two wardrobes. I always keep my arty things in the same corner on my desk. I always keep my DVDs and games in the same area. I never mix up where things go.

Advice for Someone with Asperger's — How I Tidy

1. I always tidy while listening to music. I find it helps make the chores more fun. Make sure you don't get too distracted though.
2. I always give myself a time limit. This is ridiculous but having a time limit of say five minutes to tidy away my clothes into the right compartments can actually be quite helpful because it gets the job done quicker and takes the edge off actually doing the job in the first place.
3. I often dance while tidying as well, if I have to cross the room to put something away, anyone watching would see me twirling, leaping and pointing my toes as I do so. Goodness knows why, I must look ridiculous. I just enjoy and take every opportunity to do dances and things like that. It makes the actual activity of tidying a bit more enjoyable rather than the usual boredom it entails. I find myself competing against myself; can I twirl more than six times while crossing my room to put my clothes away? I think so. Yes, for those of you who couldn't tell already, I really am, as mad as a hatter.
4. It helps me to have a timetable, stating clearly when I am tidying which area of the room, with a description of the time limit I have to complete this task in. I always try to stick to this timetable as much as possible.

Advice for Parents

It may be an idea to have a small treat if your child does all tidying for a week. Just something small so it does not count as bribery. Giving a treat at the end of the week simply means you are acknowledging and rewarding good behaviour (which is vital for any healthy relationship with your child) thus, the child is more likely to continue with wanted behaviour if you acknowledge them. I'm not saying you treat your child even when they have not done something good or tried to, I do not believe rewarding bad behaviour is good in the short or long run at all. A treat could be anything from a favourite food or dinner, a favoured activity and playtime, one to one special activity time or a trip to the park.

Earlier I mentioned time limits to help productivity. Unfortunately, they can be stressful and can lead to feelings of disappointment and lack of self belief.

If the child is tired, upset or stressed, completing the task within a time limit may not be achievable. Time limits have to be tailored to your child — depending on their current mood.

Money and finances

I earn pocket money through working in the Nursery with my mum. I have always had lots of help with managing my finances and this is purely because I would have less than no idea of how to organise them myself. I don't know how banks work, how to pay in cheques; I'm utterly oblivious about every aspect of the entire 'financing' system. The whole concept of banking renders me positively clueless… So here's the thing; my mum has a joint savings account with me, all my money gets paid into this account (it is still my money though). Only my mum has access to this account and only she can access the money for me. I am then able to spend my money on books, charity challenges and dresses (I'm kidding, I don't spend my money, ever. I prefer to save money and spend very little).

The rather embarrassing truth is, is that if my family did not sort my finances out, I would not even know how to go into a bank (or which bank to choose) to enquire about a bank account because I just would not know what was necessary. As unpractical as it is not to be able to access my own money, it is much preferable to spending all my money on goodness knows what without even realising it; at least this way, my money remains safe, until I really need it. Having support with my finances has proved invaluable to me. Not only because I don't understand the banking process; but also because some people have preyed on me before and taken advantage of my good nature. Some people have taken my money; short changed me and not paid back loans, and often, I don't know how to change that, I'm just too nice and gullible or naive to know when someone may be trying to take advantage of me.

Advice to Someone with Asperger's

I highly recommend asking for help from a very trusted person like a parent or sibling to aid you with setting up a system that works well for you, and your needs.

Even though I have a lack of understanding of the banking system does not mean you should give up trying. As I said before ask a very trusted person to teach you the process.

Summary

When most people think of Asperger's they tend to think of the difficulties with communication and reading facial expressions. Even people who have an understanding of Asperger's can forget that there is so much more to it. One of the main areas I have difficulty with is 'normal' daily tasks, aka cooking, answering the phone etc.

It has been absolutely paramount that I learn these basic skills to make life easier for me and everyone around me. It has taken a lot of work, over many years and to be honest I have only scratched the surface (started to learn the basics) but it is worth trying.

Advice to Someone with Asperger's
If you feel you would like to learn more life skills, perhaps you could ask a trusted adult or sibling to either teach you themselves or find someone who can. There may be youth groups that could help, or maybe groups set up in schools or colleges that could assist you in your life skills journey.

Good luck.

Many years ago, I was humiliated in public for not being able to complete a basic Life Skill; and the stress and overloads that followed gave me a meltdown and shutdown that lasted for weeks. That humiliation, and teasing was enough to make me never want to try that Life Skill again, I was humiliated, pained and it made to feel worthless. Yet, despite those horrendous feelings, I never gave up. Guess what that Life Skill was? It was performing and communicating my voice; public speaking; on second thoughts maybe it wasn't such a basic skill! Communicating my voice as a motivational speaker, as you may already know, is something I adore, with a passion that explodes with reels of inspiration from within my mind every day. Never giving up on that Life Skill, of communication, was probably one of the best things I could have done, because I wouldn't be in a position of happiness without it. It could have been so easy to give up; To allow those memories of humiliation whilst I cowarded, trembling on the stage, cloud my abilities and my wish to continue trying. It would have been easier to let everyone else communicate on my behalf; never trying to stand up on stage again. For a few years I did. Yet I have discovered that, as much as people in my family and voluntary sector know and understand me well, only I, can truly express my voice, in a way to help others.

Having such a hidden disability does mean that often you don't get a lot of support because people simple don't know how to help you. It's not like they can try to provide an accessible door and ramps, and some of the physical needs are catered for… having a hidden disability on the spectrum is more complicated for those trying to help. Due to this inability to see how people can help us, it does also mean that they feel useless, and they lose hope in us, to live normal, independent lives. There is, however, hope…

Autism and Living Independently

Disability or not, I believe that most of us can be empowered to become independent, providing we have support, and all of our government and council entitlements. Actually, I have some exciting news for you; I am beginning the very start of a terrifying new chapter of my life. That is, I am finally moving out of home, into my own flat, and becoming a strong, independent, super woman! I'm kidding about the last part, no magical powers have surfaced yet, but I guess with all these overloads and stress, I need to make jokes about it. I'm struggling to cope with all these changes and new demands, in all honesty. Yet the truth is, I am moving out in a matter of weeks (by the time you read this I would be 'independent' already… Crikey, that is a scary thought). My partner and I have a nice cosy little flat in a nice convenient location, and soon I'll be expected to live… independently. Something I always doubted I could do, no matter how supported I was. You see I always did require 121 support for every task or life skill I complete. Yet as I grow older, I am improving, and with my confidence growing, and being better able to manage my disabling shutdowns, I am able to do much more than before, even though in reality, that is still very little. The changes in routine will be scary, of course they will be, I will struggle with the usual hidden hardships of my disability, but I am honestly so excited about the prospects of independence. The flat itself, is in a great location for us; very familiar and safe. I can catch familiar buses, from familiar places, I can go to familiar shops and familiar places of interest near-by. Best of all, I'm just a short, familiar walk from my parents house. All of this may not seem like much, but it's almost vital to the successful independence training for autistic individuals, like myself.

My family and partner have done so much to help me on my journey. Starting with role modelling and guiding me through Life Skills, to helping and allowing me to make my own choices and do for myself. I am ever so grateful for their support in making these transitions easier for my partner and I. My family and my partner have created routines for me to follow; some which are really basic, to include my general well being, health and happiness (Medication, gentle exercise, organising myself to go out, volunteering and autism activism, social life and seeing / phoning family), other routines including house keeping, chores, bins, and other more general routines including food, bills, finances and survival. As a result, I feel kind of calm about it all now, I feel so much more empowered thanks to my family's 121 support an guidance.

Which leads me on to my next section of advice.

Autism and Independence Training – Advice for Parents

I believe that as much as all disabilities on the spectrum are all completely different, and that each individual is affected in a different way due to their own diversity and their environment. However, I also think that it is possible for people on the spectrum to learn to live independently or / half independently, in a location, and with support that is appropriate to their individual needs. It is necessary that the location is appropriate and familiar, and that these new changes are slow, well adjusted, maybe with trial runs and appropriate to the individuals needs.

In order to realise how we can help teach life skills, we need to first establish what the barriers are for people on the spectrum to become independent with life skills; So I have created yet another list because, well, I just like lists, don't you know?

Barriers of people with Autistic disabilities becoming independent with life skills:

A. Psychological barriers of those teaching them, and the individual (I.E, "I don't have time, to be with my child all the time teaching Life Skills. I have to work, and it takes so long for them to remember or process anything she's learnt")
B. Methods in teaching 'Life Skills'
C. Assuming you should start teaching life skills, when they need to learn them (in their teens)
D. No one wants to / can help my child / me

I believe that, such barriers can be mostly overcome, in most generalised cases. I also think, that 'Life Skills' can be taught at any age, the younger the better, as long as they are age and ability appropriate, and fully supported with hopefully 121 care, and structured safely into routines. From experience, I have seen a lot of people on the spectrum who have 'learnt helplessness' from their parents, custodians or carers doing everything for them, all the time, with never allowing them to make choices or actions for themselves. I understand how as parents or carers do almost too much, to compensate for their child's delay in learning by doing for them, rather than teaching them "how to." It is not a problem but I think that instead of this, it may be more helpful to always "assume" there is an ability to learn, it just may need lots of different techniques, and endless patience to be enabled to develop. In order to enable those on the spectrum to live independently, I think you should teach these basic Life Skills that will be necessary, earlier on, practising slowly, with 121 support.

Advice for parents; How to teach Life Skills for Independence:
Make a list of skills see, I told you I like lists. If you make a list of skills, easily accessible and understandable, your child always knows what's expected

of them, decreasing pressure of anxiety over un expected changes. Again, do this together, communication is key to deciding with your child where to start, and what to prioritise

Create a 'no pressure' syllabus for home learning Ensure you try and get schools to participate and use school learning to also implement these skills. After looking at your list, and the skills that have been learnt, you then need to really think about how to continue implanting these skills into normal life. To do this, you need to think about the over all purpose of each skills. In order not to overwhelm, you need to keep it simple, so all basic skills, like drawing, reading, speaking, numbers etc, need to have a direct purpose for the child to fully understand, and be able to do such skills to the best of their abilities. I recommend you keep it simple, don't overload or pressure your child. Avoid making a big deal out of what you are learning together, for instance "Now it's time for life skills!". It becomes an additional pressure, just like school. Instead try to implement basic life skill teaching into general routines. Sometimes children learn better when they feel better, comfortable; when they don't realise they need to learn, you remove the pressure of learning, and instead enable them to concentrate on what they need to. I also recommend you keep such a schedule simple with maybe 3 skills at a time, obviously depending on routines and children's ability, ability to cope and support systems.

Make an "Independence tracker" to, yes, you guessed it, keep track of your child's progress. Make an easily accessible list of skills you are both working towards, just as I mentioned before. Also, keep this list and tracker as visual as possible, and make it fun to complete. I suggest you have photos and other visual reminders, of how your child once completed a task. Document with film, photos. Make a visual entry of dos and don't lists, to make it simpler for your child to remember, and do visual safety pages, for each skill. I know it goes without saying, but make sure you keep track within the tracker. Checking off the list helps remind children of what they have learned, enhancing confidence, self-esteem and wellbeing.

Become a Life Skills Role Model As an Autism Activist who focuses on role modelling in my own services, I am a great believer that role modelling really helps. Use yourself as a role model and teach your child Life Skills by doing activities together, making sure that if there is failure, you handle it in the most helpful, and non harmful way. Teaching side by side, and getting them involved in the "how to" is much more effective than "showing" how to do skills. Try to avoid instructing and doing these tasks for them, do the tasks together; take your time and give plenty of 121 support. 121 support here is vital, and learning how your child best learns and develops is also necessary to enable your child to progress.

Practising Life Skills Regularly within Childs Current Routines If you learnt these skills together, within a routine, you then need to make sure that the skill is practised regularly because it's very hard remembering life skills when there is so much else going on in your life. Build practise sessions into routines, and then build these skills into normal daily routine. Within the safe structure of a routine, the child will be able to remember and cope a lot easier. Your child will start to function through this routine, and slowly begin to adapt and imitate back these methods you have taught through this type of role modelling. slowly, but surely. Maybe take time out of every week, or other day, when your child is in the best frame of mind, and not too overloaded, and work together, start with something of interest to your child, and work your way up, trying to keep lesson plans interesting and effective as possible.

Rewards systems If you can implement a rewards system, (not bribery) for completing, or trying to learn, each skills, it will really help. It's important to remember that the sole focus is not the child learning the skills, but simply that they are trying, don't get all wrapped up in what they have and haven't achieved, because that applies too much pressure, which could be counter-productive. Just know that your child is trying, amongst a hectic world of autism, and that deserves rewards too. Rewards could include anything to do with their specialised topic or specific narrow interests, or it could be quality time some where they like, less chores, a favourite game or movie time, inviting friends over for socialisation. If you are really clever with it, you could turn rewards into a lesson plan too – Together go to the shop and choose a movie, give them money and show how much it is, help them through it, and encourage them to go and pay and ask a question, and listen / remember response.

As a parent or carer you it would be helpful to think about
A. Repeated 121 Role Modelled learning set within a routine. To become independent, people on the spectrum need to learn by doing and thinking their way through things (rather than just allowing them to watch.)
B. Remember what works for you, might not work for them, encourage

them to try different ways of doing things, they might find it easier to do something completely different to how you would do something.

C. Trial runs of real life situations on a daily basis, with your supportive guidance. Enable them to think about how and when to do things, how to organise themselves and allow them to make their own choices (within safety reasons, of course).

D. Give them time to adjust and do new skills. Take your time with your child and try to avoid un-necessary pressure or rushing them, because that would be counter productive.

E. Contacting your local council and researching various ways in which you can support your child into independent living. Find out what funding might be available, and access support from charities and support networks.

Life's Game of Snake and Ladders

Having no support is a bit like playing life's game of Snakes and Ladders, alone. You struggle forward, terrified of the outcome of hourly life, as you play Life's Game of Snakes and Ladders. 'Snakes' in this case, can be anything from bullying, a tough boss or a negative change in the direction of your life. You roll the dice of choice, take a turn, not sure where you are going or what you are supposed to be doing, not even understanding the rules for this game... hey, adult life is hard, right?!

But then suddenly you are cornered by a large snake. You stop in your tracks, entranced by this giant, jeopardising creature. His tongue whips out, that horrible hiss escapes his mouth, scales glisten in the cold light... and the fear grips your heart. You become paralyzed with fear as you realise you shouldn't have tried to play this game alone... but there's no where you can run to, no support to help you out. Not a ladder in sight. The Snake's eyes glint as he suddenly strikes. The scream escapes your mouth as panic consumes your soul... it's happening again. You're being swallowed and taken back down to square one again, back to the beginning, as if all your progress means nothing. You land on the floor; tears stream down your face as everything within you aches, negativity corrodes you. All that progress for nothing. Chilled to the bone, you sit there, consumed by the emotional rollercoaster that is life's game of Snakes and Ladders... you tremble, you shake, your brain hurts... you were so sure you were on the right path, so sure the dice of choice was correct...

where did that Snake even come from?! How can people expect you to get back up again, after a fall like that? Hopelessness encircles you, and as you sit, huddled all alone, on square one, you feel just as trapped as you did when that snake struck you down. How can you move on without support?

On the other hand, having support, is like playing life's game of Snakes and Ladders, with a manual and Ladders. Phew; what a relief!

You step forward confident that if anything goes wrong you have a safety net; you have supportive ladders who can help you out. You roll the dice of choice, the dice stumbles and stops on a path that your supporters helped you see. You take your turn, you're on the right track, supportive ladders have saved you before; you feel at ease and reassured. Here it comes, up ahead of you a giant snake looms, she's ready to strike, venom glistens from her mouth. The fear hits you then, shaking you, seizing you, but still you travel forward, having to complete your journey. You're in her square now, her territory, she rises up tall, threatening, ready. Your heart in your mouth, desperation bubbles with your blood, shaking you, paralyzing you with fear; you just can't go back to square one again... she slithers around you, her tail whips around your feet. Her mouth stretches, red torn white, grotesque, fangs dripping with venom, when you notice something ahead of you...

It's hope, it's support; It is a Ladder!

Breathing fast, you run forward, narrowly missing the snakes lunging bite, and you grasp the ladder as if your life depends on it. Heck, sometimes it does! You climb the ladder, up, up, higher than you ever had been before. And suddenly your feet are on firm ground again, and you could weep with relief. The ladder has taken you up a few levels, and you realise that although you can see snakes, the ladder has provided you with new and exciting journey, it has taught you how to try and escape, enabled you with skills you didn't realise you had; if you knew how to climb a ladder before you would have done it a long time ago!

But best of all, there are ladders... ladders of hope, to help you out of any sticky situation. If that ladder had not of been there, where would you be now? How long would it have been before you had the strength to push forward, and try life's game of Snakes and Ladder's, again?

It's important to realise what the Ladders are in your own game of Snakes and Ladders; for me, and thousands others nationwide, the ladders are the voluntary sector, and family, friends, professionals, charities and the incredible support they provide. Support can build you up, take you to places you never before thought was possible; skills emerge you did not realize were there and you are confident in your ability; all because support has enabled you to think clearly. The brilliance of realising how truly blessed I am to be surrounded by ladders (how odd!) and to have support from my voluntary family has proved completely invaluable in shaping me to be the person I am today. Do you think I would have achieved half of my dreams if I did not have such royal support from my families? No; I doubt I would have had the opportunity, nor the ability.

When things went wrong, when snakes would corner me and threaten to swallow me back down to square one, I was not embarrassed or ashamed of my so called 'failings'. This is a big achievement in itself, because after being bullied and gaslighted for so long, you have no self belief or self value, you begin to see yourself as making mistakes all the time, you feel belittled, worthless; like you have done something wrong. Yet, support changes those negative feelings, and can help push away negativity, enabling you to move forward, with positivity. This is because the voluntary sector and my family have always made it clear, that I did not fail; rather the lack of education of my disability in people, and their lack of understanding of how to help, had failed me; which was not my fault at all. Volunteering also provides ladders for other people, to rise above their own misunderstandings and misconceptions, by learning to improve their communities / their work practises or their attitudes; in turn, creating ladders for others in need by being supportive, understanding and accepting of diversity.

Just like a real game of Snakes and Ladders, life can change at any moment, so you should always live a life that you won't regret; follow your dreams as much as possible. Build a future that you can be proud of and make those dreams happen – never forget that volunteering can open doors to a future of incredible measures; you just have to open those doors, climb those ladders and take a peek! Remember to only say "Yes" to others if you are not saying "No" to yourself. If you are dedicated enough, to the right project, change can happen one tiny little step at a time. The beautiful thing about volunteering is that whilst you are helping other people, and helping yourself, you are simultaneously building the experience, confidence, happiness, wisdom, life skills and abilities that can aid in future ambitions. Not to mention you will meet many supportive 'ladders'! I love volunteering, volunteering has enabled me with life skills and happiness. I adore making concrete change and achieving my dreams; that is why I volunteer. My family and voluntary group know how without support and understanding, I shrivel up like an old dark autumn leaf and fail to show the world my usual bright colours, instead they know how to let my colours shine and how to enable me to succeed in this difficult game of Snakes and Ladders, we call life... and I'm sure, that ladders like this, can help you too. You just need to find your ladders to reach infinity and beyond! Volunteer; Change lives, to change your life.

The End

Thank you to my friends and family for aiding me in my journey from childhood through to adulthood. Special thanks for all the endless help I received at My Linwood Special Needs Primary School where all the dedication and support from staff gave me the vital support necessary that enabled me to leave so soon, to go to a main stream Primary school. Linwood staff aided me, and shaped me in my life long journey of skills and happiness, for which I will be forever grateful. Thank you, also for my main stream secondary school, although difficult it was made bearable and hugely helped by the wonderful S.E.N.C.O, the superb Helen Pike. Thank you Helen for fighting for my rights and putting up with the daily phone calls from my family, and sorting the system out so that I got what I was entitled to. Thank you Helen, for being so patient, understand and supportive of me and never giving up on me, even during my struggles. Also, Jean Allwyn, my connections advisor who helped me in so many ways along my rollercoaster journey through mainstream secondary school, finding a brilliant transition course from school to college and showed me that I was good enough for college. Thank you to Jean to opening up the hidden world of possibilities that volunteering brings, if it was not for Jean, I would not have started my volunteering adventure at all. (You'll soon discover volunteering is my lifeline, so I can't thank her enough). If it was not for those two lovely ladies I would not be in such a position of happiness today. Thank you also, to Poppy Sargeaunt, a brilliant youth worker, (the best) for supporting me as I developed my skills and discovered my love of volunteering and helping out. Poppy nurtured me and my little tiny talents and made them into something rather brilliant (I'm now happy as a result). My love of public speaking and educating others about disabilities became a huge passion of mine. I am forever grateful to Poppy for opening my eyes to my hidden abilities, and also, for never giving up, even when I was ill or having breakdowns. I could not have holistically developed to become the person I am today without their support, all three of them. Thank you all, so much, for making me happy and helping me to develop me to try to be the best that I can possibly be.

Last, but not least, thank you to my family and friends for constantly supporting, understanding and nurturing my abilities, and my disability. Thank you for those who have stuck by me through thick and thin, making happiness a very real possibility. All of the people who have helped me, my friends, family and support workers are all stars to me. Stars that have each individually shone their beautiful light onto my life's path. Allowing me to see through the blackness of despair and confusion and brush away the fears blocking my path. Despite my countless difficulties, I know, my disability has many positives and I know with certainty that I am lucky to be alive. For this reason, I have never been happier. I have been working my way through every dream I have ever had. I have succeeded and have achieved so much in making my dreams of helping a reality- and it's all down to my disability, my wonderful gift of a disability and the support I have received. If it was not for the immense support I have received, realising such truths could have been more difficult and I thank you all for helping me realise my true potential.

Why I Want to Make a Positive Change for Disabled People

I am really passionate about making changes for those with disabilities. I strive to do everything I can to make my dreams of helping to make positive change become reality. I have three key reasons for this motivation.

Reason 1

One day, it was pouring with rain and I was walking to a restaurant to get some dinner for my family. As I walked, I saw that there was a lady in a wheelchair, waiting outside the restaurant on the other side of the road, trying to open the door to enter. She could not quite reach the door handle. As I approached, I remember thinking, 'Surely there is someone there who would help this lady?' However, it appeared not, as she continued struggling all the way until the point where I had walked over to her. I then saw that there were 10 or so people inside the restaurant, all discretely watching her lack of progress, but none of whom attempted to help her. Not only was it very shocking to me that they all completely ignored her, but they also seemed to purposely avoid any type of contact- eye contact, nothing.

I felt horrified at their behaviour towards this lady; they were treating her as if she did not exist and as if she had some deadly contagious disease. She was only trying to enter the restaurant. Why is society so uncaring that there are so few ramps and little understanding from others, when it is clearly needed? Of course I felt I had to help, I couldn't just witness such a struggle and not try to help due to my own feelings of misunderstanding. So, I smiled, said and signed 'hello' to the lady, she signed 'hello' back. I did not use sign language as an assumption that she could not speak, but only because I had been learning sign language at the time and used it at every given opportunity. However, it appeared she had difficulty talking, so I then signed and said 'help' and 'open' 'door', she nodded her head against the head rest of her wheel chair so I opened the door and supported her up the step and through the door.

Once the lady was in the restaurant, I did not want to assume that she would need any more help so I stood close by to her, in sight, to allow her time to try and do whatever it was she needed to do (I had no idea how independent she was so I couldn't judge how much support she needed, hence why I stood in sight and paying attention in case she did need more help). After a while she brought her hand out, and appeared to be gesturing to me, banging her head on the head rest, her eyes were on me. Luckily, I can read some types of body language, and noticed straight away, I smiled and walked over signing and saying 'hello' again. I then supported her through speech and sign language and smiles to find out what she wanted to do. It turned out she wanted to order a bottle of water, get a menu and leave.

All of this happened, while everyone just stared at me and a fellow human being as if we were an alien species. I felt almost disgusted that no one seemed to care; no one moved or attempted to help. I remember really hoping that any assumption about them not caring or wanting to help was wrong. Thankfully I was right, later I found that they wanted to help – but did not know how to. After the lady left, I was thanked by a staff member for helping the lady in the wheelchair. Also, someone else then said they had no idea what to do or say to help and that they felt ashamed at not trying to help. It then became clear that no one in the restaurant knew how to handle the situation, they did not know how to act, what to say, how to behave- and so logically because they did not know what to do; they did nothing at all. So my assumption of them not meaning to appear uncaring was right. They wanted to help, but did not know how to.

There are people out in our big wide world that do care and want to make positive change but simply didn't know how. I want to assist those people who are not quite sure how to help by teaching them and giving them an insight to life with a disability. Although I am no expert in Autism let alone physical disabilities, I have been told my 'ramblings' and public speeches have been very insightful, helpful, empowering, inspiring and intellectual. I wish to help by giving teaching presentations, speeches and disability awareness workshops to professionals and young people. This should aid in their personal understanding of disability, so they too, can help.

Reason 2

Everyone I have met with a disability has been a very genuine person, good at heart, quirky and kind. A lot of people don't see this, but have a very, dare I say it, narrow minded view on disabilities. Such people only look at the negative side, not the positive. This negativity can really hinder a person living with a disability. Simply because, if they are not expected by society to do well, they won't believe that they can and so they won't strive for such a goal. Yet, if society believed in disabled people and supported them correctly, they would be able to achieve their full potential, which would have a positive impact on everybody.

Reason 3

This is the most important reason as it was the main thing that drove me to write this book.

I am very lucky to receive so much amazing support and to be surrounded by people that try to understand, and want to learn more, about my difficulties. This realisation of how lucky I am got me thinking about other disabled people, and how much support they have. It worries me that other disabled people may not have support or understanding networks to help them through life. I am concerned that this could lead to them being very unhappy, and unable to reach their full potential.

In an ideal world everyone would have in-depth understanding of Autistic Disorders. As we do not live in an ideal world, I want to do my bit to educate people who are willing to learn, whether those people are:

1. Somebody learning about their own disability
2. A parent seeking knowledge to help their Autistic child
3. A teacher wishing to make school learning more bearable

4. Anyone who wants to gain an understanding of someone with Autistic Disorders.

I would love to be able to create an understanding of Autistic Disorders, so that more people are aware of the difficulties, but more importantly, the positives of the disability. My reasoning is that if more people understand and accept such difficulties as those with Autism / Asperger's have, then they may become more accepting of differences. I hope that with the knowledge people will grow in patience, develop more understanding and be supportive. This understanding could help disabled people get the right support they need, and grow to their full potential.

Even if one person reads this book and could take something positive away from it, then it's been well worth my time.

Finding beauty in disability

I want to aid people with disabilities in finding beauty within themselves. Help them find their hidden talents and find the beauty inside their quirks and 'Aspergery moments' as I like to call it. If I can help people to do that, their confidence, self esteem and self image will grow which in turn will help change others' attitude towards them. All in all it will help change a bigger picture of people's outlook on disabilities, such as A.S.D.

We must try to understand our

DIFFERENCES

Crystal analogy

I can see my disability as a gift, but not everybody can. This is because not all gifts are apparent from the start. Imagine you have received a gift. You may un-wrap the gift from its presence in a tiny box and to your puzzlement you find a small, complicated little crystal sitting in its bed of tissue paper. You look closer to see the crystals hostile angles and transparent glass. You carefully take the crystal out the box, hoping to find something of more interest, but you are somewhat disappointed by the angled prism. Confusion settles in, for, why is a crystal special enough to be a gift? Of course, it is all too easy to throw aside this crystal as you don't yet see the beauty, or purpose of the crystal at all. Yet, all it takes is a bit of patience, understanding and education for the true purpose and brilliance of the complexities of a crystal to come to light. It has to be shown to you the precise and wondrous majesty of simply tying a bit of thread to the crystal and allowing sunlight to beam through. Suddenly, with the powerful rays of the sun, this tiny crystal showers magnificent rainbow colours across the surface of its surroundings. Upon doing so, suddenly this hidden gem, with its hostile angles and complicated surfaces is abruptly transformed into something so much more, this crystal is a home for so many intriguing and beautiful colours. You glance around, a smile finding its way upon your lips, and you gaze in awe at the colours dancing upon the pale walls. Colours of different shades, depths and contrast, sprinkled around upon the dull surfaces brightening up and making their surroundings quite colourful, quirky and fun. Watching in confused splendour, a simple question drifts through to your mind – how is it that I managed to miss the curious gift, and beauty this crystal possesses? With that intriguing and enchanting discovery, you may be charmed to find that a crystals prism that hangs so delicately from a thread within a window has an astonishing realm of beauty enraptured within its province.

I feel this is much the same for those with disabilities on the Autistic spectrum. Often support, acceptance and understanding is essential to show why, and how, their disability is a gift. With the right support their true, amazing, talented and kind colours can shine through.

There are many things that those with Asperger's syndrome find difficult. However such things can also be used strongly to our advantage; while we don't understand language, we are also finely tuned to our surroundings, always learning, and trying to improve, always honest and speaking in a precise and exact manner. We are the ones who are less likely to use sarcasm deliberately, or use mean, untrue language. In an Asperger's world, where everything is exact, honest and true, those with Asperger's find it super hard to tell lies, and simply don't understand how to mislead, or perhaps, manipulate with lies. A beautiful thing in my disability is I just don't know how to lie. It renders my mind with so much confusion because every fibre of my being screams at me that I can't consider lying because it is not real, or true. You see lying goes against every fibre of our biological makeup; we can't cope with lies, untruth or unjustifications, especially if we speak it.

Where we find it difficult to cope without routine, we thrive fabulously in the comfort of routine, structure and specific instructions. We can do things really well, if we are simply given a supported chance. Where problem solving is an issue in times of sensory overloads and distractions, problem solving and our social imagination can be improved with being in an environment that allows our minds the time, and ability to think.

We have highly alert senses, and notice, often too much so, we will be the ones who can give you precise figures, facts and remember details that others would swiftly forget. We could be the ones who are more likely to pick out one person out of a line up of people who we met once ten years ago. We remember faces, (as much as we don't understand how to read faces or what they are telling us), and most aspects and characteristic of the face. Therefore we are more likely to be able to give clear descriptions of what someone looked like, even if we met them once many years ago.

I love knowing the number plates of every car (in my lifetime) my parents have driven, on holiday, or in the UK, it has become my little party trick. My memory is like a sponge, I can hold so much information in my mind, but often lose the 'useful' things (like life skills) in the process. I remember facts, figures and precise dates so although I may forget various life skills, because my brain is too busy remembering useless or helpful facts, I still have essentially a beautiful memory. For example: Even if I don't remember how to catch a train, at least I know what I wore, and why, on Monday the 17th of April 1998. What I m trying to say is that, where us Aspies find it hard to do certain things, with patience and understanding, we can practise and improve.

I love my disability because it has taught me understanding and allows me to notice many things from my environment. It allows me to learn so much more from my surroundings, simply because I take in so much more than most people. It took me many years to be able to accept my disability; the difficulties, people's judgements and the brilliance of it. I love my disability now, I see it as a huge part of my life that will never go away, but I don't want it to. I don't want a cure for my wonderful disability; because if there was a cure, it would strip me bare of everything that has ever made me myself. I would no longer be unique, quirky, and totally honest and I would no longer be a beautiful and caring person. As a friend once told me, 'I have taken what society sees as a weakness, and made it my biggest strength and selling point'. My disability is what I have made it with support; the very best.

List of why I love my disability:

1. **I like lists**, they are very helpful and very Aspergery
2. **My disability makes me very motivated, passionate and intelligent** about certain subjects, particularly specialist topics of interest. This means I can excel in any area of specialised interested if I have the support and time to research them.
3. **My disability makes me honest**, something that is somewhat rare in society today, considering honesty to be vitally important. My honesty is something I have always been very proud of
4. **My disability allows me to be very creative**; I love art and have a brilliant imagination. As a child I could play with a bubble wand (instead of real toys) for hours. My imagination allowed me to remain motivated to play and to learn so much more because I was so creative. My creativity has allowed me to come up with original ideas of how to help with my volunteering. It is also the reason I have come up with loads of events and fundraising ideas of how to help build an understanding of Autism in a fun, easy and understanding way. I am very proud of how my creativity allows me to help.
5. **Despite having empathy issues, I feel that I care very much about everyone around me.** I love this aspect of myself. For instance if a stranger I meet tells me about a little problem they're having, I would worry about that problem and how they are all day because I care too much
6. **My disability enables me to see/hear details others often miss out on.** This can lead to sensory overloads; but when it does not it really is quite a rare, precious moment of clarity and beauty to be able to witness

so much that others don't see or notice. For this reason, I feel like I can learn so much from my surroundings because of this amazing disability that I have

7. **My disability allows me to understand the differences in other people.** This helps me be less judgemental and more accepting

8. **My disability makes me a genuine character,** a good person who will always be honest, loyal and care for you

9. **My disability makes me strong,** resilient and inspiring (apparently) and dedicated to making change to help others, because of my obsession with helping, routines and my specialist topics

10. **My disability makes me happy** – I love my AspergerWorlds Fairy Jam Jar!

Book Reviews and Endorsements

Professor Simon Baron-Cohen, FBA
Professor of development Psychopathology,
A world Leading Expert in Autism Research

"Joely Colmer's beautiful book is a valuable contribution: We learn most about autism from those with autism who can communicate their experience of what helps and what make things worse. Joely's attractive illustrations and clear writing is an inspiring account of how to feel proud of one's autism and one's difference. She explains how others can either compound the disability, or minimise it. And she reminds us that we can change our perception of autism to reveal each person's talents"

Dave Howard
BBC Television and Radio Producer
BBC Generation
(Personal Endorsement)
Dave and Joely worked together on the nationally awarded BBC Radio 1 documentary, where Joely shared her story on "Stories from the Autistic Spectrum" with George the Poet.

"Joely Colmer's strength of personality shines. Saying that she 'loves' her disability and that it is 'a gift' is a powerful and important message to send to peers and younger people with similar conditions. Joely also has a rare talent, in that she is exceptionally good at articulating what it's like to have Asperger's Syndrome. Joely's extraordinary ability to describe the condition she has so that others may understand it and empathise with it is extremely rare and valuable. I was blown away by the candid, honest, and positive insight that she was able to provide; So much of the content she provides is so compelling and insightful. She so clearly has a passion for positivity representing her disability, and for putting herself 'out there' as a role model to others"

John Bercow

Head Speaker at Houses of Commons
Father of Autistic Child
(Personal Endorsement)

'I have been hugely impressed hearing about the work of Joely Colmer. She is an excellent example of someone who has used her diagnosis with Asperger Syndrome to great effect.

Her commitment to voluntary work has made a huge contribution to her community. She is an inspiring figure and I wish her will"

Jeffrey Newman

Independent Educating Management Professional
Founder of The Earth Charter UK

We all know the word 'Autism' and maybe even the word 'Asperger's' but it's likely that most of us have never met anyone with that disability. Joely Colmer has written a book to help us understand. She knows all about it – not, like an expert form the outside, but with the knowledge that only an 'insider' can provide. And, Joely writes, not only for those of us who want to know more, but also for those who have the disability and needing practical guidance. Central to her writing – and her attractive drawings – is Joely's humour and humanity. As we read the book, we pick up more and more, through Joely's stories and honest personal examples.

So, who is Joely? True, she is quite an exceptional young woman. She was diagnosed with an Autistic Spectrum Disorder at the age of two, couldn't speak till she was seven (which was connected with her deafness) or tie her shoelaces until she was eighteen. But she no has three A levels and in 2013, at the age of 21, won the national YMCA 'Youth Volunteer' Award.

Joely and I met at the Explore Diversity Conference for young people form all over Dorset (where we both did a speech). The diversities including every sort of disability, as well as race and sexual differences. Her talk was inspiring. I was there, a rabbi, representing www.

EarthCharter.org, speaking about the issue facing out worlds. Our thinking and experience connected us with one another – the need, for example, to eliminate discrimination in all its forms, such as that based on race, colour, sex, sexual orientation, religion, language, and national, ethnic or social origin and to honour and support the young people of your communities, enabling them to fulfil their essential role in creating sustainable societies.

'My Fairy Jam Jar : Life A.S We See It' is of importance to everyone, not only for the people with a disability but also parents, doctors, carers and the Government. The book is more like a person than a manual; human and lovable. Perhaps one day, the other sort of 'Expert' might compile and 'guide' to Joely's material for teaching. Joely and I agree about so much and I very much look forward to working together. More than anything else, we agree that:

"Life is incredible, to be alive, disabled or not, is an amazing adventure – this is why all life deserves the right to be listen to, respected, understood and helped, to aid in making life's adventures as supported and wonderful for everyone as one can."

Denis-Marie McIntosh
Producer and Host of Award Winning American TV series
"Fairy Tale Access" at "Access Mashua"

"I highly recommend 'My Fairy Jam Jar'. More often than not we've heard about Autism and Asperger's from those who have done clinical observations and/or form the parent's perspective. Miss. Colmer has Asperger's and her book gives us the tools to understand the sensations of actually living in her world. Written as a first hand account and completed in a way that others who haven't actually been inside her world, can only speculate at.

As parents you understand your child the best; but until a child can get to a point of articulating what they are actually feeling or experiencing in life, it's hard to understand the why.

Miss Colmer, invites you into her world a world that is amazing and frightening. But it puts things in perspective, helping anyone understand what a child and/or adult on the spectrum might be going through.

'My Fairy Jam Jar', it's one of the best books on the subject and I've read in a decade."

Lorraine Peterson OBE
Trustee of Charity "Ambitious about Autism"
Educational consultant

"A Truly inspirational book that gives a passionate and insightful view of life with Asperger Syndrome. Joely describes the first 22 years of her life in a very down to earth, highly descriptive and often humours dialogue reflecting on endless difficulties that she has encountered and the strategies she has developed to support her AS. Joely has used her life experiences to share the difficulties that people with Asperger's Syndrome encounter every day and given us a reflective and passionate story that we can all learn from.

Every person who cares for or works with children and young people would benefit from reading this book. Many of the situations that Joely describes and the stratergies she suggests to overcome her difficulties could be used to support any child or young person with additional needs to just those with AS.

Although Joely has encountered endless negative experiences she has remained incredibly positive and used her strengths to support and help other people as well as enjoying her own life to the full.

Although at times the descriptions are long, Joely admits that she "rambles", they capture your imagination and make you think about times when you may have no identified a hidden disability" in someone and therefore not fully appreciated the need to adapt the way you communicate with them.

As someone who has worked with children with SEN for the last 30 years I wished I had has this book at the start of my career – it would have really influences the way I might have interacted with some of the children I have had the pleasure to teach.

Joely gas captured the true essence of how someone with a disability can overcome their difficulties and live a fully inclusive life with their family and friends. I am sure Joely will have many more stories to tell in the future,"